A New Star-Rating System & Other Exciting News from Frommer's!

In our continuing effort to publish the savviest, most up-to-date, and most appealing travel guides available, we've added some great new features.

Frommer's guides now include a new **star-rating system.** Every hotel, restaurant, and attraction is rated from 0 to 3 stars to help you set priorities and organize your time.

We've also added **seven brand-new features** that point you to the great deals, in-the-know advice, and unique experiences that separate travelers from tourists. Throughout the guide look for:

Finds	Special finds—those places only insiders know about
Fun Fact	Fun facts—details that make travelers more informed and their trips more fun
Kids	Best bets for kids—advice for the whole family
Moments	Special moments—those experiences that memories are made of
Overrated	Places or experiences not worth your time or money
Tips	Insider tips—some great ways to save time and money
Value	Great values—where to get the best deals

Frommer's®

Yellowstone & Grand Teton National Parks

3rd Edition

by Eric Peterson

Hungry Minds™

Best-Selling Books • Digital Downloads • e-Books
Answer Networks • e-Newsletters • Branded Web Sites • e-Learning
New York, NY • Cleveland, OH • Indianapolis, IN

ABOUT THE AUTHOR

Eric Peterson is a Denver-based freelance writer who has contributed to numerous travel publications, including *Frommer's National Parks of the American West, Frommer's Texas,* and *Frommer's Colorado.* He also covers Colorado's high-tech economy and punk-rock underground for local periodicals, makes a mean chicken chili, and takes as many hiking and camping treks into the Rockies as possible.

Published by:

HUNGRY MINDS, INC.

909 Third Ave.
New York, NY 10022

ISBN 0-7645-6573-7
ISSN 1093-9792

Editor: Kimberly Perdue
Production Editor: M. Faunette Johnston
Cartographer: Roberta Stockwell
Photo Editor: Richard Fox
Production by Hungry Minds Indianapolis Production Services

SPECIAL SALES

For general information on Hungry Minds' products and services, please contact our Customer Care department, within the U.S. at 800-762-2974, or outside the U.S. at 317-572-3993 or fax 317-572-4002. For sales inquiries and reseller information, including discounts, bulk sales, customized editions, and premium sales, please contact our Customer Care department at 800-434-3422.

Manufactured in the United States of America

5 4 3 2 1

Contents

List of Maps

An Invitation to the Reader

In researching this book, we discovered many wonderful places—hotels, restaurants, shops, and more. We're sure you'll find others. Please tell us about them so that we can share the information with your fellow travelers in upcoming editions. If you were disappointed with a recommendation, we'd love to know that, too. Please write to:

Frommer's Yellowstone & Grand Teton National Parks, 3rd Edition
Hungry Minds, Inc. • 909 Third Avenue • New York, NY 10022

An Additional Note

Please be advised that travel information is subject to change at any time—and this is especially true of prices. We therefore suggest that you write or call ahead for confirmation when making your travel plans. The authors, editors, and publisher cannot be held responsible for the experiences of readers while traveling. Your safety is important to us, however, so we encourage you to stay alert and be aware of your surroundings. Keep a close eye on cameras, purses, and wallets, all favorite targets of thieves and pickpockets.

What the Symbols Mean

The following abbreviations are used for credit cards:

AE American Express	DC Diners Club	V Visa
DISC Discover	MC MasterCard	

FROMMERS.COM

Now that you have the guidebook to a great trip, visit our website at **www.frommers.com** for travel information on nearly 2,000 destinations. With features updated regularly, we give you instant access to the most current trip-planning information available. At Frommers.com, you'll also find the best prices on airfares, accommodations, and car rentals—and you can even book travel online through our travel booking partners. At Frommers.com, you'll also find the following:

- Daily newsletter highlighting the best travel deals
- Hot Spot of the Month/Vacation Sweepstakes & Travel Photo Contest
- More than 200 travel message boards
- Outspoken newsletters and feature articles on travel bargains, vacation ideas, tips and resources, and more!

Here's what critics say about Frommer's:

"Amazingly easy to use. Very portable, very complete."

—*Booklist*

"The only mainstream guide to list specific prices. The Walter Cronkite of guidebooks—with all that implies."

—*Travel & Leisure*

"Complete, concise, and filled with useful information."

—*New York Daily News*

"Hotel information is close to encyclopedic."

—*Des Moines Sunday Register*

"Detailed, accurate, and easy-to-read information for all price ranges."

—*Glamour Magazine*

Introducing Yellowstone & Grand Teton National Parks

Long before you reach the entrance to Grand Teton National Park, your sights will be set on the towering spires of the Teton Range— those signature hornlike peaks made famous through countless photographs. From afar, Yellowstone is not as dramatic because much of the parkland is comprised of heavily forested mountains and arid, high-country plateaus. However, at closer glance, Yellowstone's natural marvels are startlingly amazing: hundreds of geysers, scores of inspiring waterfalls, and a gorge carved by time and water that rivals the Grand Canyon. Both parks command the imagination and will envelop your senses from the moment you arrive.

Creatures both great and small thrive in Yellowstone and Grand Teton national parks. In the wilderness of Yellowstone's southern corners, grizzlies feed on cutthroat trout during their spawning run to the Yellowstone headwaters. In the soft blue depths of Octopus Pond, microbes of enormous scientific value are incubated and born; in the mountain ridges, wolves make their dens and mountain lions hunt bighorn sheep. Bald eagles and osprey soar above the banks of the Snake River in Grand Teton, moose munch their way through meadows of native foliage, and elk and buffalo lazily traverse the park on the same roads as visitors.

When John Colter, a scout for Lewis and Clark, first wandered this way in 1807, his descriptions of geysers and sulfurous hot pools and towering waterfalls drew jeers and suspicion. No one doubts him now, but these are still places you should see for yourself. The explorers of today come in minivans and on bicycles, aboard snowmobiles and telemark skis, and in such numbers that the parks sometimes groan under the strain.

In the early days of Yellowstone, first established as a national park in 1872, visitors were so sparse that the things they did— catching a string of 100 trout, washing their underwear in the hot pools—left few noticeable scars. Now, with millions of people visiting the parks annually, the strain on everything from sewer systems to fish populations is immense.

While there are problems, these parks still radiate with extraordinary beauty: the jagged Tetons, the glass surface of Jenny Lake, the Grand Canyon of the Yellowstone, the towering Obsidian Cliff, the steaming meandering of the Firehole River. Wildlife that most Americans see only in zoos wanders freely here, from the grizzly to the river otter, the trumpeter swan to the rufous hummingbird. Aspen groves, fields of lupine, the howls of coyotes and reintroduced wolves—all these testify to the resilience and vitality of the "Greater Yellowstone Ecosystem," which extends beyond the borders of the park to include Grand Teton, and much more.

This is not just a paradise for sightseers—it's a scientific preserve as well. The hot pools have produced unique microbes useful in everything from gene splicing to laundry detergents; studies of the elk herds and grizzly have yielded crucial information on habitat needs and animal behavior; and the rocks of Yellowstone are like the earth turned inside out, a treasure trove for geologists.

Most visitors will see or know little of this. They park in a pull-out on U.S. Highway 191/89/26 to pose in front of Grand Teton, or they sit on the crowded benches to watch Old Faithful erupt. However, if you have more time, I suggest that you take little sections of these parks—just the Jenny Lake area, say, or Yellowstone's northeast corner, the Lamar Valley—and savor them in all their fine detail rather than embark on a madcap race to see every highlight.

Definitely get out of your car and away from the road, into the wild heart of the parks' backcountry. These parks embody our country's beginnings: a nation of wilderness, of challenging and rugged extremes, and a landscape of extraordinary bounty and beauty. Use this guide as a set of footprints to help you find your way there.

1 The Best of Yellowstone & Grand Teton National Parks

A "best of" list could never do justice to Yellowstone and Grand Teton. These are just starting points, the best of the excellent accommodations and food the parks offer, as well as of the virtually unique sightseeing and recreational opportunities. Some involve backcountry expeditions; others can be enjoyed from behind the steering wheel. In the wildly diverse environments of these two parks, you can be as adventurous as you want, climbing peaks and spending the

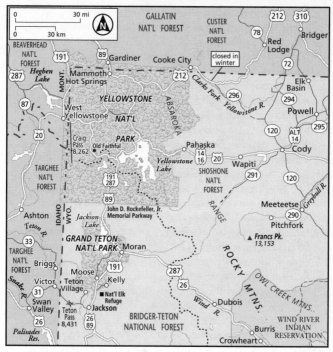

night deep in the wilderness, or simply enjoy the more civilized side of the park at grand lodges and enchanting roadside overlooks.

THE BEST VIEWS

You'll never get it all in a camera lens, but you'll undoubtedly try. Don't let that viewfinder get attached to your face; take a few shots, or run a little videotape, and then put it down so you can enjoy this place with all your senses.

- **Grand Canyon of the Yellowstone River** (Yellowstone): The waterfalls are spectacular, especially the 308-foot Lower Falls (twice the height of Niagara), and the steeply cut canyon walls are colorful and alive with life. Take the short, easy hikes to **Inspiration Point** or **Artist Point,** and you'll see the falls that stimulated Thomas Moran's creativity. If you're in reasonable shape, hike down the short but steep trail to the **Brink of the Upper Falls** or the 328-step steel staircase known as

Uncle Tom's Trail. (Be careful of slick spots in the spring and following afternoon thundershowers.) See "Yellowstone: The Extended Tour," in chapter 3.

- **Lamar Valley** (Yellowstone): Bring your telephoto lens or binoculars to the northeast corner of the park, one of the best spots to spot wildlife: **bison** and **elk** grazing along the Lamar River, **wolves** at Slough Creek and among the big ungulates, and the occasional **grizzly bear** on its never-ending quest for food. Best of all, it's less crowded than the rest of the park. See "Yellowstone: The Extended Tour," in chapter 3.

- **Yellowstone Lake** (Yellowstone): Sunrise over Yellowstone Lake is stunningly beautiful, especially if there's fog on the lake, whether you watch it from the sunroom at the Lake Hotel or (better) from a campsite along the southern wilderness shore. See "Yellowstone: The Extended Tour," in chapter 3.

- **Cathedral Group** (Grand Teton): The three central mountains in the Teton range rarely disappoint, except on the rare occasions when weather gets in the way—clouds tend to accent rather than obscure their majesty. You'll need a wide-angle lens to get it all in from the valley floor (there are pullouts along the highway between Moran Junction and Jackson), but if you want a panoramic shot, drive east on U.S. Highway 287/26 toward Togwotee Pass. See "The Highlights," in chapter 5.

- **Elk** (Grand Teton): Visiting the Jackson/Grand Teton area during the winter, take the opportunity to ride a horse-drawn sleigh out among thousands of elk on the **National Elk Refuge.** You'll get close-up shots of some of the biggest antler racks in the world, and you'll probably see coyotes and sometimes wolves. See "Jackson, Wyoming," in chapter 8.

THE BEST THERMAL DISPLAYS

Yellowstone has more thermal features—geysers, mud pots, steam vents—than the rest of the world combined. When you're angling for a good shot of a colorful pool or a belching mud pot, obey the signs—otherwise, you could find yourself, literally, on shaky ground.

- **Old Faithful Geyser** (Yellowstone): While not quite as faithful as it used to be—the intervals average 85 minutes but sometimes stretch as long as 120 minutes—it's still the most predictable geyser on the planet, blasting water 130 feet into the air more than 20 times a day. How could you skip this one? See "Yellowstone: The Extended Tour," in chapter 3.

- **Echinus Geyser** (Yellowstone): This is the most aesthetic, liveliest spouting tub of water in the Norris Geyser Basin, which gets fewer visitors than other thermal areas but has an incredible variety of hot spring activity. See "If You Have Only 1 or 2 Days (the Short Tour)," in chapter 3.
- The **Riverside Geyser** (Yellowstone): This beauty sits on the bank of the Firehole River and sends 75-foot columns of water arching over the river. See "Yellowstone: The Extended Tour," in chapter 3.

THE BEST DAY HIKES

Just a few hundred yards off the road, things get a lot less crowded, and you'll have the views and the wildlife (almost) to yourself. The hikes described have an easy rating, but you'll find more challenging options later in the book.

- The **Mount Washburn Trail** (Yellowstone): Starting at Dunraven Pass south of Tower Junction, this walk offers unsurpassed views of both parks plus the opportunity to see mountain wildlife such as bighorn sheep. See "Day Hikes," in chapter 4.
- The **Lonestar Geyser Trail** (Yellowstone): This gentle, 5-mile (8km) hike along the Firehole River presents several places to stop and take in the scenery, fish, and view this medium-size geyser. In the winter, this is a popular ski trail. See "Day Hikes," in chapter 4.
- **Cascade Canyon** (Grand Teton): This hike can be short and sweet or long and rewarding. Make a day of it, or simply take a boat ride across the lake and hike to Hidden Falls, and you'll barely break a sweat. See p. 131.
- **Signal Mountain Summit Trail** (Grand Teton): The hike from Signal Mountain to the Summit is rewarding for its solitude. While everyone else drives to the top, you'll have the same views and be closer to the greenery and wildlife. See p. 128.

THE BEST BACKCOUNTRY TRAILS

- The **Thorofare Trail** (Yellowstone): This hike will take you deeper into roadless wilderness than you can get anywhere else in the lower 48 states. You'll spend a few nights on the trail, climbing up to the park's southern border and beyond to the Yellowstone River's headwaters, a high valley bursting with wildlife. The cutthroat spawning run early in the summer attracts grizzlies and fishers if the snow has melted. It's not for the faint of heart. See "Exploring the Backcountry," in chapter 4.

- **Cascade Canyon Loop** (Grand Teton): Perhaps the most popular trail in Grand Teton, the Cascade Canyon loop, which starts on the west side of Jenny Lake, winds northwest 7¼ miles (12km) on the Cascade Canyon Trail to Lake Solitude and the Paintbrush Divide, and then returns past Holly Lake on the 10¼-mile (17km) Paintbrush Canyon trail. The payoff comes at the highest point, Paintbrush Divide, with marvelous views of the Jackson Hole Valley and Leigh Lake. See "Exploring the Backcountry," in chapter 6.

THE BEST CAMPGROUNDS

If you stay in developed campgrounds in the parks, the outdoor life is pretty civilized. You'll have running water and, in most cases, flush toilets, plus, there are opportunities to meet fellow campers.

- **Canyon Campground** (Yellowstone): Although it's among the parks' busiest, the Canyon Campground has excellent sites with a little elbow room, as well as well-maintained flush toilets. The site of numerous ranger talks, the campground is close to the Grand Canyon of the Yellowstone River and just a stone's throw from Canyon Village (especially handy when you crave an ice cream cone). See "Where to Camp in Yellowstone," in chapter 7.

- **Slough Creek Campground** (Yellowstone): Another favorite is out in the Lamar Valley. The campground is smaller, but it's away from the crowds (and other services) yet close to fishing and wolf-viewing. See "Where to Camp in Yellowstone," in chapter 7.

- **Signal Mountain** (Grand Teton): Situated near the edge of Jackson Lake, camping slots are nestled among spruce and fir trees for privacy with great views of the mountains on the other side. It's the perfect place to spend the night if you plan to launch your canoe or Hobie Cat the next morning. The only problem is, there are no site reservations, and sites are usually taken early in the morning. See "Where to Camp in Grand Teton," in chapter 7.

THE BEST PLACES TO EAT IN THE PARKS •

Don't expect five-star dining (with one exception) or a great variety, but the food is well prepared, the servers are cheerful, and the dining rooms are mostly big, convivial gathering places. All of these are detailed in chapter 7.

- The **Old Faithful Inn,** Yellowstone (© **307/545-4999**): Can't beat the ambience: a grand stone-and-timber lodge perched next to the most famous geyser in the world. The food's pretty good, too. See p. 147.

- The **Lake Yellowstone Hotel,** Yellowstone (© **307/344-7901**): Enjoy a bit of Victorian-era hospitality (without dressing up) and the finest food in the Wyoming wilderness. There are views of the lake from the dining room and the comfortable lounge area off the lobby. See p. 146.

- **Jenny Lake Lodge,** Grand Teton (© **307/543-3300**): This place gets my five-star award: Dine where presidents have dined on five-course meals with such delicacies as smoked sturgeon ravioli. Breakfast and dinner are included in the price of a room, but nonguests can call for reservations. But it's not cheap. See p. 159.

- **Signal Mountain Lodge,** Grand Teton (© **307/543-2831**): Not everyone wants a fancy, sit-down meal, and the **Cottonwood Cafe** or appetizers in the bar here make great snacks, with a view of Jackson Lake or, in the lounge, a view of several sports-tuned televisions. See p. 159.

THE BEST PLACES TO SLEEP IN THE PARKS

My Yellowstone favorites are both grand hotels, but they're very different. In Grand Teton, I lean toward the rustic option. All of these are detailed in chapter 7.

- The **Lake Yellowstone Hotel,** Yellowstone (© **307/344-7311**): Try this recipe for a great vacation: a quiet drink in the sunroom overlooking the lake, a friendly meal in the big dining room, a walk by the lake, and then a comfortable bed in one of the big wings. See p. 146.

- The **Old Faithful Inn,** Yellowstone (© **307/344-7311**): As if the wonders outside aren't enough, this is an architectural gem, a huge open ceiling 85 feet high with lodgepole balconies inside and out. Get a room in the old lodge, not the wings, even if the bathrooms are down the hall. See p. 147.

- **Jenny Lake Lodge** (© **800/628-9988**): Solitude, great food, and beautifully appointed cabins with porches have one downside: the high prices. See p. 159.

- **Colter Bay Village,** Grand Teton (© **800/628-9988** or 307/543-2855): Rough it in a roomy canvas tent with a stove and bunk beds, and firewood delivered to your door (or flap). The rates are inexpensive, and the fresh air is free. For a step up, try the rustic cabins. See p. 158.

THE BEST PLACES TO EAT OUTSIDE THE PARKS

This is food so good that you won't mind spending $15 to $30 for entrees. These are detailed in chapter 8.

- **In Jackson, Wyoming: Nani's Genuine Pasta House** (© **307/733-3888**) offers fare from a featured region of Italy, as well as a menu featuring traditional pasta favorites, and it's all good. See p. 195. Mornings, though, you'll find me at **Nora's Fish Creek Inn** (© **307/733-8288**), at nearby Wilson, with a bottomless cup of coffee and a huge plate of huevos rancheros. See p. 195.
- **In Cody, Wyoming: The Gardens** (© **307/587-1101**) melds Wyoming's wild game with Mediterranean culinary traditions in what could just be the snazziest-looking eatery in the entire state. Have some antelope sausage or pheasant ravioli in the cowboy-cosmopolitan dining room, or just sip on a cocktail in the sinful red wine bar. See p. 206.

THE BEST PLACES TO SLEEP OUTSIDE THE PARKS

All of these are detailed in chapter 8.

- **In Jackson, Wyoming: Rusty Parrot Lodge and Spa** (© **800/458-2004**) brings luxurious country inn charm to a downtown location; it's hip and expensive, like most things in Jackson. See p. 187.
- **In Gardiner, Montana:** The **Absaroka Lodge** (© **800/755-7414**) has modern rooms and decks overlooking the Yellowstone River, near the center of town. See p. 172.
- **In West Yellowstone, Montana:** The individually decorated cabins of **Hibernation Station** (© **800/580-3557** or 406/646-4200), just a stone's throw from the west entrance, are the most distinctive lodgings in the chain-dominated town. See p. 169.
- **In Cody, Wyoming:** The **Mayor's Inn** of Cody's Guest Houses (© **888/217-0890** or 307/587-0887), a historic A-frame inhabited by the mayor in 1905, was spared the wrecking ball 90 years later, with good reason: It's now a delightful B&B

with a cozy enclosed back porch that doubles as a cocktail lounge. See p. 204.

THE BEST THINGS TO SEE & DO OUTSIDE THE PARKS

Don't assume that all the best scenery, best snow, or best fishing waters are in the parks. Here are a few attractions worth highlighting in the area. See chapter 8 for more information.

- **In Cody, Wyoming:** The **Buffalo Bill Historical Center** is the best museum in the region; don't miss its art, gun, and Indian artifact collections. See p. 201.
- **In Jackson, Wyoming:** Glimpse some of the finest artistic interpretations of the natural world in existence at the fantastic **National Museum of Wildlife Art,** which houses 1,300 pieces within its red sandstone walls. See p. 184.
- **In West Yellowstone, Montana:** For a postmodern approach to visiting Yellowstone, sit in a dark room and watch the film *Yellowstone* on a 57-foot-high screen at the **Yellowstone IMAX Theater.** See p. 168.

THE BEST SCENIC DRIVES

Roll down the windows, crank up your favorite music, and take time to relax as you travel these byways.

- Every stretch along the figure eight of roads at the center of Yellowstone has some scenic allure, but my favorite is the part along the western and northern shores of **Lake Yellowstone.** There's less traffic than around Old Faithful or the Grand Canyon of the Yellowstone, and you have a good chance of seeing wildlife east of **Fishing Bridge,** as well as steaming geothermal features near **West Thumb.** The drive is best in the morning, when the sun is rising over the steaming lake. See chapter 3.
- From the northeast entrance of Yellowstone, head across the Beartooth Highway (U.S. 212) to Red Lodge, Montana; at Red Lodge, head southeast toward Cody (MT 308 to WY 120), and then catch the **Chief Joseph Highway** (WY 296) and return to the park. Imagine this: dramatic mountain peaks, river valleys, painted landscapes, and two Old West towns, all on this 155-mile (249km) drive. See chapter 3.
- A twisting, narrow road climbs **Signal Mountain** to a fine 360° view of the valley and the mountains. On the way up you'll see wildflowers and birds, and from the top you can study the moraines and potholes left by retreating glaciers. See chapter 5.

2 A Look at Yellowstone

Think about this: What other national park boasts an assortment of 10,000 thermal features, including 300 geysers? Even when the rest of North America was largely a wilderness, Yellowstone was unique. The geothermal area is greater than any other in the world, with mud pots, geysers, and hot springs of all colors, sizes, and performances. Plus, there's a waterfall that's twice as tall as Niagara Falls and a canyon deep and colorful enough to fall into the "grand" category. Sure, other parks have great hiking trails and beautiful geologic formations—Grand Teton is pretty spectacular in its own right, as is Yosemite—but virtually all of the geology in Yellowstone is reachable by anyone in average shape.

Wildlife? Ever focus your telephoto lens on a wild, untamed grizzly bear? Or a bald eagle? What about a wolf? Thousands of visitors have these experiences here every year. Protected by the national park and surrounding forests from development, Yellowstone is home to herds of bison, elk, grizzly bears, trumpeter swans, Yellowstone cutthroat trout, and more subtle beauties such as wildflowers and hummingbirds.

And the park doesn't appeal solely to the visual senses; you'll smell it, too. By one biologist's estimate, Yellowstone has more than 1,100 species of plants. When wildflowers cover the meadows in spring, their fragrances are overpowering. The mud pots and fumaroles have their own set of odors, although many are less pleasing than a wild lily.

Your ears will be filled with the sounds of geysers noisily spewing forth thousands of gallons of boiling water into the blue Wyoming sky. After sunset, coyotes break the silence of the night with their high-pitched yips.

You can spend weeks hiking its backcountry or fishing its streams, but the park's road system makes it easy to tour in a day or two from behind the windshield. Yes, *really.* It's possible to see the highlights of Yellowstone without ever leaving your car. Park roads lead past most of the key attractions and are filled with wildlife commuting from one grazing area to another. There's no doubt you will return home with vivid memories if you approach your visit of the park in this fashion, but you'll be shortchanging yourself.

Yellowstone is just as active when summer ends, when the park is open for snowmobiling and skiing for 3 months during the winter. (However, the snowmobiles have emerged as a major bone of contention and might well be banned as soon as 2003.)

3 A Look at the Grand Tetons & Jackson Hole

Because the Grand Tetons stand so tall, with the park curling snugly at their feet, visitors sometimes fail to appreciate this surrounding environment of rivers and high valley floor. The Tetons are a young range of old pre-Cambrian granite, abrupt and sharp-edged as they knife up from the Snake River valley, sliding upward along a 40-mile-long (64km) fault sculpted 15,000 years ago by retreating glaciers and erosion. The result is a masterpiece. Many visitors regard Grand Teton National Park as more dramatically scenic than its northern neighbor, with its shimmering lakes, thickly carpeted forests, and towering peaks blanketed with snow throughout most of the year.

It's also a very accessible park. You can appreciate its breathtaking beauty on a quick drive-by, or take to the trails and waterways in search of backcountry lakes and waterfalls. The Tetons themselves are especially popular with mountain climbers, who scale them year-round.

There's a dynamic relationship between the Tetons and the valley below. The elk and other wildlife migrate from the high country down to the open grasslands to forage during the winter, when the snowmelt curls across the valley floor and west through a gap in the mountains, and the moraines and alluvial soils that slough off the mountains provide rich soils for the pastures below.

Visitors can float and fish the lively Snake River, visit the National Elk Refuge in the winter, hike in nearby ranges such as the Wind Rivers or the Gros Ventre, or play cowboy at one of the dude and guest ranches that dot the valley of Jackson Hole. Skiers and snowboarders have a blast at the resorts here, as well as at Grand Targhee on the other side of Teton Pass. And the snug town of Jackson, with its antler-arched town square and its busy shops, offers everything from classy art galleries to noisy two-step cowboy bars.

4 Making the Most of Your Trip

Yellowstone and Grand Teton are more than photo ops and zoos where the animals roam free. They aren't museums, either, where magnificent scenery is merely on display. Both parks, unlike a picture hanging lifelessly on the wall of a museum, are works in progress; they are living, breathing wilderness areas. Plant your feet in a comfortable pair of walking or hiking shoes, find a trailhead, and head into the woods with a sack lunch and big bottle of water.

Better yet, if you can afford the time, plan an excursion around Shoshone Lake or to the south end of Yellowstone Lake by boat to areas few visitors ever see. There are isolated areas in Grand Teton, too—even on the far shore of popular Jenny Lake—where, with a little hiking, you'll be rewarded by a pristine, forested glade with nothing to distract your attention but an awe-inspiring mountaintop.

If you're more adventurous, take a white-water trip down the canyon, or let a guide take you up to Grand Teton's summit. In Yellowstone, sleep under the stars and listen to the wolves howl at Slough Creek Campground, or backpack for a week on the Thorofare Trail.

You will never plumb the absolute depths of these parks—no one ever will. You can spend your whole life trying, though, and have a great and illuminating time doing it.

5 Some Historical Background

YELLOWSTONE NATIONAL PARK

Before the arrival of European settlers, the only residents on the plateau were small bands of Shoshone Indians known as "Sheepeaters," who lived on the southern fringe. Three other Indian tribes came and went: the Crows (Absaroka), who were friendly to the settlers; the Blackfeet, who lived in the Missouri Valley drainage and were hostile to both whites and other Indians; and the Bannocks, who largely kept to themselves. The nomadic Bannocks traveled an east-west route in their search for bison, from Idaho past Mammoth Hot Springs to Tower Fall, and then across the Lamar Valley to the Bighorn Valley, which is outside the park's current boundaries. Called the Bannock Trail, it was so deeply furrowed that evidence of it still exists today on the Blacktail Plateau near the Tower Junction. (You'll be able to see remnants of the trail if you take Blacktail Plateau Drive, described in chapter 3, "Exploring Yellowstone.")

The first white explorer to lay eyes on Yellowstone's geothermal wonders was probably John Colter, who broke away from the Lewis and Clark expedition in 1806 and spent three years wandering a surreal landscape of mud pots and mountains and geysers. When he described his discovery on his return to St. Louis, no one believed him. Miners and fur trappers followed in his footsteps, reducing the plentiful beaver of the region to almost nothing, and occasionally making curious reports of a sulfurous world still sometimes called "Colter's Hell."

The first significant exploration of what would become the park took place in 1869, when a band of Montanans led by David Folsom completed a 36-day expedition. Folsom and his group traveled up the Missouri River and then into the heart of the park, where they discovered the falls of the Yellowstone, mud pots, Yellowstone Lake, and the Fountain Geyser. The very next year, an expedition led by the director of the U.S. Geological Survey, Ferdinand Hayden, brought back convincing evidence of Yellowstone's wonders, in the form of astonishing photographs by William H. Jackson and sketches by famed Western artist Thomas Moran.

A debate began over the potential for commercial development and exploitation of the region, as crude health spas and thin-walled "hotels" went up near the hot springs. There are various claimants to the idea of a national park—members of the Folsom party later told an oft-disputed story about thinking it up around a campfire in the Upper Geyser Basin—but the idea gained steam as Yellowstone explorers hit the lecture circuit back East. In March 1872, President Ulysses S. Grant signed legislation declaring Yellowstone the nation's first national park.

The Department of Interior got the job of managing the new park. There was no budget for it and no clear idea how to take care of a wilderness preserve; many mistakes were made. Inept superintendents granted favorable leases to friends with commercial interests in the tourism industry. Poachers ran amok, and the wildlife population was decimated. A laundry business near Mammoth went so far as to clean linens in a hot pool.

By 1886, things were so bad that the U.S. Army took over control of the park; its iron-fisted management practices resulted in new order and protected the park from those intent upon exploiting it. (However, the military did participate in the eradication of the plateau's wolf population.) By 1916, efforts to make the park more visitor-friendly had begun to show results: Construction of the first roads had been completed, guest housing was available in the area, and order had been restored. Stewardship of the park was then transferred to the newly created National Park Service.

GRAND TETON NATIONAL PARK

Unlike Yellowstone, Grand Teton can't boast of being the nation's first park and a model for parks the world over. This smaller, southern neighbor was created as the result of a much more convoluted process that spanned 50 years.

The first sign of human habitation in the Grand Teton region points to people being here around 12,000 years ago. Among the tribes who hunted here in the warmer seasons were the Blackfeet, Crow, Gros Ventre, and Shoshone, who came over the mountains from the Great Basin to the west. Summers were spent here hunting and raising crops, before heading to warmer climes.

The trappers and explorers who followed them into the valley were equally distressed by the harsh winters and short growing season, which made Jackson Hole a marginal place for growing crops or ranching. Among these early visitors were artist Thomas Moran and photographer William Henry Jackson, whose images awoke the country to the Tetons' grandeur. Early homesteaders quickly realized that their best hope was to market the beauty of the area, which they began doing in earnest as early as a century ago.

The danger of haphazard development soon became apparent. There was a dance hall at Jenny Lake, hot dog stands along the roads, and buildings going up on some prime habitat. In the 1920s, Yellowstone park officials and conservationists met to discuss how the Grand Teton area might be protected and then went to Congress. Led by local dude ranchers and Yellowstone superintendent Horace Albright, the group was able to protect only the mountains and foothills, leaving out Jackson Lake and the valley; Wyoming's congressional delegation—and many locals—were violently opposed to enclosing the valley in park boundaries.

Then, in 1927, something called the Snake River Land Company started buying up ranches and homesteads along the base of the Tetons. It was a front for John D. Rockefeller Jr., one of the richest men in the world, working in cahoots with the conservationists. He planned to give the land to the federal government, while keeping a few choice parcels for himself. But Congress wouldn't have it, and Rockefeller made noises about selling the land, about 35,000 acres, to the highest bidder. In the 1940s, Pres. Franklin D. Roosevelt created the Jackson Hole National Monument out of Forest Service lands east of the Snake River. That paved the way for Rockefeller's donation, and in 1950 Grand Teton National Park was expanded to its present form.

6 Issues Facing the Parks Today

After spending 32 years with the National Park Service, former Yellowstone superintendent Michael Finley left his post for the private sector in 2001. As he departed, he fired off a few parting shots, warning the public that the park's future might be in jeopardy. "At some point, you just can't keep dumping people into the parks," he told Montana's *Livingston Enterprise* in May 2001. "The park's mission is not to sell more motel rooms in an adjacent community or more rubber tomahawks."

This viewpoint has its supporters and detractors, but the schism is hardly new. The struggle to balance recreation and preservation is as old as the park itself, and it's an issue that continually comes to a boil when long-standing park policies, such as the use of snowmobiles, are revisited with a critical eye. The mission of the Park Service hasn't gotten any easier since poachers ran rampant more than 100 years ago, but numerous issues continue to emerge and evolve.

BISON, BEARS & WOLVES

In the frontier West, where bison seemed to be everywhere, grizzly bears were fearsome, and wolves regularly raided livestock, wildlife was treated as more of a nuisance than a national treasure. Eventually, the bison and grizzly populations around Yellowstone and Grand Teton were whittled down to near extinction, and wolves were completely eradicated by the 1930s.

It took some intensive management to bring grizzlies and bison back to reasonably healthy numbers in the area, and now the wolves, which were reintroduced from Canada in 1995, are reaping the benefits of the huge ungulate herds that have enjoyed a nearly predator-free environment for quite some time. But these high-profile species—called "charismatic megafauna" by biologists—are not out of the woods yet. Given the pressures of development around the parks, they might never be secure again.

There are now some 3,000 bison in Yellowstone and Grand Teton, and, naturally, they are entirely disrespectful of the park's invisible boundary line. In the winter, when snows are deep, they leave the park to forage at lower elevations, sometimes in ranch pastures shared with domestic cattle. The ranchers fear that the bison will spread brucellosis, a virus that can be transmitted to cattle, causing infected cows to abort their unborn calves. While there have been only six documented cases of bison-cattle transmission, because of the perceived threat to livestock, Montana officials allow them to be shot once they wander outside the park. Animal rights activists are outraged, and park and state officials continue to search for some middle ground.

Wolves are another sore point with area ranchers. The reintroduction has been astonishingly successful. Rapidly reproducing, feeding on abundant elk in the park's Lamar Valley, there are now more than 150 wolves, and the packs have spread as far south as

Grand Teton, where several have denned and produced pups. Although the Defenders of Wildlife have set up programs to compensate ranchers for livestock lost to wolves, the ranchers have gone to court seeking to have the wolves removed. The wolves have indeed been implicated in the deaths of sheep and cattle, and a federal judge in Wyoming ruled in 1998 that all reintroduced wolves should be removed. This decision was overturned in 2000, and the wolves are finally entrenched in Yellowstone for the long haul.

Grizzly bears once teetered on the brink of extinction in the parks, but they've made a slow comeback to a healthier population of around 600. Unfortunately, the habitat that they need so much of keeps shrinking, as more and more development takes place around the plateau.

A MULTIPLE USE PARK

Grand Teton National Park is much more than just a preserve of mountains and lakes and wildlife. Its land is used for all sorts of things that most people don't expect of a national park. There's a big dam holding irrigation water for potato farmers in Idaho; commercial climbing businesses charge big bucks to take climbers up the peaks; cattle graze on seeded, irrigated pastures; and there's even a commercial airport and a country club.

Each year, one of these conflicting uses makes headlines. Lately, it's the cattle, which graze in the fall only a short lope from a den of young wolves. What's the purpose of this park, critics ask, to feed a rancher's cattle or to protect wildlife?

As park spokesperson Joan Anselmo points out, these are the sort of public lands conflicts that arise more often in modern times. With its pockets of private land, uses that predate the creation of the park, and heightened debate between park purists and multiple-use advocates, Grand Teton is a prime example of the difficulty of modern park management.

A BURNING ISSUE

Yellowstone's park managers faced the ultimate test of their non-interference philosophy of fire management in 1988, when nearly one-third of Yellowstone was burned by a series of uncontrollable wildfires. These violent conflagrations scorched more than 700,000 acres, leaving behind dead wildlife, damaged buildings, injured firefighters, and ghostly forests of stripped, blackened tree trunks.

The debate over park and public land fire policies still rages, although things have quieted down some. After years of suppressing every fire in the park, Yellowstone in 1988 was operating under a new "let it burn" policy, based on scientific evidence that fires were regular occurrences in nature, part of the natural cycle of a forest.

What you will see as you travel Yellowstone today is a park that could be healthier than it was before. Saplings have sprouted from the long-dormant seeds of the lodgepole pine (fires stimulate the pine cones to release their seeds), and the old, tinder-dry forest undergrowth is being replaced with new green shrubs, sometimes as thick as one million saplings per acre. Visitors who want to better understand the effects of the fires of 1988 should visit the exhibit *Yellowstone and Fire* at the Grant Village visitor center; its coverage is the best in the park.

SNOWMOBILES: TO BAN OR NOT TO BAN?

Winter in Yellowstone is a time of silent wonder, with fauna descending from the high country in search of warmth and food. The only dissonance to this winter wilderness tableau is the roar of snowmobiles, which inhabit the park's snow-packed roads in ever-growing numbers. The noisy, pollution-heavy engines are not exactly ecologically friendly, but the gateway towns are staunch snowmobile proponents because the activity boosts their economies in the moribund winter.

Before President Clinton left office in 2001, he "ended" the ongoing controversy by establishing a ban on snowmobiles in Yellowstone, effective beginning the winter of 2003–04. For the winter of 2001–02, the Clinton administration established a quota equal to the total number of snowmobiles that entered the park the previous winter (about 66,000) with a limit of 33,000 for the winter of 2002–03.

However, gateway communities and snowmobile manufacturers filed lawsuits in 2001, throwing the situation into limbo until another environmental study is completed in 2002. The Bush administration has also indicated that it opposes a total ban, delighting the outfitters in West Yellowstone and Cody. At press time, the National Park Service, the pro-snowmobile forces, and the Bush administration were awaiting the results of this new study (the NPS was also conducting a supplemental study) because it will likely shape the future winter landscape in Yellowstone, whether it is punctuated by the wail of snowmobiles or not. For the time being, it is business as usual, but snowmobilers might have to settle for the trails in surrounding federal lands instead of those in Yellowstone in coming years.

2

Planning Your Trip to Yellowstone & Grand Teton National Parks

It's no one's idea of a fun vacation to end up sucking exhaust behind a long line of cars waiting for a break in construction at Yellowstone's east entrance, or wearing a T-shirt in a Montana snowstorm. Few things can ruin a much-anticipated vacation more than poor planning. So look over some of the crucial information in this chapter before you hit the road—it might be the difference between a trip you'll never forget and one you'd rather not remember.

1 Getting Started: Information & Reservations

The primary entries to Yellowstone and Grand Teton are through Montana and Wyoming, so if you want information about the surrounding areas, contact these states' travel services: **Travel Montana,** P.O. Box 200533, 1424 9th Ave., Helena, MT 59620-0533 (© **800/ VISIT-MT** or 406/444-2654; www.visitmt.com); and the **Wyoming Business Council Tourism Division,** I-25 at College Drive, Cheyenne, WY 82002 (© **800/225-5996** or 307/777-7777; www. wyomingtourism.org).

YELLOWSTONE NATIONAL PARK   To receive maps and information before your arrival, contact Visitors Services, Box 168, **Yellowstone National Park,** WY 82190 (© **307/344-7381;** www. nps.gov/yell).

Information regarding lodging, tours, boating, and horseback riding is available from **Yellowstone National Park Lodges,** P.O. Box 165, Yellowstone National Park, WY 82190 (© **307/344-7311;** www.travelyellowstone.com). You'll find complete information about lodging both inside the park and in the surrounding communities in chapters 7, "Where to Stay & Dine in the Parks," and 8, "Gateways to Yellowstone & Grand Teton National Parks."

For information about educational programs at the Yellowstone Institute, contact **The Yellowstone Association,** P.O. Box 117, Yellowstone National Park, WY 82190 (📞 **307/344-2293;** www.yellowstoneassociation.org). The association also operates bookstores in park visitor centers, museums, and an educational facility open to the public; contact them for catalog of the books they offer.

GRAND TETON NATIONAL PARK   To receive park maps and information before your arrival, contact **Grand Teton National Park,** P.O. Drawer 170, Moose, WY 83012 (📞 **307/739-3600;** www.nps.gov/grte).

Lodging information is available from three park concessionaires: **Grand Teton Lodge Company,** P.O. Box 240, Moran, WY 83013 (📞 **800/628-9988**); **Signal Mountain Lodge Co.,** P.O. Box 50, Moran, WY 83013 (📞 **307/543-2831**); and **Flagg Ranch Village,** Box 187, Moran, WY 83013 (📞 **800/443-2311**). You'll find complete information about lodging both inside the park and in the surrounding gateway communities in chapters 7 and 8.

Educational and field trips are offered by the **Teton Science School,** P.O. Box 68, Kelly, WY 83011 (📞 **307/733-4765;** www.tetonscience.org). The school's **Wildlife Expeditions** (📞 **307/773-2623**) offers tours that bring visitors closer to the park's wildlife.

The **Grand Teton Natural History Association** is a not-for-profit organization that provides information about the park through retail book sales at park visitor centers; you can also buy books about the park from the organization by mail. Contact the association at P.O. Drawer 170, Moose, WY 83012 (📞 **307/739-3403;** www.grandtetonpark.org).

National forests and other public lands surround the parks. For information about national forests and wilderness areas in Montana, as well as **Bridger-Teton National Forest** in Wyoming, contact the **U.S. Forest Service Northern Region Office,** Federal Building, 200 E. Broadway, P.O. Box 7669, Missoula, MT 59807 (📞 **406/329-3511;** www.fs.fed.us/r1). The rest of Wyoming's forests, including the **Shoshone National Forest** east of the Tetons over Togwotee Pass, are covered by the **Rocky Mountain Region Office,** P.O. Box 25127, Lakewood, CO 80225 (📞 **303/275-5350;** www.fs.fed.us/r2).

The federal **Bureau of Land Management** also manages millions of acres of recreational lands and can be reached at its Wyoming state office, 5353 Yellowstone Rd., P.O. Box 1828 Cheyenne, WY 82003 (📞 **307/775-6256**); or its Montana state office, 5001 Southgate Dr., P.O. Box 36800 Billings, MT 59107 (📞 **406/896-5004**).

What Things Cost in Yellowstone & Grand Teton	U.S.$
Double motel room in or around the parks, peak season	$60–$250
Double motel room, winter season	$50–$138
Cabin with bed and bathroom	$68–$116
Dinner in a full-service hotel restaurant	$12–$30
Dinner in a coffee shop	$6–$15
Horseback riding for 1 hour	$18
Stagecoach ride	$7
1-hour lake cruise	$9
Bus sightseeing tour (Yellowstone)	$26–$40
1-day snowmobile rental	$115–$150
Snowcoach round-trip to Old Faithful	$99

GENERAL TOURIST INFORMATION   Other sources of information include **Yellowstone Country,** P.O. Box 1107, Red Lodge, MT 59068 (© 800/736-5276); **Gardiner Chamber of Commerce,** 222 Park St., P.O. Box 81, Gardiner, MT 59030 (© 406/848-7971); **Colter Pass/Cooke City/Silver Gate Chamber of Commerce,** Box 1071, Cooke City, MT 59020 (© 406/838-2395); **West Yellowstone Chamber of Commerce,** 100 Yellowstone Ave., West Yellowstone, MT 59758 (© 406/646-7701); **Jackson Chamber of Commerce,** P.O. Box E, Jackson, WY 83001, (© 307/733-3316); **Jackson Hole Central Reservations** (© 800/443-6931); **Cody Country Chamber of Commerce,** P.O. Box 2777, Cody, WY 82414 (© 307/587-2777); and the **Park County Travel Council,** P.O. Box 2454, Cody, WY 82414 (© 307/587-2297).

2 When to Go

Summer, autumn, and winter are the best times to visit the Northern Rockies. The days are sunny, the nights are clear, and the humidity is low. A popular song once romanticized "Springtime in the Rockies," but that season lasts about 2 days in early June. The rest of the season formally known as spring is likely to be chilly and spitting snow or rain. Trails are still clogged with snow and mud.

From mid-June on, you can hike, fish, camp, and watch wildlife, and if you come before July 4 or after Labor Day, you won't have to share the view much. The great wildflower season? The flowers actually bloom at these elevations in early summer—beginning in May in the lower valleys and plains, while in the higher elevations they open up in July.

Autumn is not just the time when the aspen turn gold—it's also the time when gateway motel and restaurant rates are lower and the roads are less crowded. That allows you to pay attention to the wildlife, which is busy fattening up for the winter.

Winter is a glorious season here, although not for everyone. It can be very cold, but the air is crystalline, the snow is powdery, and the skiing is fantastic. If you drive in the parks' vicinity in the winter, *always* carry winter clothing, sleeping bags, extra food, flashlights, and other safety gear. Every resident has a horror story about being caught unprepared in the weather.

THE CLIMATE   The region is characterized by long, cold winters and short, relatively mild summers. There is not a lot of moisture, winter or summer, and the air is dry, except for the brief wet season in March and April.

I've already warned you about the brief glimpse of spring in these parts. Cold and snow can linger into April and May—a blizzard hit the area in mid-June 2001—although temperatures are generally warming. The average daytime readings are in the 40s to 50s (F), gradually increasing into the 60s to 70s (F) by early June. So, during **spring,** a warm jacket, raingear, and water-resistant walking shoes could be welcome traveling companions.

The area is never balmy, but temperatures during the middle of the **summer** are typically 70° to 80°F in the lower elevations and are especially comfortable because of the lack of humidity. Remember, too, that the atmosphere is thin at this altitude, so sunscreen is a must. Nights, even during the warmest months, will be cool, with temperatures dropping into the low 40s, so you'll want to include a jacket in your wardrobe. Because summer thunderstorms are common, you'll probably be glad you've included a waterproof shell or umbrella.

As **fall** approaches, you'll want to have an additional layer of clothing because temperatures remain mild but begin to cool. The first heavy snows typically fall in the Valley by November 1 (much earlier in the mountains) and continue through March or April. Aspen trees turn bright yellow; cottonwoods turn a deeper gold.

During **winter** months, you'll want long johns, heavy shirts, vests, coats, warm gloves, and thick socks. Temperatures hover in single digits, and subzero overnight temperatures are common. Ultracold air can cause lots of health problems, so drink fluids, keep an extra layer of clothing handy, and don't overexert yourself.

Montana's Average Monthly Temperatures (High/Low) °F

	Jan	Feb	Mar	Apr	May	June	July	Aug	Sept	Oct	Nov	Dec
Billings	32/14	38/19	45/25	57/24	67/44	77/52	86/58	85/57	72/47	61/37	45/26	36/18
Bozeman	33/13	38/18	44/23	55/31	64/39	74/46	82/52	81/51	70/42	59/33	43/23	34/15
Butte	29/5	34/10	40/17	50/26	60/34	70/42	80/46	78/44	66/35	56/26	39/16	29/6
Dillon	32/11	39/16	44/21	55/28	64/36	73/44	83/49	81/48	69/39	58/31	42/21	33/12
Glasgow	20/0	27/7	39/18	56/31	68/43	77/51	85/57	84/55	71/44	59/33	40/19	26/7
Great Falls	31/12	37/17	43/22	55/32	65/41	78/49	83/54	81/53	71/44	59/36	44/25	35/16
Havre	24/3	32/10	43/20	57/31	68/41	77/49	84/54	84/52	71/42	60/31	41/18	29/7
Helena	29/9	36/15	44/22	56/31	65/40	74/47	85/52	82/51	70/41	58/31	42/21	32/12
Kalispell	28/13	35/18	43/23	55/31	65/39	72/45	81/48	80/47	69/39	55/30	39/24	31/17
Lewistown	31/9	36/14	41/20	53/29	63/37	72/45	81/50	80/49	68/40	58/32	44/21	34/12
Libby	29/13	36/17	43/21	52/27	62/33	70/40	78/43	78/42	67/35	54/28	37/22	29/15
Miles City	25/5	33/11	43/21	58/33	69/44	79/53	89/60	87/58	73/46	61/35	43/21	31/11
Missoula	30/15	37/21	47/25	58/31	66/38	74/46	83/50	82/49	71/40	57/31	41/24	30/16
Sidney	24/2	32/8	44/19	60/30	72/42	80/51	86/55	85/53	73/42	61/33	41/19	28/6
W. Yellowstone	24/0	30/4	37/10	46/20	58/29	69/37	79/41	76/39	65/31	52/23	34/12	23/1

Wyoming's Average Monthly Temperatures (High/Low) °F

	Jan	Feb	Mar	Apr	May	June	July	Aug	Sept	Oct	Nov	Dec
Casper	33/12	38/16	45/22	56/30	67/39	78/48	87/54	86/53	74/43	61/33	44/22	35/15
Cheyenne	38/15	41/18	45/22	55/30	65/40	74/48	82/55	80/53	71/44	60/34	47/24	39/17
Cody	34/12	40/17	47/23	56/31	64/40	75/48	84/55	82/54	71/43	61/35	45/24	36/15
Devils Tower	34/4	39/10	48/18	60/28	70/38	80/47	88/53	87/50	76/39	64/28	46/17	35/7
Dubois	35/13	38/14	43/18	52/25	62/32	71/39	80/43	79/41	68/34	58/28	43/19	36/14
Gillette	30/10	36/15	44/21	55/30	64/39	76/49	85/55	84/53	71/43	60/33	43/21	33/12
Jackson	26/4	32/7	41/16	51/24	62/30	72/37	82/41	80/39	70/31	58/23	39/16	27/5
Kemmerer	28/5	32/6	39/13	50/22	62/32	72/39	82/45	79/43	69/34	56/25	40/15	30/6
Lander	32/8	37/14	45/21	56/31	66/40	77/49	86/55	84/54	73/44	60/33	43/19	33/11
Rawlins	30/11	33/14	40/20	52/28	63/36	75/45	83/52	80/50	69/41	56/31	41/21	31/13
Riverton	29/2	37/6	48/18	59/28	69/38	80/46	89/51	87/48	75/38	62/27	43/13	30/0
Rock Springs	30/11	34/14	42/21	53/28	64/37	75/46	83/53	81/51	70/41	57/31	41/20	31/12
Sheridan	33/9	38/15	46/22	57/31	67/40	76/48	86/53	85/52	73/41	62/32	45/20	35/10
Thermopolis	35/6	42/13	51/22	61/31	71/39	82/47	90/54	88/51	76/41	65/31	47/19	36/8
Yellowstone	29/9	34/13	38/15	50/25	61/33	68/40	80/45	78/44	67/37	56/29	39/20	31/13

Tips Road Openings & Closings

In Yellowstone Traveling Yellowstone's roads during spring months can be a roll of the dice because openings can be delayed for days (sometimes weeks) at a time, especially at higher altitudes. There is always some section of road in Yellowstone under reconstruction, with projects for Dunraven Pass (closed for summer 2002) and the stretch between Madison and Norris being the current hotspots, so call ahead and get a road report (© **307/344-7381**). It's irritating, but don't take it out on the road workers: They often labor through the night to cause as little inconvenience as possible.

The only road open year-round in the area is the north entrance to **Mammoth Hot Springs.** From Mammoth, a winter access road to the northeast entrance and **Cooke City** is plowed throughout the winter. This service for Cooke City residents gives visitors a great opportunity to watch wildlife in winter in the Lamar Valley. Just be watchful of the weather; the road is often slick with ice.

Snowplowing begins in early March. In Yellowstone, the first roads open to motor vehicles usually include **Mammoth–Norris, Norris–Canyon, Madison–Old Faithful,** and **West Yellowstone–Madison.** These roads might open by the

AVOIDING THE CROWDS Between the Fourth of July and Labor Day, the Northern Rockies come to life. Flowers bloom, fish jump, bison calves frolic—and tourists tour. The park roads are crowded with trailers, with the well-known spots jammed with a significant portion of the millions who make their treks to Montana and Wyoming every year. Your best bet: Travel before June 15, if possible, or after Labor Day. If you can't arrange that, then visit the major attractions at off-peak hours when others are eating or sleeping, and you'll have the park more to yourself. Or, as I suggest over and over, abandon the pavement for the hiking trails.

Whenever you come, give these parks as much time as you can; you'll experience more at an unhurried pace.

3 Special Permits

BACKCOUNTRY PERMITS If you want to sleep in the Yellowstone or Grand Teton backcountry, you have to get a permit, end of April. If the weather cooperates, the east and south entrances, as well as roads on the east and south sides of the park, will open early in May. Opening of the road from **Tower–Roosevelt** to **Canyon Junction,** however, might be delayed by late season snowfall on Dunraven Pass.

The **Sunlight Basin Road** (which is also called the **Chief Joseph Highway**), connecting the entrance at Cooke City, Montana, with Cody, Wyoming, often opens by early May. The **Beartooth Highway** between Cooke City and Red Lodge, Montana, is generally open by Memorial Day weekend.

Road closures begin in mid-October, when the Beartooth Highway closes. Depending upon weather, most other park roads remain open until the park season ends on the first Sunday in November.

In Grand Teton   Because Grand Teton has fewer roads and they're at lower elevations, openings and closings are more predictable. **Teton Park Road** opens to conventional vehicles and RVs around May 1. The **Moose–Wilson Road** opens to vehicles about the same time. Roads close to vehicles on November 1 and open for snowmobiles in mid-December, although they never close for nonmotorized use.

follow limits for length of stay and campfires, and stay in a designated area. The permit is free if you pick it up at the park during the final 48 hours before you begin your trip or on the day of your trip. Or, you can reserve a site in advance by paying a $15 fee to Grand Teton or $20 to Yellowstone. If you wish to reserve in advance, you must do so in writing, and you still need to pick up your permit in person upon your arrival in the park. Yellowstone reservations can be made starting on April 1 of the current year and are generally not accepted after early November. In Grand Teton, you can reserve a permit from January 1 to May 15; thereafter all permits are first come, first served. If you're going during the parks' busy season, you'd be wise to reserve in advance.

In Yellowstone, permits can be obtained at any ranger station, most of which are open from 8am to 7pm. To make a reservation, you must contact the park more than 48 hours in advance. You can request one by writing the **Backcountry Office,** P.O. Box 168, Yellowstone National Park, WY 82190, or by stopping in at a ranger station. Phone reservations are not accepted, but if you want information about the system, call ℂ **307/344-2160.**

In Grand Teton, permits are issued at the Moose and Colter Bay Visitor Centers and the Jenny Lake ranger station. Reservations can be made by writing the **Permits Office,** Grand Teton National Park, P.O. Box 170, Moose, WY 83012, or by sending a fax to 307/739-3438. Phone reservations are not accepted.

BOATING PERMITS   For motorized craft, the cost is $20 for annual permits and $10 for 7-day permits. Fees for nonmotorized boats are $10 for annual permits and $5 for 7-day permits. See the "Regulations" section later in this chapter for more information. Boating permits are required for all vessels. Motorized boating is restricted to designated areas. Boating is prohibited on all of Yellowstone's rivers and streams except for the Lewis River Channel, where hand-propelled vessels are permitted. The fees are the same in Grand Teton, where powerboaters are permitted on Jenny, Jackson, and Phelps lakes; nonmotorized boats are allowed on most park lakes and the Snake River. Sailboats, windsurfers, and jet skis are allowed only on Jackson Lake. U.S. Coast Guard–approved personal flotation devices are required for each person boating.

FISHING PERMITS   In **Yellowstone,** park permits are required for anglers 16 and over; the permit costs $10 for 10 days and $20 for the season. Youths 12 to 15 years of age also must have a permit, but it's free. Children under 12 may fish without a permit. Permits are available at any ranger station, visitor center, Hamilton store, and most fishing shops in the gateways. The season usually begins on the Saturday of Memorial Day weekend and continues through the first

---

Driving Distances to Yellowstone National Park*

Denver	563 miles (900km)
Las Vegas	809 miles (1,294km)
Salt Lake City	390 miles (628km)
Portland	869 miles (1,399km)
Seattle	827 miles (1,331km)
Omaha	946 miles (1,523km)
Washington, D.C.	2,081 miles (3,350km)

*The difference in distance to Grand Teton is about 70 miles (113km), depending on your route.

Sunday in November. Exceptions to this rule are Yellowstone Lake, its tributaries, and sections of the Yellowstone River.

In **Grand Teton,** State of Wyoming fishing licenses are required for anyone over 14 years of age. An adult nonresident license costs $10 per day and $65 for the season. Youth fees (ages 14 to 18) are $3 per day and $15 for the season. The river season generally opens April 1 and ends on October 31; Jackson Lake is closed all of October.

4 Getting There

If interstate highways and international airports are the measure of accessibility, then Yellowstone is as remote as Alaska's Denali National Park. But three million people make it here every year, on tour buses, in family vans, on bicycles, and astride snowmobiles, even from the other side of the world.

Grand Teton's gateways are from the north, south, and east. Drivers naturally enter from whichever side they approach the parks, but fliers have some choices to make.

THE NEAREST AIRPORTS

The closest airport to Yellowstone is the **West Yellowstone Regional Airport** (© **406/646-7631**) in Montana, where the airport sits just 1 mile (1.5km) north of town (and the west entrance) on Highway 191. The airport has commercial air service seasonally, from June through September only, on Delta's commuter service, **SkyWest** (© 800/453-9417).

Visitors can land right in Grand Teton National Park when they fly to **Jackson,** Wyoming, and will be only 56 miles (90km) of scenic driving from the southern entrance of Yellowstone. **American Airlines** (© 800/433-7300), **Delta** (© 800/221-1212), **SkyWest** (see above), and **United Express** (© 800/241-6522) all have flights to and from **Jackson Airport** (© 307/733-7682).

To the north, **Bozeman,** Montana, is 87 miles (140km) from the West Yellowstone entrance on U.S. 191. Or, you can drive east from Bozeman to Livingston, a 20-mile (32km) journey on Interstate 90, and then south 53 miles (85km) on U.S. 89 to the northern entrance at Gardiner. Bozeman's airport, **Gallatin Field** (© 406/388-8321), provides daily service via **Delta** (see above), **Northwest** (© 800/225-2525), and **United** (© 800/241-6522), as well as **Horizon** (© 800/547-9308) and **SkyWest** (see above) commuter flights.

Also to the north, **Billings,** Montana, is 129 miles (207km) from the Cooke City entrance. Billings is home to the Montana's busiest airport, **Logan International** (© 406/238-3420), 2 miles (3km)

Tips **Driving Suggestions**

The speed limit in Yellowstone and Grand Teton parks is 45 mph (except on U.S. 191 through the east side of Grand Teton), but drivers go faster and sometimes much slower, often without any thought to the cars backed up behind them, the bicyclists trying to survive on the narrow shoulder, or the risks to their own passengers. In the winter, snowmobilers, too, must take it slow, or risk an accident or a ticket.

Wildlife such as bison often use the roads as well, especially during the winter—don't crowd them or try to pass. Drivers who gaze around at the sights risk running into a "bear jam" where people have pulled partway off the road, or simply slowed to a crawl. Use the pullouts and walk back to the view—it's safer, and you won't cause any road rage.

Larger vehicles such as RVs can also be a big irritation. They move slower than other traffic, and they block the view from smaller vehicles behind them. If you drive an RV, make a point of using the pullouts so that folks behind you can have an unimpeded view.

north of downtown. Daily intrastate service is provided by **Big Sky Airlines** (© 800/237-7788 or 406/245-2300), and regional daily service is provided by **Delta, Horizon, Northwest,** and **United** (see phone numbers above). From Billings, it's a 65-mile (104km) drive south on U.S. Highway 212 to Red Lodge, and then 30 miles (48km) on the Beartooth Highway to the northeast entrance to the park.

From **Cody,** Wyoming, it's a gorgeous 53-mile (85km) drive west along U.S. Highway 16/14/20 to the east entrance of the park. Cody's **Yellowstone Regional Airport** (© 307/587-5096) serves the Bighorn Basin as well as the east and northeast entrances of Yellowstone National Park with year-round commercial flights via **SkyWest** and **United Express** (see phone numbers above).

Airfares to the small airports surrounding the parks can be pricey, so if you like to drive, consider flying in to **Salt Lake City,** Utah, and driving 280 miles (450km) to the park, a drive that has some nice scenic stretches. Even **Denver,** a much longer drive of more than 400 miles (643km), is an alternative for some, although it's a less beautiful drive than from Salt Lake.

RENTING A CAR   Most of the major auto-rental agencies have operations in the gateway cities. **Avis** (© 800/831-2847), **Budget**

(© 800/527-0700), **Thrifty** (© 800/367-2277), and **Hertz** (© 800/654-3131) all have operations in **Bozeman, Billings,** and **Jackson. National** (© 800/227-7368) has locations in **Bozeman** and **Billings,** while **Cody** is served by **Thrifty, Avis, Hertz,** and **Budget. Alamo Auto Rental** (© 800/327-9633) serves **Jackson.**

5 Tips for RVers

You love 'em or you hate 'em—the large, lumbering vehicles that serve some travelers as both transport and home. There are some retirees, self-named "full-timers," who sell their homes and their possessions and spend the rest of their lives chasing comfortable weather down the highway. Others might see it as a cost-saving way to vacation in the West, by renting a rolling room for the whole family at perhaps $1,000 per week plus gas. Is that a better deal than an economy car and less expensive motels? You do the math.

But you don't have to carry your bags, or even unpack them, and you'll sleep in campgrounds instead of motels, hear the sounds of the night outside, and have great flexibility in planning your itinerary. The trade-off will be making your own beds, doing without cable television, and making your own breakfast most of the time.

A few years back, Yellowstone officials considered closing the RV campground at Fishing Bridge, on the north end of Yellowstone Lake. The outcry was enormous, testimony to the immense popularity of RV travel, so the Fishing Bridge facility remains open today. You can drive most of the major roads in both parks with an RV or trailer, but there will be some areas where large vehicles are prohibited, and most of the camping areas don't provide hookups—Colter Bay, Flagg Ranch, and Fishing Bridge are the exceptions.

For details on rentals, contact **Cruise America,** a nationwide company that rents all sorts of RVS (© **480/464-7300;** www.cruise america.com).

6 Learning Vacations & Special Programs

One of the best ways to turn a park vacation into an unforgettable experience is to join an educational program. There are no finals in these courses; they're just a relaxed, informative way to spend time outdoors.

The **Yellowstone Association Institute** ★★, P.O. Box 117, Yellowstone National Park, WY 82190 (© 307/344-2294; www. yellowstoneassociation.org), operates at the historic Lamar Buffalo Ranch, on the road through the Lamar Valley to the park's northeast entrance. It offers more than 100 courses, winter and summer, covering everything from wildlife tracking in the snow, to wilderness medicine, to the history of fur trappers on the plateau. The courses, some of which are offered for college credit, run from 1 to 5 days, with forays into the field, and lectures and demonstrations at the Institute's cozy quarters. The classes are a study in camaraderie as well as natural history, with participants sharing meals and stories in the common kitchen. Prices are reasonable (around $60 a day for tuition), and some classes are specifically oriented to families and youngsters. To make the most of a class, you'll want to stay at the ranch itself, where simple, comfortable cabins are available for $20 a night per student.

New as of 2001, the Institute teamed with Yellowstone National Park Lodges to offer the best of two worlds: days spent exploring little-seen trails with knowledgeable and witty guides, and nights at the comfortable Mammoth Hot Springs Hotel. This four-night package, called "Trails Through Yellowstone," is an excellent option for those who want to delve into the park without too much of the traditional "roughing it." Rates (around $500 per person) include box lunches, breakfast, and in-park transportation. Contact the Yellowstone Association Institute (see above) or **Yellowstone National Park Lodges** (© **307/344-7311;** www.travelyellowstone. com) for reservations.

The **Teton Science School,** P.O. Box 68, Kelly, WY 83011 (© **307/733-4765;** www.tetonscience.org), is a 30-year-old institution, with a cabin campus in the park near the little town of Kelly, that offers summer and winter programs for students and adults. Classes cater to different ages, and the emphasis is on experiential, hands-on learning. College credit is available. Long and short classes review the ecology, geology, and wildlife of the park, with workshops in photography and tracking as well.

The school's **Wildlife Expeditions** (© **307/773-2623;** www. tetonscience.org) offers trips on open-roof vans, rafts, and sleighs and by foot. These tours bring visitors closer to the wildlife than they're likely to get on their own, and guests sometimes participate in radio tracking and other research projects. The institute offers trips from a half-day sunset safari to week-long trips through the park, usually lodging in park hotels. Adult seminars usually run $45 or $65 per day, but more inclusive ones cost $120 per day. Residential offerings for middle and high school students range from $1,100 for a 10-day course to $2,800 for a 5-week course. Elementary-age students can take nonresidential courses for $180 per week. Two-day Wildlife Expeditions run $350 per person, which includes some meals and accommodations.

7 Clothing & Equipment

Nothing will ruin a trip to the parks faster than sore or wet feet. Take some time planning your travel wardrobe. Bring comfortable walking shoes, even if you plan to keep walking to a minimum. Bring shoes that are broken in, and if you plan to do some serious hiking, get sturdy boots that support your ankles and wick away water. Early in the season, trails might be wet or muddy; late in the fall, you can get snowed on. The more popular trails are sometimes also used by horses, which can make stream crossings a mucky mess.

Wear your clothing in layers, and bring a small backpack or fanny pack so that you can take those layers off and on as temperature, altitude, and your physical exertion change. Gloves or mittens are useful before the park heats up, or in the evening when it cools down again, *even in summer.*

The atmosphere is thin at higher altitudes, so protect your skin. Bring a strong sunblock, a hat with a brim, and sunglasses. I also recommend bringing insect repellent, water bottles, and a first-aid kit (recommendations for its contents are discussed under "Protecting Your Health & Safety," below).

Take into account that elevations at the parks are between 5,000 and 11,000 feet; so, in campgrounds and on hiking trails, you'll want clothing appropriate to the temperatures—40°F in the evening, 75°F during the day.

8 Tips for Travelers with Special Needs

FOR TRAVELERS WITH DISABILITIES

In recent years, both parks have become more user-friendly for travelers with disabilities.

YELLOWSTONE   Accessible accommodations are located in the Cascade Lodge at Canyon Village, in Grant Village, in the Old Faithful Inn, and in the Lake Yellowstone Hotel. For a free *Visitors Guide to Accessible Features in Yellowstone National Park,* write to the **Park Accessibility Coordinator,** P.O. Box 168, YNP, WY 82190, or pick up the guide at the gates or visitor centers. There are **accessible campsites** at Madison, Canyon, and Grant campgrounds, which can be reserved by calling © 307/344-7311.

Accessible restrooms with sinks and flush toilets are located at all developed areas except West Thumb and Norris. Accessible vault toilets are found at West Thumb and Norris, as well as in most scenic areas and picnic areas.

Many of Yellowstone's **roadside attractions,** including the Grand Canyon of the Yellowstone's south rim, West Thumb Geyser Basin, much of the Norris and Upper Geyser Basins, and parts of the Mud Volcano and Fountain Paint Pot areas, are negotiable by wheelchair.

Visitor centers at Old Faithful, Grant Village, and Canyon are wheelchair-accessible, as are the Norris Museum and the Fishing Bridge Visitor Center.

Accessible parking is available at Old Faithful, Fishing Bridge, Canyon, Norris, and Grant Village, although you'll have to look for it; at some locations, it is near a Hamilton store.

GRAND TETON Campsites at Colter Bay, Jenny Lake, and Gros Ventre campgrounds are on relatively level terrain; Lizard Creek and Signal Mountain are hilly and less accessible. Picnic areas at String Lake and Cottonwood Creek are both accessible, although the toilet at Cottonwood is not.

Accessible dining facilities are located at Flagg Ranch, Leek's Marina, Colter Bay Village, Jackson Lake Lodge, and Jenny Lake Lodge.

Visitor centers at Moose, Colter Bay, Jenny Lake, and Flagg Ranch provide interpretive programs, displays, and visitor information in several formats, including visual, audible, and tactile. Large-print scripts, Braille brochures, and narrative audiotapes are available at Moose and Colter Bay.

Accessible parking spaces are located close to all visitor center entrances; curb cuts are provided, as are **accessible restroom facilities.**

More information is available by contacting **Grand Teton National Park,** Drawer 170, Moose, WY 83012 (© **307/739-3600;** www.nps.gov/grte).

FOR TRAVELERS WITH PETS

Domestic animals and wild animals don't mix well, and park regulations reflect that. So, as much as you might like traveling with Fido, don't bring him unless he likes the inside of a car and the end of a leash an awful lot. Pets must be leashed and are allowed only 25 feet away from roads and parking areas. They are prohibited on trails, in the backcountry, on boardwalks, and in thermal areas.

FOR TRAVELERS WITH CHILDREN

The best general advice I've discovered is in Lisa Evans's book *An Outdoor Family Guide to Yellowstone and Grand Teton National Parks*

(The Mountaineers, 1996). Another useful guide to consult is the latest edition of *Frommer's Family Vacations in the National Parks.* Both guides are easy to find in bookstores.

Older children will be entertained (distracted) and receive a nature lesson by enrolling in the **Yellowstone Junior Ranger Program** (no specific age restrictions) at any visitor center or ranger station. The $3 fee covers the cost of the activity paper for Junior Rangers, *Yellowstone's Nature,* which describes the requirements for attaining Junior Ranger status. Activities include attending a ranger-led program, hiking, and keeping a journal. When participants complete the program, it's announced to the public with great fanfare, and a patch is awarded.

The **Young Naturalist** program at **Grand Teton** provides children with a similar opportunity to explore the natural world of the park, following an activity brochure. It costs $1 to participate; when you complete the course, you're awarded a patch.

9 Protecting Your Health & Safety

Health hazards range from mild headaches to grizzly bear attacks, with their attendant high levels of pain and suffering.

Because most of us live at or near sea level, the most common health hazard is discomfort caused by **altitude sickness** as we adjust to the parks' high elevations, a process that could take a day or more. Symptoms include headache, fatigue, nausea, loss of appetite, muscle pain, and lightheadedness. Doctors recommend that, until acclimated, travelers should avoid heavy exertion, consume light meals, and drink lots of liquids, avoiding those with caffeine or alcohol.

Two waterborne hazards are **giardia** and **campylobacter,** with symptoms that wreak havoc on the human digestive system. If you pick up these pesky bugs, they might accompany you on your trip home. Untreated water from the parks' lakes and streams should be boiled for 3 to 6 minutes before consumption or pumped through a fine-mesh water filter specifically designed to remove giardia.

To be on the safe side, you might want to keep a **first-aid kit** in your car or luggage and have it handy when hiking. It should include, at the least, butterfly bandages, sterile gauze pads, adhesive tape, an antibiotic ointment, pain relievers for both children and adults, alcohol pads, a knife with scissors, and tweezers.

10 Planning a Backcountry Trip

While I've given the particulars for both Yellowstone and Grand Teton national parks in their respective chapters (see chapters 4,

Tips Bear Encounters

Most people have a healthy respect for bears, content to view them from a distance, but a close encounter can happen unexpectedly, and you need to know how to handle yourself. First, be aware that what matters most to a bear are food and cubs. If you get between a sow and her cubs, you could be in trouble. If a bear thinks that the food in your backpack is his, you have a problem.

Unless bears have already developed a taste for human food, though, they won't come looking for you. Make a lot of noise on the trail through bear habitat, and *Ursus horribilus* will give you a wide berth. Don't camp anywhere near the carcass of a dead animal; grizzlies sometimes partially bury carrion and return to it. Hang your food bag high in a tree, keep your cooking area distant from your campsite, and don't keep any food or utensils in your tent—or even clothes worn while cooking. Soaps and other perfumed items can also be attractants.

Avoid hiking at night or in meadowy mountain areas if visibility is poor. Bears have an extremely good sense of smell but poor eyesight.

If you encounter a bear, here are some things you should and should not do:

"Hikes & Other Outdoor Pursuits in Yellowstone National Park," and 6, "Hikes & Other Outdoor Pursuits in Grand Teton National Park"), there are some general things to keep in mind when planning a backcountry trip.

REGULATIONS   The theme in the backcountry is "leave no trace," and that means packing out any garbage you take in, not taking pets, and avoiding leaving scars on the landscape by staying on designated trails and reusing existing, designated campsites. Fires are allowed only in established fire rings, and only dead and downed material may be used for firewood; fires are prohibited in some areas, but backpacking stoves are allowed throughout the parks. You must have a park permit for overnight stays in the backcountry. The complete lists of do's and don'ts is available in the *Backcountry Trip Planner,* available at most visitor centers. For more information on "leave no trace" ethics, surf to **www.lnt.org**.

- **Do not run.** Anything that flees looks like prey to a bear, and it might attack. Bears can run at more than 30 mph. The bear might bluff charge, but you're best off holding your ground.
- **Avoid direct eye contact.**
- If the bear is unaware of you, **stay downwind** (so that it can't catch your scent) and **detour away from it slowly.**
- If the bear is aware of you but has not acted aggressively, **slowly back away.**
- **Do not climb a tree.** Although black bears have more suitable claws for climbing, grizzly bears can climb trees, too.
- If you're attacked, drop to the ground face down, clasp your hands over the back of your neck, tuck your knees to your chest, and **play dead.** Only as a last resort should you attempt to resist an attack and fight off a bear.
- If you carry **pepper spray,** be sure that it's handy when you're in potential bear habitat, not buried in your backpack. If you use it, aim for the bear's face and eyes. After you use it, leave the area: Bears have been seen returning to sniff about an area where spray has been used.

BACKPACKING FOR BEGINNERS   Be sure to wear comfortable, sturdy hiking shoes that will resist water if you're planning an early season hike; cotton socks are not a good idea because the material holds moisture, whereas wool and synthetics such as fleece "wick" it away from your body. Your sleeping bag should be rated for the low temperatures found at high elevations; if you bring a down bag, keep it dry or suffer the consequences. Most campers are happy to have a sleeping pad. The argument rages about the merits of old-fashioned, external-frame packs and the newer, internal-frame models. Over the long run, the newer versions are more stable and comfortable, but a big frame pack can shoulder bigger loads. Good padding, a lumbar support pad, and a wide hip belt are pluses. Be sure that you've tried out the pack—wear it around the house!—before you take it on a long trip with heavy loads, so that your body and the pack frame have a chance to adjust to each other.

PERSONAL SAFETY ISSUES   It's best not to hike alone, but if you must, be sure that you have told both park rangers and friends where you'll be and how long you'll be gone. Don't leave the parking lot without the following gear: a compass, topographical maps, a first-aid kit, bug repellent, toilet paper and a trowel of some sort, a flashlight, matches, a knife, a rope for hanging food supplies in a tree, and a bell or other noisemaker that hopefully will alert any bears in the neighborhood to your presence, as well as a tent, a stove, and a sleeping bag. At this altitude, sunscreen and sunglasses with UV protection are a wise addition. A recently developed bear repellent generically referred to as "pepper spray," available in most sporting goods stores, has proven successful in countering bear attacks. You'll also need iodine pills or a good water filter because that seemingly clear stream is filled with parasites that are likely to cause intestinal disorders. If you don't have iodine or a filter, boil water for at least 5 minutes before you drink it.

11 Recommended Reading

The following books are interesting, informative, and easy to find: *Yellowstone, A Visitor's Companion,* by George Wuerthner, Stackpole Books, Harrisburg, PA; *The Yellowstone Story* (2 volumes), by Aubrey Haines, Colorado Associated University Press; *Searching for Yellowstone,* by Paul Schullery, Mariner Books, New York; *Yellowstone Trails: A Hiking Guide,* by Mark C. Marschall, Yellowstone Association, Yellowstone National Park; *Exploring the Yellowstone Backcountry,* by Orville Bach Jr., Sierra Club Books, San Francisco; *Grand Teton National Park,* available from the Grand Teton Natural History Association; *A Guide to Exploring Grand Teton National Park,* by Linda L Olson and Tim Bywater, RNM Press, Salt Lake City, Utah; *Crucible for Conservation,* by Robert Righter, Grand Teton Natural History Association, Moose, Wyoming; and *Teton Trails: A Guide to the Trails of Grand Teton National Park,* by Katy Duffy and Darwin Wile, Grand Teton Natural History Association. Falcon Press (Helena, Montana) also publishes a long list of hiking, fishing, climbing, and other guides to the Yellowstone/Grand Teton region.

   If you cannot find these publications in your local bookstore, many can be ordered from either the **Yellowstone Association** (✆ 307/344-2293; www.yellowstoneassociation.org) or the **Grand Teton Natural History Association** (✆ 307/739-3403; www. grandtetonpark.org).

3

Exploring Yellowstone

You can sample the park in bite-size sections, or you can devote an entire summer to it. One trip, however long, never feels adequate; there's always a road not traveled. You can focus on the roadside highlights or venture deep into the backcountry. You can enjoy the old-style park hotels or pitch your own tent. You can learn about the geology and flora and fauna in visitor center exhibits or take an in-depth class with expert naturalists.

There are 370 miles (595km) of paved roadway in Yellowstone, with a figure-eight loop at the center that takes you to some key attractions: You can cover that ground in one long day. This is a common strategy, but it hardly scratches the surface. Ultimately, those who embark on it are selling the park short.

Give yourself a minimum of 3 days. Despite the crowds, you should check the famous sites because they're deserving of all the attention: **Old Faithful,** the **Grand Canyon of the Yellowstone, Fishing Bridge,** and **Washburn Peak.** If you're seeking knowledge, take a class at the **Yellowstone Association Institute,** or follow one of the rangers on a nature hike. If you want solitude, go early in the morning up one of the less trafficked trails, such as **Bunsen Peak** or **Mystic Falls.**

You'll find more details in the chapters that follow on where to hike, fish, sleep, and enjoy yourself in the park.

1 Essentials

ACCESS/ENTRY POINTS   Yellowstone has five entrances. The **north entrance,** near Mammoth Hot Springs, is located just south of Gardiner, Montana, and U.S. Highway 89. In the winter, this is the only access to Yellowstone by car.

The **west entrance,** just outside the town of West Yellowstone on U.S. Highway 20, is the closest entry to Old Faithful. Inside the park, you can turn south to Old Faithful or north to the Norris Geyser Basin. This entrance is open to wheeled vehicles from April to

Yellowstone National Park

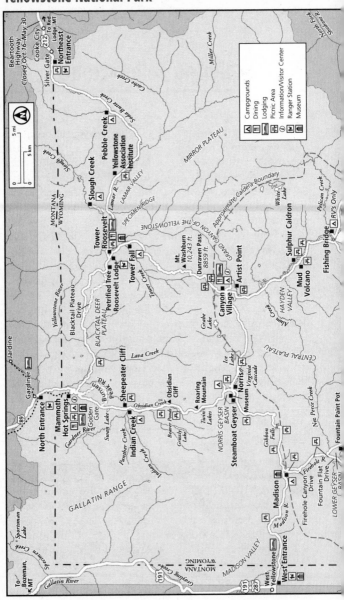

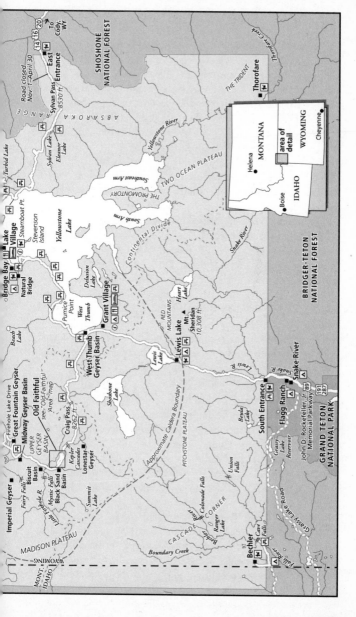

November and during the winter to snowmobiles and snow-coaches.

The **south entrance,** on U.S. Highway 89/191/287, brings visitors into the park from neighboring Grand Teton National Park and the Jackson area. On the way to Yellowstone, drivers get some panoramic views of the Teton Range. Once in the park, the road winds along the Lewis River to the south end of Yellowstone Lake, at West Thumb and Grant Village. It's open to cars from May to November and to snowmobiles and snowcoaches from December to March.

The **east entrance,** on U.S. Highway 14/16/20, is 52 miles (83km) west of Cody, Wyoming, and is open to cars from May to September and to snowmobiles and snowcoaches from December to March. The drive up the Wapiti Valley and over Sylvan Pass is especially beautiful, when not marred by road repair delays.

The **northeast entrance,** at Cooke City, Montana, is closest to the Tower-Roosevelt area, 29 miles (46km) to the west. This entrance is open to cars year-round, but beginning on October 15, when the Beartooth Highway closes, until around Memorial Day, the only route to Cooke City is through Mammoth Hot Springs. When it's open, the drive from Red Lodge to the park is a grand climb among the clouds.

Regardless of which entrance you choose, you'll be given a good map and up-to-date information on facilities, services, programs, fishing, camping, and more.

VISITOR CENTERS　There are five major visitor and information centers in the park, and each has something different to offer. Unless otherwise indicated, summer hours are 8am to 7pm.

The **Albright Visitor Center** (✆ **307/344-2263**), at Mammoth Hot Springs, is the largest and is open year-round. It provides visitor information and publications about the park, has exhibits depicting park history from prehistory through the creation of the National Park Service, and houses a wildlife display on the second floor.

The **Old Faithful Visitor Center** (✆ **307/545-2750**) is another large facility. An excellent short film describing the microscopic inhabitants of the geysers, *Yellowstone Revealed,* is shown throughout the day in an air-conditioned auditorium. Rangers dispense various park publications and post projected geyser eruption times here. By 2003, the Park Service hopes to open a state-of-the-art $15-million visitor education center in place of the current architecturally maligned building.

The **Canyon Visitor Center** (© 307/242-2550), in Canyon Village, is the place to go for books and an informative display about bison in the park. It's staffed with friendly rangers used to dealing with crowds.

The **Fishing Bridge Visitor Center** (© 307/242-2450), near Fishing Bridge on the north shore of Yellowstone Lake, has an excellent wildlife display. You can get information and publications here as well.

The **Grant Village Visitor Center** (© 307/242-2650) has information, publications, a video program, and a fascinating exhibit that examines the effects of fire in Yellowstone.

All five of the major visitor centers began screenings of a new Discovery Channel–produced film, *Hidden Yellowstone,* in fall 2001.

Helpful staff and park literature can also be found at a trio of small information stations: the **Madison Information Station** (© 307/344-2821); the **Museum of the National Park Ranger** (no phone; open daily in summer 9am–6pm) and the **Norris Geyser Basin Museum** (© 307/344-2812; open daily in summer 10am–5pm), both at Norris; and the **West Thumb Information Station** (no phone; open daily in summer 9am–5pm). These don't have the museum-quality exhibits that you'll find at the larger centers, but they are well equipped to answer questions and offer advice on almost any subject about Yellowstone.

ENTRANCE FEES   Park users are now asked to share more of the burden of park costs with taxpayers, but fees are still moderate: A 7-day pass costs $20 per automobile and covers both Yellowstone and Grand Teton national parks. A snowmobile or motorcycle costs $15 for 7 days, and someone who comes in on bicycle, skis, or foot pays $10. If you expect to visit the parks more than once in a year, buy an annual permit for $40. And if you visit parks and national monuments around the country, purchase a **Golden Eagle Passport** for $65 (good for 365 days from the date of purchase at nearly all federal preserves) or a $50 **National Parks Pass.** Anyone aged 62 or older can get a **Golden Age Passport** for a one-time fee of $10, and blind or permanently disabled people can obtain a **Golden Access Passport,** which costs nothing. All passes are available at any entrance point to Yellowstone. While the Golden Age and Golden Access passports must be purchased in person (to verify age or disability), the National Parks Pass and the Golden Eagle Passport are also available online at **www.nps.gov** or by phone at © **888/ GO-PARKS.**

CAMPING FEES   Fees for camping in Yellowstone range from $10 to $15 per night, depending on the number of amenities the campground offers. The RV Campground at Fishing Bridge charges $28 per night and has full hookups; while other campgrounds have sites suitable for RVs, this is the only one with hookups, and only RVs are allowed here. Flagg Ranch, just outside the south entrance, also has an RV camp with hookups.

For more information on camping, see the "Where to Camp in Yellowstone" section in chapter 7, "Where to Stay & Dine in the Parks." It is possible to make advance reservations at some campgrounds in both parks.

SPECIAL REGULATIONS & WARNINGS   More detailed information about these rules can be requested from the park rangers or at visitor centers throughout the parks or at **www.nps. gov/yell**.

- **Bicycles**   Bicycles are not allowed on the park's trails or boardwalks, but there are some designated off-pavement bicycling areas—contact the park for more information. Helmets and bright clothing are recommended because of the narrow, winding nature of park roads and the large recreational vehicles with poor visibility.

- **Camping**   In any given year, a person may camp for no more than 30 days in the park, and only 14 days during the summer season. Food, garbage, and food utensils must be stored in a vehicle or container made of solid material and must be suspended at least 10 feet above the ground when not in use.

- **Climbing**   Because of the loose, crumbly rock in Yellowstone, climbing is discouraged throughout the park and is prohibited in the Grand Canyon of the Yellowstone.

- **Defacing park features**   Picking wildflowers and collecting natural or archaeological objects, is illegal. Only dead-and-down wood can be collected for backcountry campfires.

- **Firearms**   Firearms are not allowed in either park. However, unloaded firearms may be transported in a vehicle when cased, broken down, or rendered inoperable, and on certain trails for access to areas outside the park, with a special permit. Ammunition must be carried in a separate compartment of the vehicle.

- **Littering**   Littering in the national parks is strictly prohibited—remember, if you take it in, you have to take it out. Throwing coins or other objects into thermal features is illegal.

- **Motorcycles** Motorcycles, motor scooters, and motorbikes are allowed only on park roads. No off-road or trail riding is allowed. Operator licenses and license plates are required.

- **Pets** Pets must be leashed and are prohibited in the back-country, on trails, on boardwalks, and in thermal areas, for obvious reasons. If you tie up a pet and leave it, you're breaking the law.

- **Smoking** No smoking is allowed in thermal areas, visitor centers or rangers stations, or any other posted public areas.

- **Snowmobiling** Pending litigation, snowmobiling in Yellowstone could be banned by 2003. Regardless, snowmobilers must have valid drivers licenses, stay on the designated unplowed roadways, and obey posted speed limits.

- **Swimming** Swimming or wading is prohibited in thermal features or in streams whose waters flow from thermal features in Yellowstone. (One exception is the "Boiling River" near Mammoth, where visitors can take a warm soak between dawn and dusk except during spring runoff.) Swimming in Yellowstone Lake is discouraged because of the low water temperature and unpredictable weather.

- **Wildlife** It is unlawful to approach within 100 yards of a bear or within 25 yards of other wildlife. Feeding any wildlife is illegal. Wildlife calls such as elk bugles or other artificial attractants are forbidden.

 FAST FACTS: Yellowstone

ATMs There are numerous ATMs in the park: at Old Faithful Inn, Old Faithful Snow Lodge, Old Faithful Upper Store, Grant Village General Store, Canyon Lodge, Canyon General Store, Fishing Bridge General Store, Lake Hotel, and Mammoth Hot Springs Hotel and General Store.

Car Trouble/Towing Services If you have car trouble, you'll find car repair shops in Old Faithful, Canyon Village, Fishing Bridge, and Grant Village. Call the park's main information line (✆ 307/344-7381) 24 hours a day if you need to be towed.

Emergencies Call ✆ 911 or the park's main information number (✆ 307/344-7381), which is staffed 24 hours a day.

Gas Stations You can purchase gasoline at Old Faithful, Canyon Village, Grant Village, Mammoth Hot Springs, Fishing Bridge, and Tower Junction.

Laundry There are laundry facilities at Fishing Bridge RV Park, Canyon Village campground, and Grant Village Campground.

Medical Services There are three **medical clinics** in the park: at Mammoth Hot Springs (© **307/344-7965**), Old Faith-ful (© **307/545-7325**), and the Lake Hotel (© **307/242-7241**), where there is a pharmacy and a small hospital. The Lake and Old Faithful clinics are open daily from May to early fall, while the Mammoth clinic is open weekdays year-round.

Permits You can obtain fishing and backcountry permits at most visitor centers. See "Special Permits," in chapter 2, "Planning Your Trip to Yellowstone & Grand Teton National Parks," for more information.

Post Offices All of the major visitor centers in Yellowstone have post offices (Mammoth, Old Faithful, Grant Village, Lake Village, and Canyon Village).

Supplies Hamilton stores are located in all the park villages, with groceries, film and camera supplies, camping gear, and souvenirs.

Weather Updates For weather updates and road conditions, call the park's main information number (© **307/344- 7381**), which has recorded information.

2 The Highlights

This is a wonderland that you can return to again and again, sampling a different pleasure each time. All the sites mentioned here are easily accessible along the loop roads of the park. But the farther you get from the pavement, and the farther from July and August you schedule your visit, the more private your experience will be.

THE UPPER LOOP

MAMMOTH HOT SPRINGS   Here, 5 miles (8km) south of the park's north entrance at Gardiner, Montana, you'll find some of the park's spectacular thermal areas, including unique limestone terraces (the **Upper and Lower terraces** ⊕, which are described in section 4, "Yellowstone: The Extended Tour"). The Albright Visitor Center is here, with some interesting exhibits and a bookstore, as well as the

---

Tips **Choosing Your Route**

If you are considering making your trip to the parks before mid-June, think about beginning your exploration in Grand Teton and working north to Yellowstone. Elevations in Grand Teton are slightly lower and snow melts earlier, so accumulations on trails are reduced and temperatures are more moderate.

Mammoth Hot Springs Hotel. Your best bet: Follow the interpretive trail through the terraces.

NORRIS GEYSER BASIN 🐾🐾 South of Mammoth Hot Springs, you'll find several impressive **geysers,** geothermal areas of different type and age, as well as two museums. Norris is conveniently close to the west entrance of the park at West Yellowstone. You can follow boardwalks north and south (the south has more activity, but the north takes you across the dramatic Porcelain Basin). Best bet: Tour both of them.

CANYON VILLAGE AREA East of Norris, the **Grand Canyon of the Yellowstone River** 🐾 provides some of the park's best views. There are hikes of all lengths and for all abilities here. Canyon Village is one of the most developed sections of the park, with lots of facilities, including comfortable new lodges. The canyon might not be as big as the Grand Canyon in Arizona, but it's got its own dynamic beauty.

TOWER-ROOSEVELT AREA The closest of the major park areas to the northeast entrance (which is near Cooke City, Montana), this is also one of the most easygoing areas of the park, away from the big crowds and a short drive from the beautiful **Lamar Valley** 🐾🐾. The Roosevelt Lodge Cabins are a good budget lodging if you want to rough it, and **Tower Falls** provides a dramatic backdrop for photos. Your best bet: Try the buckboard ride from Roosevelt Lodge to the **evening Old West cookout.**

THE LOWER LOOP

OLD FAITHFUL AREA **Old Faithful** remains an enduring symbol of Yellowstone, even as it slows down with age, and you'll find the benches filled for each eruption. The historic **Old Faithful Inn** (with its fine restaurant) is located here, and the new **Old Faithful Snow Lodge** is a great addition. The most convenient access is from West Yellowstone and the park's west entrance. And don't miss the **Riverside Geyser.** Your best bet: Climb to the top of **Observation Point** for a lesser-seen view of Old Faithful's classic burst.

LAKE VILLAGE AREA   On the north shore of Yellowstone Lake you'll find many fishing and boating opportunities, as well as fine dining and lodging choices. The **Lake Hotel** is one of the two best choices in the park. This area is the closest to Yellowstone's east entrance, which is about 50 miles (80km) from Cody, Wyoming. The **Hayden Valley** is nearby. You can rent a boat at Bay Bridge to get out and try to catch one of those intrusive lake trout. Best bet: Take a sunset tour from Lake Hotel in one of Yellowstone National Park Lodges' classic 1930s touring buses.

GRANT VILLAGE/WEST THUMB AREAS   Grant Village is the southernmost of the park's developments, a nondescript collection of modern buildings on the south end of Yellowstone Lake. The **West Thumb Geyser Basin** and the Grant Village Visitor Center are nearby. West Thumb has a lakeside boardwalk that allows views of geysers that are on both sides of the water's edge. Best bet: Take an afternoon stroll on the boardwalks and gander at some of the jewels of Yellowstone's geothermal wonders.

3 If You Have Only 1 or 2 Days (the Short Tour)

If you are so pinched for time that you have only 1 or 2 days to tour Yellowstone, here's an itinerary that highlights the best of the best. If you'll be spending the night, your best bets are to reserve a room at either Old Faithful Inn or the Lake Hotel—if those are booked, try the new Old Faithful Snow Lodge, or get a campsite at Norris or Indian Creek. Other options along the itinerary route are given below.

The quickest route to the inner road loops of the park is by the west entrance road, so come in that way, stopping perhaps for a stroll along the banks of the **Madison River,** where you can see the forest recovering from the 1988 fires. You'll also spot wildlife: ducks and trumpeter swans on the river, and grazing elk and bison. Turn north at Madison Junction to **Norris Geyser Basin,** where there are two boardwalk tours; take the southern one, if you're in a hurry, because there you can wait for the **Echinus Geyser** pool to fill and erupt.

You're now driving the **upper loop,** which goes north to **Mammoth Hot Springs,** east to **Tower-Roosevelt,** south to **Canyon Village,** and west again to Norris, finally returning to Madison

Junction, a circuit of about 85 miles (137km) . If you go south rather than west at Canyon Village, you'll be on the southern loop, which will take you to **Fishing Bridge** and **Lake Village,** then by **West Thumb,** west over Craig Pass to **Old Faithful,** and back to the Madison Junction. The entire lower loop covers 96 miles (154km).

Altogether, this 2-day circuit is called the **Grand Loop,** taking you through all the major areas of the park except the road between Norris and Canyon Village. You could do it in a day—it's only 120 miles (193km) long—but you'd scare a lot of other travelers as you sped by.

THE UPPER LOOP   If you're pressed for time, the Norris Geyser Basin is a major concentration of **thermal attractions,** including Porcelain Basin, and has a nice museum that explains the park's red-hot underpinnings. Mammoth has one of the park's major attractions, the ever-growing **terraces** of Mammoth Hot Springs. In addition to the natural attraction, the **Albright Visitor Center** provides excellent historical background for everything you'll see in the park. There is a fine old hotel at Mammoth and lodging just outside the park in Gardiner, too, but I recommend that you continue farther around the loop on your first day.

From Mammoth, the route winds through forested areas that lead to the edge of the **Lamar Valley,** a deep, rounded path for the Lamar River that is a prime haven for wolves, bison, elk, and grizzly bears. If you want to spend a quiet night out here, a rustic option, especially good for families, is the nearby Roosevelt Lodge. Otherwise, you can continue south to Yellowstone's **Grand Canyon,** one of the most dramatic sights in the park.

THE LOWER LOOP   This is the better way to go if you have only a day. You'll also see the two largest geyser areas in Yellowstone—**Norris** to the north and the park's signature attraction, **Old Faithful,** to the south. On the eastern side of this route, you'll find the **Grand Canyon of the Yellowstone** and **Hayden Valley,** where you'll find resident herds of buffalo. Farther south, the **Yellowstone Lake** area is a haven for water-sports fans: There's fishing, boating, and places for picnicking on the shore of the lake.

4 Yellowstone: The Extended Tour

Stretching your visit to 4 or 5 days has several advantages. You'll have more time to visit the roadside highlights, plus you can walk a few of the trails and actually learn from the exhibits at the visitor centers instead of just blasting by them.

The **visitor centers** are a good source of information about the ecosystem, the flora and fauna, and the history of the park; knowledgeable rangers are on hand who can answer your questions. There are eight altogether (see section 1, "Essentials," earlier in this chapter, for a complete list), but some might be closed if you visit the parks during the off-seasons. The **Albright Visitor Center** is open year-round, and the **Old Faithful Visitor Center** is open during summer months and December to March. The others usually open concurrently with the lodging facilities in their area of the park. Ask the rangers about programs in their area, and check whether any geothermal features have undergone a change in their activity recently—geysers have been known to revive suddenly after years of quiescence.

The roads in Yellowstone are organized into a series of interconnecting loops, which you can come into from any of the park's five entrances. To simplify things, I will discuss attractions and activities going clockwise along each section of the **Grand Loop Road,** beginning at the **Madison Junction.** But you can enter the loop at any point and pick up this tour as long as you are traveling clockwise. I haven't suggested an optimum amount of time to spend on each leg of the loop because that will depend on your particular interests. If you want to get away from the crowds, take your time and try to get off the pavement and out into the park away from the main roads.

WEST YELLOWSTONE TO NORRIS
Closest entrance: West Yellowstone (west entrance).

Distances: 14 miles (22km) from West Yellowstone to Madison; 14 miles (22km) from Madison to Norris.

Because the largest percentage of visitors to Yellowstone enter at the **west entrance,** I'll use that as a jumping-off point to begin an extended tour of the park. As you travel the 14 miles (22km) from the gate to **Madison Junction,** you will find the **Two Ribbons Trail,** which offers an opportunity to walk through and inspect the effects of the 1988 fire. The trailhead is 3 miles (5km) east of the West Yellowstone entrance at a well-marked turnout. Along this ¾-mile (1km) loop trail, you'll see a mosaic of blackened, singed, and unburned timber—charred snags and green trees side by side among boulders shattered by the heat. A testament to the regenerative effects of fire, millions of bright green saplings have emerged from the soil that surrounds the scraggly, deformed branches and piles of rock.

Park maps don't identify all the observation points and side roads in the area, so now is the time to begin forming the habit of driving off the beaten path, even when you might not know where you're going. Keep a sharp eye peeled for the poorly marked **riverside turnout** on the Madison River side of the road; it's a paved road on the north side of the highway about 6 miles (9.5km) from the entrance. This back road takes you along a river, removed from most traffic, with a number of turnouts perfectly situated to look for resident swans, enjoy a picnic, or test your fly-fishing ability.

As you continue toward Madison Junction, you'll see more vivid evidence of the 1988 fire and, odds are, a herd of bison that frequents the area during summer months. As frightening as the fire was, it had its good points: There is evidence that the 1988 fire burned hotter here because the old lodgepole pines had been infected by beetles, decimating the trees long before the fires blazed. The good news is that the fire killed the beetles and remineralized the soil. When temperatures exceeded 500°F, pine seeds were released from fire-adapted pinecones, quickening the rebirth cycle. The hundreds of tiny trees poking through the soil are evidence that the forest is recovering quickly.

The ½-mile (1km) round-trip **Harlequin Lake Trail,** located 1½ miles (2.5km) west of the Madison campground on the West Entrance Road, offers an excellent, easy opportunity to explore the area. It winds through the burned forest to a small lake that is populated by various types of waterfowl. Regardless of the trail's moniker, however, sightings of the rare harlequin ducks are uncommon.

An alternative hike, one of the best in the area, is up the **Purple Mountain Trail,** which begins ¼ mile (0.5km) north of the Madison Junction on the Norris Road. This hike requires more physical exertion because it winds 6 miles (9.5km) (round-trip) through a burned forest to the top of a large hill, with an elevation gain of 1,400 feet.

Madison Junction is a focal point of the most widely known Yellowstone myth, namely that, in September 1870, Cornelius Hedges and a group of explorers agreed that the land should be protected from those who would exploit its resources and began making plans to promote the creation of a national park. In reality, this conversation never happened. Madison Junction is also the confluence of the Gibbon and Firehole rivers, two famous trout streams that meet to form the Madison River, one of three that join to form the Missouri.

The **Madison Campground,** one of the largest and most popular in the park, is situated at the junction, with hiking trails and sites in view of the river. If you're planning a stay here, it's wise to arrive by 8am or you might be disappointed.

This is where you'll enter the northern loop toward Norris Junction, along a windy 14-mile (22km) section of road that parallels the **Gibbon River.** The river was named for Gen. John Gibbon, who explored here in 1872 but whose main, dubious, claims to fame were as the cavalry leader who buried Custer's army and who chased Chief Joseph and the Nez Perce Indians from the park as they attempted to escape to Canada.

At 84-foot **Gibbon Falls,** you'll see water bursting out of the edge of a caldera in a rocky canyon, the walls of which were hidden from view for several hundred years until being exposed by the fire of 1988. There's a delightful **picnic area** just below the falls on an open plateau overlooking the Gibbon River.

Before arriving at Norris Junction, you'll discover the **Artist Paint Pot Trail** in Gibbon Meadows, 4½ miles (7km) south of the Norris Junction, an interesting, worthwhile, and easy ½-mile (1km) stroll that winds through a lodgepole-pine forest to a gurgling mud pot at the top of a hill. This thermal area contains some small geysers, hot pools, and steam vents.

Across the road from the trailhead is **Elk Park,** where you can expect to see a large resident herd of the majestic ungulates.

NORRIS GEYSER BASIN
Closest entrances & distances: 28 miles (45km) from West Yellowstone (west) entrance; 26 miles (42km) from Gardiner (north) entrance.

Perhaps more than any other area in Yellowstone, this basin is living testimony to the park's unique thermal activity. It is never the same, changing from year to year as thermal activity and the ravages of wind, rain, and snow create new and different ponds and landscapes. Trees fall, slides occur, and geysers erupt. The **Norris Geyser Basin** 🎯🎯 was named for the second superintendent of the park, the outgoing Philetus Norris whose name graces many park roads and attractions. It is also the location of one of the park's highest concentration of thermal features, including the most active geysers, with underground water temperatures that reach 459°F.

There are two loop trails here, both fairly level with wheelchair access, to the Porcelain Basin and the Back Basin. If you complete both of them, you'll see most of the area's interesting thermal features. If you're pressed for time, take the shorter **Porcelain Basin Trail,** a ¾-mile (1km) round-trip that can be completed in 45 minutes. Along this boardwalk are Black Growler Steam Vent, Ledge Geyser, and descriptively named Whale's Mouth. To me, this area is especially spectacular on summer days when thermal activity takes place on the ground and thunder and lightning storms boom overhead.

The 1½-mile (2.5km) **Back Basin Loop** is easily negotiable in 1 hour and passes by **Steamboat Geyser,** which has been known to produce the world's highest and most memorable eruptions. However, these 400-foot waterspouts occur infrequently, so it will take some luck to see one—the last two eruptions were in 1991 and 2000. Conversely, **Echinus Geyser** farther down the trail erupts several times a day.

Among the many highlights of the area is the **Norris Geyser Basin Museum,** a beautiful single-story stone-and-log building, the stone archway of which leads to an overlook of the Porcelain Basin. The museum houses several excellent exhibits that explain the nature of the area; with luck, you'll arrive in time for a ranger-led tour. In the past, ranger programs have been scheduled four times a day; ask at a visitor center for current schedules.

Also nearby is the **Museum of the National Park Ranger,** which is little more than a room full of artifacts in a small building near the Norris Campground (see below).

Both museums open in mid- to late May, weather permitting, and are open until September; hours vary by season, but you can expect the museums to be open from 9 or 10am to 5 or 6pm during the busiest times (roughly Memorial Day to Labor Day, but, again, weather is a factor here).

The **Norris Campground,** which is just slightly north of the Norris Junction, is another very popular campground, so plan an early arrival or be prepared to look for an alternative site, which isn't

---

Tips **Watch Your Step!**

In thermal areas, the ground might be only a thin crust above boiling hot springs, and there's no way to guess where a safe path is. New hazards can bubble up overnight, and pools are acidic enough to burn through boots; so, you must stay in designated walking areas.

easy during the peak season. Part of the appeal of the campground is its proximity to the Gibbon River and to an old cavalry building from the 1880s, which houses the Museum of the National Park Ranger.

NORRIS TO MAMMOTH HOT SPRINGS

Closest entrances: Norris is 28 miles (45km) from the West Yellowstone (west) entrance; Mammoth Hot Springs is 5 miles (8km) from the Gardiner (north) entrance.

Distance: 21 miles (34km) from Norris to Mammoth Hot Springs.

From Norris Geyser Basin, it's a 21-mile (34km) drive north to Mammoth Hot Springs, past the **Twin Lakes,** beautiful, watery jewels surrounded by trees. During the early months of the park year, the water is milky green because of the runoff of ice and snow. This is an excellent place to do some bird watching.

This stretch of road between Norris Junction and Mammoth Hot Springs presents yet another excellent opportunity to see the effects of the 1988 fire. Try to use one of the turnouts to avoid blocking the roads. The large **meadow** on the west side of the highway that begins 3 miles (5km) from Norris is popular with moose, thanks to water from bogs, marshes, and a creek. As you travel alongside **Obsidian Creek,** you'll notice the smell of sulfur in the air, olfactory evidence of thermal vents.

On the east side of the road 4 miles (6.5km) from Norris is **Roaring Mountain,** a patch of ground totally devoid of brush and plant life, covered with trees and stumps from the fire. Its bareness is attributed to the fact that, as steam vents developed here, the ground became hot and acidic, which bleached and crumbled the rock, taking the undergrowth with it. Historians say that the noise from the Roaring Mountain was once so loud that it could be heard as far as 4 miles (6.5km) away; these days, it is very quiet.

Just up the road 2 miles (3km) is the **Beaver Lake Picnic Area,** an excellent little spot for a snack. Keep an eye out for moose.

As you wend your way a half-mile (1km) to **Obsidian Cliff,** the terrain changes quickly and dramatically, and you'll find yourself driving through a narrow valley bisected by a beautiful green stream. Obsidian Cliff is where ancient peoples of North America gathered to collect obsidian, a hard, black rock that was used to make weapons and tools.

If you didn't stop at Beaver Lake, consider taking time for a short (3-min.) detour on the road to **Sheepeater Cliffs** (unless you're driving an RV or pulling a trailer), which, like most park attractions, is in a well-marked area just off the pavement. Though close to the main road, this quiet, secluded spot sits on the banks of the Gardner River beside a cliff comprised of columnar basalt rock that was formed by cooling lava following a volcanic eruption. This area, once inhabited by the Sheepeater Indians, is today home to yellow-bellied marmots (nicknamed "whistle pigs") that live in the rocks, safe from flying predators and coyotes.

As you travel the final few miles to Mammoth Hot Springs, you'll be in an area whose geologic diversity is especially interesting. You'll see evidence of the fire, large springs and ponds, and enormous glaciated rock terraces and cliffs.

Exiting the valley, head north onto a high plateau, where you'll find **Swan Lake,** flanked by Little Quadrant Mountain and Antler Peak to the west, and Bunsen Peak to the north.

At the northernmost edge of the Yellowstone Plateau, you'll begin a descent through **Golden Gate.** This steep, narrow stretch of road was once a stagecoach route constructed of wooden planks anchored to the mountain by a massive rock called the **Pillar of Hercules,** the largest rock in an unmarked pile that sits next to the road.

Beyond Hercules are **The Hoodoos,** an ominous-looking jumble of travertine boulders on the north side of the road that have tumbled off the mountainside above to create a pile of unusual formations.

From the 45th parallel parking area on the North Entrance Road north of Mammoth Hot Springs, a short hike leads to the **Boiling River** 🎿🎿. Here you can take a dip during daylight hours, where a hot spring empties into the Gardner River. The best time to soak is around sunset, tending to muscles made sore by hiking, and you'll get a dramatic demonstration by the hordes of bats in the area. As far as facilities go, there is only a restroom with pit toilets here.

MAMMOTH HOT SPRINGS
Closest entrance and distance: 5 miles (8km) from the Gardiner (north) entrance.

This area might offer the best argument for getting off the roads, out of your car, and into the environment. Although it's possible to see most of the wildlife and the major thermal areas from behind car windows, your experience of the park will be multiplied tenfold through the expenditure of a small amount of energy. Most people in average shape are capable of negotiating the trails here, a signifi-cant percentage of which are level or only moderately inclined boardwalks. Even the more challenging trails frequently have rest areas where you can catch your breath or, more important, stop and absorb the magnificent views.

One of Yellowstone's most unique, beautiful, and fascinating areas is the **Upper** and **Lower terraces** . Strolling among them, you can observe Mother Nature going about the business of mixing and matching heat, water, limestone, and rock fractures to sculpt the area. This is one of the most colorful areas in the park; its tapestries of orange, pink, yellow, green, and brown, formed by masses of bacteria and algae, seem to change colors before your eyes.

The mineral-rich hot waters that flow to the surface here do so at an unusually constant rate, roughly 750,000 gallons per day, which results in the deposit of almost 2 tons of limestone every 24 hours. Contours are constantly changing in the hot springs as formations are shaped by large quantities of flowing water, the slope of the ground, and trees and rocks that determine the direction of the flow.

On the flip side of the equation, nature has a way of playing tricks on some of her creatures: **Poison Spring** is a sinkhole on the trail, so named because carbon dioxide collects there, often killing creatures that stop for a drink.

The **Lower Terrace Interpretive Trail** is one of the best ways to see this area. The trail starts at 6,280 feet and climbs another 300 feet along rather steep grades through a bare, rocky, thermal region to a flat alpine area and observation deck at the top. A park guide says that the 1½-mile (2km) round-trip walk to the Upper Terrace and back takes 2 hours, but it can be done in less.

Liberty Cap is a 37-foot-tall dome at the entrance to the interpretive trail. Once the site of a percolating hot spring, the domed Cap deposit is the result of 2,500 years of continuous gushing. The Hayden Expedition named it because of its resemblance to hats worn by Colonial patriots during the French Revolution.

After passing **Palette Spring,** where bacteria create a collage of browns, greens, and oranges, you're on your way to **Cleopatra** and **Minerva terraces.** Minerva is a favorite of visitors because of its bright colors and travertine formations, the product of limestone deposits. In nature's way, these attractions occasionally become unruly and spray deposits of water and mineral deposits large enough to bury the boardwalk.

The hike up the last 150 feet to the Upper Terrace Loop Drive is slightly steeper, although there are benches at frequent intervals. From here you can see all the terraces and several springs—**Canary Spring** and **New Blue Spring** being the most distinctive—and the

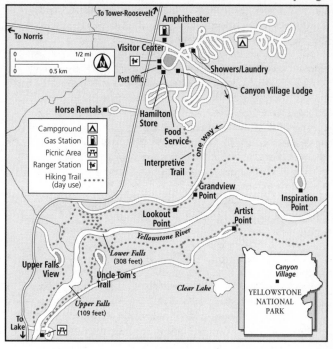

red-roof buildings of **Fort Yellowstone,** which is now the park headquarters.

Near Fort Yellowstone is the large **Albright Visitor Center** (© **307/344-2263**), which has more visitor information and publications than other centers, along with significant exhibits telling the story of the park from prehistory through the creation of the National Park Service. It's open from 8am to 8pm during peak season. Enclosed in floor-to-ceiling glass cases are uniforms, furniture, sidearms, and memorabilia that reflect the park's varied human history. There are excellent photography exhibits, much of it by the first park photographer, William Henry Jackson. A second level is filled with displays of the wildlife that inhabits the park, including wolves, mountain lions, waterfowl, and other birds. Films on the park's origin and the art that it has inspired are shown throughout the day.

If you wish, you can continue walking along **Upper Terrace Loop Drive,** which is also accessible by car. The Upper Terrace has its own unique attractions, including **New Highland Terrace,** which is a forest of tree skeletons engulfed by travertine, and **Angel Terrace,** known for its pure white formations.

Just steps from the lower terrace is the trailhead for the **Beaver Ponds Loop Trail,** a 5-mile (8km) jaunt through shaded woods along a trail that follows **Clematis Creek.** The ponds, which have been dammed by beavers, are some 2½ easy miles (4km) from the trailhead. You might be forced to adjust your body clock to catch a glimpse of these toothy engineers because they're most active early in the morning and in the evening. The area is also a hangout for elk, pronghorn, and bears, so it might be closed early in the year. If you get tired, there are several shady areas along the creek to stop and soak your feet.

MAMMOTH HOT SPRINGS TO TOWER JUNCTION

Closest entrance: Mammoth is 5 miles (8km) from the Gardiner (north) entrance.

Distance: 18 miles (29km) from Mammoth to Tower.

Heading east from Mammoth on Tower Road, a 6-mile (9.5km) drive will bring you to the **All Person's Fire Trail,** so named because this flat, easy stroll along a boardwalk offers an excellent opportunity to educate yourself about the effects of the fire on the environment.

Two miles (3km) later is **Blacktail Plateau Drive,** a 7-mile (11km), one-way dirt road that offers great wildlife-viewing opportunities and a bit more solitude. You'll be more or less following the route of the Bannock Trail, made by the long-vanished Indian inhabitants of the area. For centuries, the trail was used by Bannock Indians as they trekked from Idaho to buffalo hunting grounds in eastern Montana; scars in the land made by their travois—twin poles tied to a horse that were used as a luggage rack—are still evident along the trail. You'll emerge back onto Mammoth–Tower Road, about a mile (1.5km) west of the turnoff to the Petrified Tree.

Turn right onto this half-mile (1km) long road to the **Petrified Tree,** a redwood that, while standing, was burned by volcanic ash more than 50 million years ago. If you have the time and energy, park your car at the base of the road after you turn off Mammoth–Tower Road and hike up because the parking area is often congested. After your stop, continue on to Tower Junction.

TOWER-ROOSEVELT

Closest entrances & distances: 23 miles (37km) from the Gardiner (north) entrance; 29 miles (46km) from the Cooke City (northeast) entrance.

Just beyond the Petrified Tree, you'll come to **Tower-Roosevelt,** the most relaxed of the park's villages and a great place to take a break from the more crowded attractions. Even if you aren't going to stay, you might want to make a quick stop at the **Tower Soldier Station,** now the ranger residence at Tower Junction, one of three surviving outposts from the era of U.S. Cavalry management of the park. Also here is **Roosevelt Lodge,** a rustic building that commemorates President Theodore Roosevelt's camping excursion to this area of the park in 1903. It now serves as a dining hall, bar, and registration area for visitors staying at nearby frontier cabins. You can get into the cowboy spirit by taking a guided trail ride, a stagecoach ride, or a wagon ride. A more adventurous alternative to the rather rustic dining-room atmosphere at Roosevelt Lodge is the lodge's Old West cookout to which you will arrive by either horseback or wagon for a hearty meal (see "Where to Dine in Yellowstone," in chapter 7 for more details). There's a range of other services in this spot, including a Hamilton store if you need to buy provisions, and a gas station.

At **Specimen Ridge,** 2½ miles (4km) east of the Tower Junction on the Northeast Entrance Road, you'll find a ridge that entombs one of the world's most extensive fossil forests. Between 45 million and 50 million years ago, the mature forest that stood here was engulfed by deep volcanic ash some 27 times; subsequent erosion has exposed more than 100 different fossilized species in an area that spans 40 square miles.

A DETOUR: THE CHIEF JOSEPH HIGHWAY
Closest entrance & distance: 29 miles (46km) to the Cooke City (east) entrance.

Because all the major attractions in Yellowstone are located on the loop roads, some of the park's most beautiful and secluded areas go unnoticed by travelers. If you have an additional day or two, I suggest that you head for the eastern entrances on another loop tour. From Tower Junction, go east to Cooke City and then continue to Cody; or, from Fishing Bridge, head across Sylvan Pass to Cody. If you hurry, you can complete the trip in a day, although you'll miss the Cody rodeo.

From **Tower Junction,** you'll traverse the **Lamar Valley** ⚘⚘, one of the prettiest and lesser-traveled areas of the park. This area was covered with a thick crust of ice during the last ice age, which began 25,000 years ago and ended 10,000 years later, leaving a valley shaped by melting glaciers that is dotted by glacial ponds and strewn with boulders dropped by moving ice. Before the ice came a volcanic eruption 50 million years ago. Volcanic ash from the explosion engulfed the mature forest that once stood here., the results of which you can view at the Specimen Ridge wayside (see above). In addition to the region's natural beauty, it's the new home of packs of transplanted wolves and offers excellent fishing in the Lamar River.

Cooke City might best be described as an outpost that provides essential services including restaurants, motels, gas stations, and grocery stores, but it's a long way from being as developed as its sister gateway cities. See chapter 8, "Gateways to Yellowstone & Grand Teton National Parks," for more information about lodging and dining here.

Fourteen miles (22km) outside of Cooke City, take the **Chief Joseph Scenic Highway** ❋❋ (WY 296), which connects to WY 120 into Cody. This highway, also called the Sunlight Basin Road, offers great opportunities for viewing deer, coyotes, and other wildlife.

Cody is the quintessential Western town. Folks are friendly, accommodations are well turned out and moderately priced, and there are enough tourist attractions—the nightly rodeo and the impressive Buffalo Bill Historical Center are most famous—to make it worth the detour. See chapter 8 for more details.

From Cody, return to Yellowstone's East Entrance on U.S. 12/16/20. After you re-enter the park, you'll cross 8,541-foot **Sylvan Pass** and travel through the Absaroka mountain range, estimated to be 50 million years old. Driving along the shores of Yellowstone Lake, you'll pass **Mary Bay,** yet another crater created by a volcanic explosion. You'll return to the main area of the park at **Fishing Bridge Junction,** where you can rejoin the Grand Loop Road and continue your tour.

FROM TOWER JUNCTION TO THE GRAND CANYON OF THE YELLOWSTONE

Closest entrances: 23 miles (37km) from the Gardiner (north) entrance; 29 miles (46km) from the Cooke City (northeast) entrance.

Distance: 19 miles (30km) from Tower Junction to Canyon Village.

A few minutes' drive from the Tower area is the **Calcite Springs Overlook.** A short loop along a boardwalk leads to the overlook at the rim of **The Narrows,** the narrowest part of this northern section of the Grand Canyon. You can hear the river raging through the canyon some 500 feet below and look across at the canyon walls comprised of rock spires and bands of columnar basalt. Just downstream is the most prominent feature in this area of the canyon, **Bumpus Butte.** More noticeable than majestic, it is a box-shape outcropping between Rainy Lake and Calcite Springs.

A few footsteps from the Hamilton Store that lies farther along the road, you'll find a trail to the 132-foot **Tower Fall** and an overlook that is typically crowded with sightseers. You'll have a more interesting and photogenic view if you continue past the overlook on the fairly steep path to the base of the falls where Tower Creek flows into the Yellowstone River.

Continuing south, you'll travel through the **Washburn Range,** an area in which the 1988 fires ran especially hot and fast. The terrain changes dramatically as the road climbs along some major hills toward **Mount Washburn.** The kinkiest section of this road is the aptly named **Mae West Curve.** Just before the curve, one stretch of this highway overlooks stands of aspen trees, a favorite summer haunt of the grizzly bear. Other sections are covered with sagebrush. During the fire, the sagebrush was incinerated, but roots were uninjured, so it now grows vigorously in soil that is fertilized by ash leached into the earth by snowmelt, another example of nature's artful ways.

There are trailheads for the **Mount Washburn Trail** ★★★, one of my favorites, on each side of the summit. One is at the end of Old Chittenden Road (the turnoff to this road from the Tower–Canyon Road is well marked); the other begins at Dunraven Pass, about a mile (1.5km) farther down the highway. Both hikes take 2 to 3 hours to complete, but Old Chittenden has the larger parking lot, so it might be more crowded; it's also more scenic (although steeper).

As you approach **Dunraven Pass** (8,859 ft.), keep your eyes peeled for the shy bighorn sheep because this is one of their prime habitats.

One mile (1.5km) farther south is the **Washburn Hot Springs Overlook,** which offers sweeping views of the canyon. On a clear day, you can see 50 to 100 miles (80.5 to 161km) south, beyond Yellowstone Lake. Get out of the car and take a look. As you wander the immediate area on foot, you will often see fox and marmots amid the flower-covered alpine meadows.

CANYON VILLAGE

Closest entrances & distances: 40 miles (64km) from West Yellowstone (west) entrance; 38 miles (61km) from Gardiner (north) entrance; 48 miles (77km) from the Cooke City (northeast) entrance; 43 miles (69km) from the east entrance.

You're in for yet another eyeful when you reach the **Grand Canyon of the Yellowstone** ⋇⋇⋇, which offers a vivid example of nature unleashing its destructive power to create indescribable beauty.

The canyon has its geologic origins in the same volcanic eruptions that created Yellowstone Lake. As lava flows created lakes that overflowed their banks, walls of hard, granitelike rock remained as softer minerals eroded. This process carved the canyon, which was subsequently blocked by glaciers. Eventually, when the ice melted, floods recarved each end of the canyon, deepening it and removing sand and gravel.

The result: a 24-mile (38km) crevasse that at some points is 1,200 feet deep and 4,000 feet wide, and two waterfalls, one of which is twice as high as Niagara Falls. Even the most reluctant hiker will be rewarded with sites as colorful as those seen in "the other canyon." Compared to the Grand Canyon of Arizona, Yellowstone's Grand Canyon is relatively narrow; however, it's equally impressive because of the steepness of the cliffs, which descend hundreds of feet to the bottom of a gorge where the Yellowstone River flows. It's also equally colorful, with displays of orange, red, yellow, and gold. And you won't find thermal vents in Arizona, but you will find them here, a constant reminder of ongoing underground activity.

You should plan on encountering crowds when you reach **Canyon Village.** Although it is a bit overdeveloped, you'll find many necessary services here, including a post office, a trio of restaurants, and two stores stocked with fresh and preserved foodstuffs, camping gear, and souvenirs. Accommodations are in cabins and a large campground. Concessionaires offer horseback trail rides from a nearby stable and other guided tours. See chapter 7 for more details about lodging and dining in the area.

The **Canyon Visitor Center** (© 307/242-2550) is the place to go for books and an excellent exhibit on bison. It's also staffed with friendly rangers used to dealing with the crowds here.

An auto tour of the canyon follows **North Rim Drive,** a two-lane, one-way road that begins in Canyon Village, to your first stop, Inspiration Point. On the way, you'll pass a 500-ton **glacial boulder** that was deposited by melting ice more than 10,000 years ago. Geologists estimate that ice flows carried this chunk of rock 40 miles (64km) to its present location.

At **Inspiration Point,** a moderately strenuous descent down 57 steps takes you to an overlook with views of the Lower Falls and

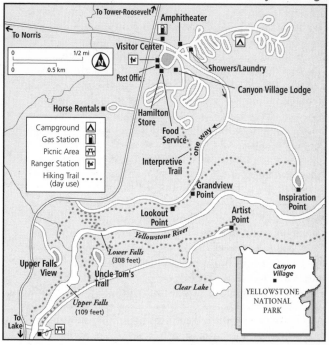

canyon. (At 8,000 feet, the hike will cause your pulse rate and blood pressure to rise, so it is wise to pause for a few extra minutes before making the return.) Evidence of current earthquake activity is beneath the soles of your shoes. The viewing platform once extended 100 feet farther over the canyon; on June 30, 1975, it was shattered by an earthquake and tumbled into the canyon. There are several other viewpoints you can stop at along North Rim Drive before you reconnect with the main Canyon Village–Yellowstone Lake Road, which will take you down to South Rim Drive.

Along the way, you can also stop at **Grand View** overlook, where the river flows some 750 feet below the observation platform. During summer months, Grand View is an excellent spot from which to view ospreys, which normally nest in this area and can be seen riding the thermals. **Lookout Point** provides a better view of the Lower Falls; however, the observation deck is at the end of a steep, 150-foot trail. Going down is the easy part; the return trip is not recommended for those with heart or lung problems.

For the adventurous, an alternative to driving from one overlook to another is to negotiate the **North Rim Trail** 🛉, which is slightly more than 2¼ miles (0.5km) long, beginning at Inspiration Point. This trail ends at the Upper Falls parking area, where the Upper Falls Trail begins; it's another ¾ mile (1km) to the bridge that connects the North and South rims. Unfortunately, the North Rim Trail is not a loop, so if you take the hike, you'll have to backtrack to get your car at Inspiration Point. The footpath brings you closer to what you want to see, and you won't be fighting for elbowroom like you will at the overlooks that are a stone's throw from the road.

Whether you drive or walk, you should go down to the **Upper Falls View,** where a ¼-mile (0.5km) trail leads down from the parking lot to the **Brink of the Upper Falls,** an overlook within splashing distance of the rushing river, and the waterfall. At this point you won't just hear the power of the river, but you'll feel it as it begins its course down the canyon.

The **South Rim Road** leads to several overlooks and better views of the Lower Falls. The most impressive vantage point is from the bottom of **Uncle Tom's Trail** 🛉🛉, a steep, 500-foot route to an unbeatable vantage point that begins at the first South Rim parking lot. The trail is named after Tom Richardson, an adventuresome early day guide who led travelers to the base of the falls with ropes and ladders; these days, the trip is down 328 steps and paved inclines. The trail is rather steep, but it can be negotiated in about an hour, although it will be challenging for the neophyte hiker (an experienced hiker might be able to negotiate this distance in somewhat less time).

South Rim Road continues to a second, lower parking lot and a trail that leads to **Artist Point** 🛉🛉. The view here is astounding, one of my favorites in the park, and is best in the early morning. It was at this point that Thomas Moran was inspired to create his famous painting of the falls, reproductions of which are seen in galleries and print shops throughout the world. This is one of the most photogenic (and most photographed) tableaus in the country: Almost every visitor snaps a shot or two.

The **South Rim Trail** is an alternative to viewing the Lower Falls and the canyon from wooden observation decks. From the first South Rim parking lot, which is just beyond the South Rim Drive Bridge, follow trail markers to the partially paved trail and then 1¾ miles (3km) to Artist Point. (The trail follows the canyon for 3¼ miles (5km) beyond Artist Point to **Point Sublime,** where you must double back along the same route.) You'll have several different views of the falls, and you can always hop off to access Uncle Tom's Trail, Artist Point, and **Lily Pad Lake.** Neither Point Sublime nor Lily Pad Lake is accessible by car.

A DETOUR: CANYON VILLAGE TO NORRIS

Distance: 12 miles (19km) from Canyon Village to Norris.

Before proceeding to the Yellowstone Lake area, consider back-tracking 12 miles (19km) on the road from Canyon Village to Norris Geyser Basin. About three-quarters of the way to Norris, you'll find a turn-off for **Virginia Cascades Drive,** a 3-mile (5km) road that winds along the Gibbon River, which flows off the Solfatara Plateau to create the 60-foot high Virginia Cascade. The road is open only to hikers and bikers, and the cascades are beautiful, so it's an excellent hideaway from the crowds and a great spot to call a timeout from your tour. Virginia Cascades Drive winds back in the direction of Canyon Village.

CANYON VILLAGE TO FISHING BRIDGE

Closest entrances: 27 miles (43km) to the east entrance; 43 miles (69km) to the south entrance.

Distance: 16 miles (26km) from Canyon Village to Fishing Bridge.

The road from Canyon Village winds through the **Hayden Valley,** which is a vast expanse of beautiful green meadows accented by brown cuts where the soil is eroded along the banks of the Yellowstone River. Imagine this: Ten thousand years before Ferdinand V. Hayden led the survey expedition of 1871, the entire Hayden Valley, except for the tallest peaks that surround it, was covered with a 4,000-foot-thick layer of ice. Today, wooded banks define what was once a shoreline. The valley is now a wide, sprawling area where bison play and trumpeter swans, white pelicans, and Canada geese float along the river. This is also a prime habitat for the grizzly, so during early spring months pay close attention to binoculars-toting visitors grouped beside the road.

Tips Photo Tip

The Hayden Valley offers excellent opportunities to photograph **bison.** They are less harassed by tourists here and less confined.

Nature is at her acidic best at the **Sulphur Caldron** and **Mud Volcano** areas, 12 miles (19km) south of the Canyon Junction, which were described by the frontier minister Edwin Stanley as "unsightly, unsavory, and villainous." While Stanley interjected human traits into natural phenomena, his appraisal is fairly accurate, so you'll certainly want to explore this area. There's nothing quite like the sound of burping mud pots.

By 1984, the vapors from Sulphur Caldron (on the east side of the road) had rotted the foundations on which the overlook was constructed, and it collapsed. The pH of the caldron is twice that of battery acid; if you stepped in one of these pools, your shoes would be reduced to ashes.

At **Dragon's Mouth Spring,** escaping steam and sulfurous gases propel turbid water from an underground cavern to the surface, where it colors the earth with shades of orange and green. The belching of steam from the cavern and the associated sound, which is due to the splash of 180°F water against the wall in a subterranean cavern, creates a aura of fantasy and medieval times; hence, the name of the spring. Nearby **Mud Volcano** is a murky mud spring, the product of vigorous activity caused by escaping sulfurous gases and steam. The youngest feature in the area is **Black Dragon's Caldron,** which is often referred to as "the demon of the backwoods"—and rightly so. The caldron emerged from its subterranean birthplace for the first time in 1948 when it announced its presence by blowing a hole in the landscape, scattering mature trees hundreds of feet in all directions. Since then, continual seismic activity and intermittent earthquakes in the area have caused it to move 200 feet south of its original position.

Le Hardy Rapids, a shaded area 2 miles (3km) farther south, is an ideal spot for a stroll along a shaded section of the river. This is a prime route for cutthroat trout in the early summer on their way to spawn. It is also popular with the shy harlequin ducks and bald eagles. The scary side of the equation is that this innocent-looking stretch of water flows across a fault in the earth. Some geologists believe that this will be the spot where the next major eruption will occur and that it will be as large as, or larger than, the eruption that created the Yellowstone Caldera 600,000 years ago. Their guess: The explosion could occur anytime in the next 100,000 years—in other words, anytime.

The road across the Yellowstone River at **Fishing Bridge** was once the only eastern exit in the park, the route leading over Sylvan Pass to Cody, Wyoming. The bridge, which was built in 1937, spans the Yellowstone River as it exits Yellowstone Lake and is another prime spawning area for native trout. As a consequence, it became so popular that as many as 50,000 fishermen would beat the water into a froth every year in their search for the perfect entree. To protect the trout, fishing was banned in the 1960s, but it remains an excellent vantage point from which to watch them as they head upstream. The bridge is also an excellent spot for observing waterfowl, especially the large, white pelicans and Canadian geese that inhabit the area, seemingly oblivious to the crowds.

The **Fishing Bridge Visitor Center** (✆ **307/242-2450**), which is open from 8am to 7pm, has an excellent wildlife display. The nearby Hamilton Store sells provisions as well as liquor. The Fishing Bridge **RV Park** is restricted to hard-sided vehicles only because this is a prime grizzly habitat. You'll find an excellent hiking trail, **Elephant Back Loop Trail,** leading off the short strip of highway between Fishing Village and the Lake Village area. The 2-mile (3km) loop leads to an overlook with panoramic views of Yellowstone Lake and its islands, the Absaroka Range, and Pelican Valley to the east. Instead of taking the entire loop around to the overlook, you can shorten the hike a half-mile (1km) by taking the left fork approximately 1 mile (1.5km) from the trailhead and doubling back after you get to the overlook.

YELLOWSTONE LAKE AREA

Closest entrances: Approximately 31 miles (50km) from Fishing Bridge to the east entrance; approximately 39 miles (63km) from Fishing Bridge to the south entrance.

Distances: The lakefront from Fishing Bridge to the West Thumb Geyser Basin is 21 miles (34km).

As if the park didn't have enough record-setting attractions, at 7,773 feet, **Yellowstone Lake** 🐾🐾 is North America's largest high-altitude lake. It is 20 miles (32km) long and 14 miles (22km) wide, contains 110 miles (177km) of shoreline, has depths ranging to 390 feet, and is *very* cold. Because the surface freezes by December and remains crusted until late May, the temperature at the bottom remains at 39°F year-round, and the surface temperature isn't a lot warmer. Considering its size relative to the entire volcanic caldera, the lake is considered by many to be just a puddle. At one point in its history, the entire area was filled with ice, most of which has since melted, so the lake relies on 124 tributaries, including the Yellowstone River, to maintain its present level.

Tips **Photo Tip**

If the weather looks promising, be certain to schedule an early morning wake-up call and then head for a scenic vantage point near the edge of Yellowstone Lake just before sunrise. If conditions are right, the surface of the lake will be flat and enshrouded in fog. As you watch, the sun heats the surface and the fog rises to reveal an island (Stevenson) that seems to have magically appeared from the sky.

The lake exhibits its multifaceted personalities every day, which range on the emotional scale from a placid, mirrorlike surface to a seething tantrum whipped by southerly winds that create 3- to 4-foot waves. Boaters should be especially cautious because of the number of boat-related fatalities related to hypothermia. Compelling evidence of the ongoing changes occurring in the park as a consequence of subsurface thermal activity is the fact that the lake bottom is rising and tilting about 1 inch per year, a veritable sprinter's pace in geologic time. Trees on the south end of the lake drown as new beaches come into being on the north end, and existing beaches are expanding.

Because the lake has the largest population of native cutthroat trout in North America, it makes an ideal fishing spot in summer. (See chapters 2, "Planning Your Trip to Yellowstone & Grand Teton National Parks," and 4, "Hikes & Other Outdoor Pursuits in Yellowstone National Park," for information on fishing regulations.) The lake is also an ornithologist's paradise; the skies are filled with osprey, bald eagles, white pelicans, and cormorants. On the shore, moose and grizzly bear are especially prevalent during the trout runs in spring.

Lake Village, on the northwest shore of the lake, offers a wide range of amenities, the most prominent of which is the regal Victorian facade of the 100-year-old **Lake Hotel.** You'll find excellent food and fine-dining ambiance in the restaurant, as well as a postage-stamp-size deli. Hamburgers and the like are available at the Hamilton Store. Lodging is in the hotel, in its motel-style annex, and at Lake Lodge, which offers sleeping accommodations in modestly priced, rustic, frontier-style cabins. See chapter 7 for more details.

Just south of Lake Village is the **Bridge Bay Marina,** the center of the park's water activities. Here you can arrange for guided

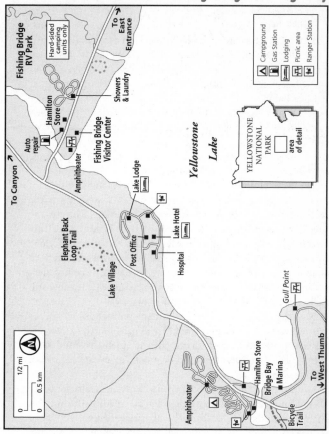

Yellowstone Lake: Fishing Bridge to Bridge Bay

fishing trips or small boat rentals, or learn more about the lake during an informative and entertaining 1-hour narrated boat tour. The views are magnificent, and the skipper shares fascinating facts about the area's history. The marina is usually open from mid-June to mid-September.

Campers will discover a large **campground** here with sites for RVs and tent campers. Although trees surround the campground area, the area itself is very large and has been cleared, so campsites here offer very little privacy.

Although the **Natural Bridge,** near Bridge Bay, is well marked on park maps, it's one of the park's best-kept secrets, and you might end up enjoying it by yourself. The mile-long (1.5km) path down to the bridge, a geologic masterpiece consisting of a massive rock arch 51 feet overhead, spanning Bridge Creek, is an excellent bike route.

Looking for a picnic area? Keep a sharp eye out for an inconspicuous paved road on the lake side of the highway 13 miles (21km) west of Fishing Bridge that leads down to a secluded spot near **Pumice Point.**

The **West Thumb** area along the western shoreline is the deepest part of Yellowstone Lake. Because of its suspiciously craterlike contours, many scientists speculate that this 4-mile-wide (6.5km), 6-mile-long (9.5km), water-filled crater was created during volcanic eruptions approximately 125,000 years ago.

The **West Thumb Geyser Basin** is notable for a unique series of geysers. Some are situated right on the shores, some overlook the lake, and some can be seen *beneath* the lake surface. Three of the shoreline geysers, the most famous of which is **Fishing Cone,** are occasionally marooned offshore when the lake level rises. (Fishing Cone was named for the park's early fishermen who used it as a combination casting spot/kitchen by immediately cooking their catch, hook still in mouth.) Fortunately, a half-mile (1km) of boardwalks crisscrosses the area, so it's easy to negotiate.

Near the center of an area that is totally surrounded by healthy growing trees is a **tree graveyard.** These pale, limbless trees were killed when thermal activity caused hot water to move toward them. When their roots absorbed the hot water, the trees were cooked from the inside out.

Details about the area, books, and maps are available at the **West Thumb Information Station,** housed in a log structure that functioned as the original West Thumb Ranger Station. The center is open daily from late May through September from 9am to 5pm.

As you depart the West Thumb area, you are presented with two choices: either to head south toward Grand Teton National Park or to head west across the **Continental Divide** at Craig Pass, en route to Old Faithful.

GRANT VILLAGE TO THE SOUTH ENTRANCE
Closest entrance and distance: 22 miles from Grant Village to the south entrance.

Located on the southern shore of Yellowstone Lake, Grant Village offers dramatic views of summer squalls and one of Yellowstone's most inspiring sunrises. Perhaps the primary appeal of the village, the southernmost outpost in the park, is its location as a jumping-off place for travelers leaving for Grand Teton National Park, or

Yellowstone Lake: West Thumb to Grant Village

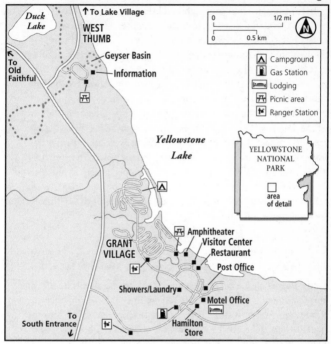

as a place for them to spend their first night in Yellowstone. Named for President Ulysses S. Grant, the village was completed in 1984. It's the newest of Yellowstone's villages and home to the park's most modern facilities.

The **Grant Visitor Center** (© **307/242-2650**) has information, publications, a slide program, and a fascinating exhibit examining the effects of fire in Yellowstone. *The Unfinished Song,* a video about the fires of 1988, is shown daily.

The **Grant Village Dining Room** is an excellent restaurant with views of the lake. Reservations are recommended. Nearby is **Lake House,** which serves less expensive pizza and pasta dinners in an informal dining room closer to the shoreline. Guest accommodations are in a motel-style building. Other services include a general store that serves light meals and fast food, a modest gift shop, and a service station. For more details about dining and accommodations in the area, see chapter 7. Given a choice, I'd head north to a different destination or continue south to Grand Teton.

In contrast to this forgettable village is the beautiful 22-mile (35km) drive to **Grand Teton** along high mountain passes and **Lewis Lake.** The lake, which is 108 feet deep, is the third largest in the park and is connected to Shoshone Lake by a narrow channel that is populated by German brown trout. After the lake loses its winter coat of ice, it is a popular spot for early season anglers who are unable to fish streams that are clouded by the spring runoff.

Beyond the lake, the road follows the Lewis River through an alpine area and along the **Pitchstone Plateau,** a pile of lava more than 2,000 feet high and 20 miles (32km) wide that was created some 500,000 years ago. A high gorge overlooking the river provides views that are different from but equally spectacular to those in other sections of the park. At its highest point, the road winds across a high plateau that is accented with forests of dead, limbless lodgepole pine—remnants of the 1988 fire.

WEST THUMB TO OLD FAITHFUL

Closest entrance: 25 miles (40km) from West Thumb to the South Entrance.

Distance: 17 miles (27km) from West Thumb Geyser Basin to Old Faithful area.

Craig Pass is an important geologic landmark because it is here, at the Continental Divide in the Yellowstone–Teton area, that the headwaters of two major rivers are formed, one emptying into the Pacific Ocean, the other into the Gulf of Mexico. The Snake River winds from Grand Teton through Idaho to meet the Columbia River in Oregon and then drains into the Pacific Ocean at Astoria, Oregon. The Yellowstone River, which begins south of Yellowstone Park, drains into the Missouri River, which drains into the Mississippi, which empties into the Gulf of Mexico.

The most interesting phenomenon on the Old Faithful route is **Isa Lake** at Craig Pass. Unlike most lakes and streams in the parks, it has both eastern and western drainages and ends up in both the Pacific Ocean and the Gulf of Mexico. Amazingly, as a consequence of a gyroscopic maneuver, the outlet on the *east* curves *west* and drains to the Pacific, and the outlet on the *west* curves *east* and drains to the Gulf.

Before you reach the Old Faithful geyser area, two additional detours are recommended. Two and a half miles (4km) south of Old Faithful is an overlook at the spectacular **Kepler Cascades,** a 150-foot stair-step waterfall on the Firehole River that is a stone's throw from the parking lot.

Near that parking lot is the trailhead for the second detour, the 5-mile (8km) round-trip **Lonestar Geyser Trail** 𝕽𝕽. The geyser erupts every 3 hours, sending steaming water 30 to 50 feet from its 12-foot cone. The hike, which winds along a gentle trail bordering the Firehole River through pastoral meadows and a forest, is a must-do. Even when others are on the trail, the area exudes a solitary air because it is possible to abandon the trail, follow the meandering stream, and find flat, open places to relax or picnic.

OLD FAITHFUL AREA

Closest entrance & distances: 16 miles (26km) from Old Faithful geyser to Madison Junction, then another 14 miles (23km) to West Yellowstone (west) entrance.

Despite the overwhelming sight of the geysers and steam vents that populate the Old Faithful area, I suggest that you resist the temptation to explore until you've stopped at the **Old Faithful Visitor Center** (© **307/545-2750**). It has a larger staff and more facilities than most of the other park visitor centers. An excellent film describing the geysers' amazing microscopic residents, *Yellowstone Revealed,* is shown throughout the day in an air-conditioned auditorium that provides relief from hot July afternoons. Various park publications and an informative seismographic exhibit are added attractions. You will also want to check the information board for estimated times of geyser eruptions, and plan your time accordingly. (At press time, fund-raising was underway to replace this center with a $15 million, cutting-edge facility that will better blend into the architectural motif of the Old Faithful Inn and Snow Lodge; the target date for ribbon cutting is 2003.)

The Yellowstone Association's guides for **Old Faithful** and the **Fountain Paint Pots** include complete maps and explanations of the 150 geysers and many hot springs in the area, which happen to be a quarter of the world's total. Priced at 50¢, they're a bargain.

The number and variety of accommodations here is greater than at any other park center. The **Old Faithful Inn** is said to be the largest log structure in the world, seven stories underneath an 80-foot ceiling. The Inn was finished in 1904 and is a National Historic Landmark. There are two other accommodations in this bustling center of activity: **Old Faithful Lodge,** which has rustic frontier cabins for rent, and **Old Faithful Snow Lodge,** which was rebuilt in 1998 and has garnered awards for its rustic, environmentally friendly design.

Several **dining** choices are available, the nicest of which is the upscale dining room in the Inn, where three meals are served daily; the requisite deli is situated off the lobby. Another good eatery is situated in Snow Lodge, as is a fast food restaurant; a cafeteria with

---

(*Tips* **Bison Crossing**

Warning: The shaded **Observation Point Trail** area is a popular spot with resident bison, so don't be surprised to find
yourself sharing the trail with them. Be sure to give the
ornery beasts plenty of room.

---

food to satisfy various ethnic palates and an ice cream stand are in
the Lodge, as is a large gift shop. Nearby are a Hamilton Store with
various provisions and souvenirs, a gas station, an auto repair shop,
a post office, and a medical clinic. For more information about
dining and lodging in the area, see chapter 7.

The Old Faithful area is generally divided into four sections:
Upper Geyser Basin, which includes Geyser Hill, **Black Sand
Basin, Biscuit Basin,** and **Midway Geyser Basin.** All of these areas
are connected by paved trails and roads. If time allows, hike the area;
it's fairly level, and distances are relatively short. Between the Old
Faithful area and Madison Junction, you'll also find the justifiably
famous **Lower Geyser Basin,** including Fountain Paint Pot and the
trails surrounding it. You can see some of these geysers on Firehole
Lake Drive.

Although **Old Faithful** 🐾🐾 is not the largest geyser in the park
and seems less inclined these days to be faithfully "regular," its image
has been seen on everything from postage stamps to whiskey bottles.
It acquired its name when the Washburn Expedition of 1870
observed its predictable pattern of eruptions. Seismic activity has
wrought changes in the geyser's habits, but it's still the most predictable geyser on the planet, erupting with an average interval of
88 minutes, although it can vary 30 minutes in either direction.
A typical eruption lasts 1.5 to 5 minutes, during which 3,700 to
8,400 gallons of water are thrust upward to heights of 180 feet. For
the best views and photo ops of the eruption in the boardwalk area,
plan on arriving at least 15 minutes before the scheduled show, to
ensure a first-row view.

An alternative to a seat on the crowded boardwalk is a stroll from
the Old Faithful Geyser up the **Observation Point Trail** to an
observation area that provides better views of the entire geyser basin.
The path up to the observation point is approximately a half-mile
(1km), and the elevation gain is only 200 feet, so it's an easy 15-
minute hike. The view of the eruption of the geyser is more spectacular from here, and the crowds are less obtrusive.

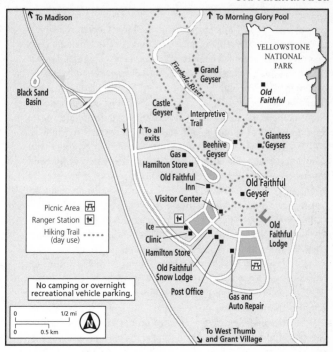

From the vantage point of the Observation Point Trail, you'll have a different perspective of the entire **Upper Geyser Basin;** it's possible to see most of the major geysers as well as inaccessible steam vents in the middle of wooded areas. On clear, sunny days, sunbeams highlight the colors of the ponds and geysers in the valleys below. Interested in continuing your hike? From the top of the boardwalk, continue to the **Solitary Geyser** on a loop that leads back to the Inn, adding only 1 mile (1.5km) to the trip on a mostly downhill trail.

Accessible by walkways from Old Faithful Village, the **Upper Geyser Basin Loop** is referred to as Geyser Hill on some maps. The 1¼-mile (2km) loop trail winds among several thermal attractions. **Anemone Geyser** might offer the best display of the various stages of a typical eruption as the pool fills and overflows, after which bubbles rising to the surface begin throwing water in 10-foot eruptions, a cycle that is repeated every 7 to 10 minutes.

The **Lion Group** consists of four geysers that are interconnected beneath the surface. The eruptions of the **Lion Geyser,** the largest of the quartet, are usually preceded by gushes of steam and a deep roaring sound, from which it derives its name. **Doublet Pool** is especially popular with photographers who are attracted by a complex series of ledges and deep blue waters. Further along the trail is **Giantess Geyser,** known for its violent eruptions, which cause the surrounding area to shake and quake as underground steam explodes before reaching the surface, where it can burst at heights of 200 feet. It erupts infrequently, at unscheduled intervals, so you should check with rangers to see if it's active. The colors of **Emerald Pool** algae—blues, greens, yellows, and oranges—offer an excellent example of the effects of water temperature and sunlight on what are actually unexpected living organisms.

Two other stars of the show in the Upper Geyser Basin are **Castle Geyser** and **Grand Geyser.** Castle Geyser, which has the largest cone of any geyser in the park, currently erupts for 20 minutes every 10 to 12 hours, after which a noisy steam phase could continue for half an hour. Grand Geyser, the tallest predictable geyser in the world, usually erupts every 7 to 15 hours with powerful bursts that produce streams of water that can reach 200 feet in height.

The **Riverside Geyser** ⚡ is situated on the bank of the Firehole River, near **Morning Glory Pool.** One of the most picturesque geysers in the park, its 75-foot column of water creates an arch over the river two to three times daily. **Morning Glory Pool** was named for its likeness to its namesake flower in the 1880s but has since lost some of its beauty. Vandals have tossed so much debris into its core over the years that it now suffers from poor circulation and reduced temperatures, which are causing unsightly brown and green bacteria to grow on its surface.

The **Black Sand Basin** is a cluster of especially colorful hot springs and geysers located 1 mile (1.5km) north of Old Faithful. It is interesting primarily because of its black sand, a derivative of obsidian. **Biscuit Basin,** located 2 miles (3km) farther up the road, was named for biscuitlike deposits that surrounded colorful **Sapphire Pool** until a 1959 earthquake caused the pool to erupt, sending them skyward. Both the Black Sand Basin and the Biscuit Basin are easily viewed from flat, interpretive boardwalks.

The **Midway Geyser Basin** extends for about 1 mile (1.5km) along the Firehole River. The major attractions here are the **Excelsior Geyser,** the third largest geyser in the world and once the park's most powerful geyser, and the well-known **Grand Prismatic Spring,** the largest hot spring in Yellowstone and the second largest in the world. A boardwalk leads to Excelsior, which in the 1880s erupted to 300 feet, creating a 300-foot wide crater in the process. Just beyond is Grand Prismatic Spring. Those colorful bands of yellow, red, and green are thermal algae.

OLD FAITHFUL TO MADISON JUNCTION

Closest entrance: 30 miles (48km) from Old Faithful area to the West Yellowstone (west) entrance; 39 (63km) miles to the south entrance.

Distance: 16 miles (23km) from Old Faithful area to Madison.

Believe it or not, there are other superb geysers and hot springs on **Firehole Lake Drive,** all viewable without leaving your vehicle, along a 3-mile (5km), one-way road that passes several of them. The turnoff for Firehole Lake Drive is about 8 miles (13km) north of the Old Faithful area. There are three geysers of particular interest on this road. The largest is **Great Fountain Geyser,** which erupts every 8 to 12 hours, typically spouting water some 100 feet high for periods of 45 to 60 minutes. However, lucky visitors might see the occasional "superburst" that reaches heights of 200 feet or more.

Estimates are that **White Dome Geyser** has been erupting for hundreds of years. Unfortunately, the age and height of this massive cone are not matched by spectacular eruptions. The vent on top of the cone has been nearly sealed with deposits of "geyserite," so eruptions now reach only 30 feet. However, the sight of the cone itself is worth a trip down this road.

Farther on, **Pink Cone Geyser** couldn't be closer to the road: Road builders cut into the geyser's mound during construction.

About a quarter-mile (0.5km) north of where Firehole Lake Drive rejoins the Grand Loop Road is the **Fountain Paint Pots** 🐾

Fun Fact **Know Your Bacteria**

Even the most casual visitor can do some scientific sleuthing at the **Fountain Paint Pots** 🐾, learning to identify water temperature by observing the colors in the pots. The colors result from different types of bacteria that survive at specific water temperatures. Some turn yellow until temperatures reach 161°F, above which bacteria cannot live. As temperatures approach boiling—199°F at this elevation—pinks begin to appear.

---

area. This is a very popular spot, so you might be forced to wait for a parking place. Although it's not large or spectacular, it's one of the most interesting areas in the park. All the various types of thermal activity are on display here, so as you stroll along the easy, ½-mile (1km) boardwalk, you'll be in an area that might have six geysers popping their lids at the same time. Though less impressive than other basins, these ponds, pots, and vents are among the most active in the park.

The first part of this natural exhibit, **Bacteria,** offers an excellent example of how algae and bacteria are at work in these thermal areas. The centerpiece, literally, of this region is **Fountain Paint Pot,** which changes character as summer temperatures increase, causing once thin, watery mud to become very thick. The mud is composed of clay and particles of silica that are trapped in the paint pots. (If you see a bubble forming on the surface, be prepared for a burst that could throw mud over the guardrail.) **Leather Pool** has undergone a transformation since the 1959 Hebgen Lake earthquake. It was once a warm, 143°F pool lined with leatherlike algae, but its temperature increased so dramatically after the quake that the algae were killed. **Red Spouter** changes its temperament with the seasons as its water table changes. During summer months, when the water table is low, it is a fumarole; from late fall through the winter, it spouts red water and mud. The Fountain Pots themselves are very colorful, with orange, yellow, blue, and green pots surrounded by bleached mud, gurgling like experiments in high school chemistry labs. All in all, it takes roughly 20 minutes to do the whole tour. Before departing, take a look across the large grassy area called **Fountain Flat.**

As you continue toward the Madison Junction, consider a detour along **Fountain Flat Drive,** a left turn about 2 miles (3km) beyond Fountain Paint Pot. This scenic paved road ends ¼ mile (0.5km) north of Ojo Caliente, after which it is open only to hikers and bikers. One mile (1.5km) south of the Firehole River bridge, you'll find the **Imperial Meadows Trailhead** (for a description, see chapter 4). Park the car and head up the 3-mile (5km) trail to the 200-foot **Fairy Falls.** This trail gets less traffic than the popular Lonestar and Dunraven trails.

Although a detour along **Firehole Canyon Drive** will require backtracking when you're approaching Madison from the south, the trip is worth the time you'll spend. There are great views of the canyon and **Firehole Falls.** The 2-mile (3km), one-way road, which is a left turn off the Grand Loop Road just before you get to the Madison Junction, skirts 800-foot lava cliffs as it meanders along the canyon of the Firehole River in the shadow of National Park Mountain before rejoining the Grand Loop Road. Like much of the park, the 1988 fire scorched this area, so it offers excellent opportunities to see how quickly new growth is reconstituting the forest.

There are excellent views of the beautiful Firehole River as it rages through this narrow canyon, highlighted by a close-up of Firehole Falls. Be sure and bring a camera. Near the end of this 2-mile (3km) road is a popular swimming hole (although you'll need to change into your swimwear before arriving). There are several places to soak weary feet during the hot days of July and August.

5 Self-Guided Driving Tours

Depending on your driving skills and your tolerance for large numbers of cars, recreational vehicles, and auto-towed trailers, there is no substitute for a self-driven tour of the park. Although roads are narrow, there are hundreds of turnouts that afford opportunities to take in the views. On the downside, the roads twist, turn, and change elevation frequently, so freeway speeds are out of the question.

6 Organized Tours

A number of tour companies offer bus tours of the park originating in gateway communities: **Powder River Coach USA** (© 800/442-3682 ext. 114; www.coachusa.com), out of Cody, offers day-long trips; **Gray Line of Yellowstone** (© 800/523-3102; www.grayline yellowstone.com) takes travelers around the park from West Yellowstone, as does **Buffalo Bus Lines** (© 800/426-7669). If you are looking for specialized guided trips—such as photo safaris or snowmobile tours—contact the chambers of commerce in the gateway community where you want to begin (see section 1, "Getting Started: Information & Reservations," of chapter 2 for contact information).

Within the park, the hotel concessionaire, **Yellowstone National Park Lodges** (© 307/344-7311; www.travelyellowstone.com), has a variety of general and specialized tours. Three different motorcoach tours are available from all of Yellowstone's villages. For $29, you can explore either the **Washburn Expedition** (Norris Geyser Basin, the Grand Canyon of the Yellowstone, and Mammoth Hot Springs) or the **Circle of Fire** (Old Faithful, Yellowstone Lake, the

---

(Tips) **Photo Tip**

Shutterbugs who want to increase the odds of taking the perfect photo can receive hands-on instruction from a professional photographer, compliments of Kodak. Beginning in mid-June, talks and **photo walks** are scheduled in the park's most photogenic areas. These no-fee programs generally last 2 hours and are conveniently scheduled throughout the day. For information, check in the Yellowstone newsletter (handed out at the entry gates) or at the Fishing Bridge Visitor Center.

Hayden Valley); or, for $33, you can do the whole thing, the **Yellowstone in a Day** tour. These are full-day tours, with stops at all the sights and informative talks by the guides. Specialty trips include photo safaris, wildlife trips up the Lamar Valley (try it in winter), and Yellowstone Lake sunset tours in historic buses from the 1930s.

At Bridge Bay Marina, 1-hour **scenicruise tours** depart throughout the day from June to the end of September for a trip around the northern end of giant Yellowstone Lake. You view the Lake Hotel from the water and visit Stevenson Island while a guide fills you in on the history, geology, and biology. Fares are $9 for adults and $5 for children 2 to 11. Guided fishing trips on 22-foot and 34-foot cabin cruisers are also available from Yellowstone Park Lodges at Bridge Bay ($55 and $72 per hour, respectively), and you can rent smaller outboards and rowboats.

Buses are replaced in the winter by **snowcoach tours.** These are closer in size to a van than a bus, mounted on tank treads with skis in front for steering. The snowcoach can pick you up at the south or west entrances, or at Mammoth, and take you all over the park. You can spend a night at Old Faithful and then snowcoach up to Mammoth the next night, or do round-trip tours from the gates or wherever you're staying in the park. One-way trips range from $46 to $51, while round-trips cost $92 to $99.

One- and 2-hour **guided horseback trail rides** are available at Mammoth Hot Springs, Roosevelt Lodge, and Canyon Village. Children must be 8 years old and at least 48 inches tall; adults cannot exceed 250 lbs. Tour prices are $23 for a 1-hour ride and $35 for a 2-hour ride, and there is no discount for children. Check any activity desk for times and dates. Reservations are recommended and can be made at **Yellowstone National Park Lodges** activity centers in the hotels, although not before you leave home.

7 Ranger Programs

Yellowstone National Park continues to offer free **ranger-led educational programs** that will significantly enhance a visitor's understanding of the area's history, geology, and wildlife. Most programs run from early June through late September. Detailed information on location and times is listed in the park newsletter, which is distributed at the entrance gates. On a more informal basis, you'll run into ranger-naturalists roaming the geyser basins and along the rim of the Grand Canyon in Yellowstone, and in areas where wildlife gather in both parks, leading informative walks and answering the questions of inquisitive visitors.

Evening campfire programs are presented nightly in the summer at Mammoth, Norris, Madison, Old Faithful, Bridge Bay, Grant, and Canyon. Many of these activities are accessible to the disabled. It's a good idea to bring a flashlight, warm clothing, and rain gear. Rangers also conduct walking, talking, and hiking programs throughout the park.

As one would expect, there are more tours and evening programs in the **Old Faithful** area than anywhere else in the park. The topics of the guided walks, which can run as long as 1½ hours, usually focus on the geysers, their fragile plumbing, and their role in the Yellowstone ecosystem.

Beginning in June, daily hikes in the **Canyon** area head out to the Hayden Valley and the rim of the Grand Canyon; a ranger talk on the art inspired by the falls is held several times a day at the lower platform of Artist Point. An explanation of the origins of the hot pools and mud pots is conducted daily beginning in June at the **Grant** area as part of a walk of the Lakeshore area of the West Thumb Geyser Basin. The **Lake/Fishing Bridge** agenda includes walking tours of the Mud Volcano area and the shores of Yellowstone Lake and Indian Pond. There is an afternoon talk at the Fishing Bridge Visitor Center about managing wildlife such as grizzlies and wolves, and a discussion of fisheries management is held on the west end of the Fishing Bridge. Many changes are made annually in these presentations; consult the park newsletter that is distributed at the entrance gates.

Mammoth Hot Springs is host to several interesting ranger-led programs, namely a pair of "Daily Special" talks on the park's natural wonders and a historical tour of the original site of Fort Yellowstone, established more than 125 years ago. There is also a guided tour of the hot springs terraces. The hottest, most dynamic, and oldest geyser basin in the park is at **Norris,** where a popular 1½-hour tour begins at the Norris museum three times daily.

4

Hikes & Other Outdoor Pursuits in Yellowstone National Park

Those who complain that Yellowstone's three million annual visitors have compromised the park's wilderness should park their car and tackle a trail because there's plenty of virtually pristine, wild country here. If you want a wilderness experience with privacy, abundant wildlife, hot springs, trout streams, and thrilling scenery, Yellowstone is, in fact, the ideal choice.

There are short hikes on which you never lose sight of the road, moderate hikes on which you might spend an afternoon penetrating the forest to visit a spot of secluded beauty, and overnight trips on which you can hike and camp for days without running into another visitor.

In fact, there's so much to see and do in Yellowstone that it's easy to get overwhelmed. I've tried to make it easier for you by describing my favorite day hikes, as well as my favorite backcountry experiences and other park activities.

For a more extensive and detailed list of trails than what follows here, pick up Mark C. Marschall's excellent *Yellowstone Trails* (Yellowstone Association, $9.95) or the maps provided by the park.

1 Day Hikes

Below is a small selection of good hikes, long and short. The **Continental Divide Trail (CDT)** links many of these individual hikes together as part of a continuous trail from Mexico to Canada, roughly following the spine of the continent. The Yellowstone Backcountry Office maintains a guide to CDT trails. The **Howard Eaton Trail** system once went all through the park but was largely supplanted by the Grand Loop Road. Sections of the old trail are still maintained and will be found in trail guides, although some of them closely parallel park roads.

Wherever you go, if you're planning to hike for more than 30 minutes, be sure to carry a supply of water and raingear.

WEST YELLOWSTONE TO MADISON

Artist Paint Pot Trail 𝄖 Free of heavy foot traffic, this interesting and easy ½-mile (1km) path winds through a lodgepole forest in Gibbon Meadows to the Amazonia Mud Pot atop a small hill. This thermal area contains some small geysers, hot pools, and steam vents, colored by hues of orange, bright red, and rust.

1 mile (1.5km) RT. Easy. Access: Trailhead is 4½ miles (7km) south of Norris Junction in Gibbon Meadow.

Harlequin Lake Trail You'll get a good look at the interior of a burned forest en route to a small lake that is populated by various types of waterfowl, although few of the harlequin ducks that inspired its name. Short and level, this hike is a good diversion for those who don't want to divert too much from the road. Be sure to bring your insect repellent.

½ mile (1km) RT. Easy. Access: Trailhead is 1½ miles (2.5km) west of the Madison Campground on West Entrance Road.

Purple Mountain Trail This hike requires more physical exertion because it winds 3 miles (5km) through a burned forest to the top of what many consider only a tall hill with an elevation gain of 1,400 feet.

6 miles (9.5km) RT. Easy. Access: Trailhead is ¼ mile (0.5km) north of the Madison Junction on the Madison–Norris Road.

Two Ribbons Trail This trail offers an opportunity to inspect the effects of the 1988 fire. Along the boardwalk, you'll see evidence of not only the blaze that ravaged the area, but also the beginning of a new cycle of life in the dense green shag of lodgepole saplings. You'll also see some of the calling cards of bison in wallows, patches of rubbed-raw earth once used to scratch an itch.

1½ mile (2.5km) RT. Easy. Access: Trailhead is 5 miles (8km) east of the west entrance at an unmarked turnout on the north side of the road.

NORRIS GEYSER BASIN

Back Basin Loop 𝄖 This level boardwalk is easily negotiable in an hour and passes by **Steamboat Geyser,** which has been known to produce the world's highest and most memorable eruptions. How often? About once a decade, with the last bursting in 2000. Wait instead by **Echinus Geyser** because its colorful pool fills and then erupts several times a day.

1½ miles (2.5km) RT. Easy. Access: Trailhead is located at Norris Geyser Basin.

Porcelain Basin Trail   You'll share this boardwalk with other folks, but it takes you across a broad, flat basin where steaming water makes colorful trails. You can complete the walk in less than an hour, but you'll probably stop to look closely at some of these geo-thermal features, a few of which periodically spit and rumble in small eruptions.

½ mile (1km) RT. Easy. Access: Trailhead is located at Norris Geyser Basin.

MAMMOTH HOT SPRINGS AREA

Beaver Ponds Loop Trail   Start at Clematis Gulch and make your way to a series of beaver ponds. Your best chance of seeing the big-tailed beasts is early morning or late afternoon, but you might spot a moose, pronghorn, or elk on the way. There are some good views coming and going, including Mount Everts.

5 miles (8km) RT. Easy. Access: Trailhead is located at Mammoth Hot Springs Terrace.

Bunsen Peak Trail *Finds*   This trail takes you up 1,300 feet in 2 miles (3km) to the 8,564-foot summit. Make the hike early, and you can watch the morning sun strike Electric Mountain; then leave your thoughts in a rusted lockbox packed with the notes of thousands of past hikers. You can take an alternate route back down to the Osprey Falls Trail (see below).

4¼ miles (7km) RT. Moderate. Access: Trailhead across the road from the Glen Creek Trailhead, 5 miles (8km) south of Mammoth on Mammoth–Norris Road.

Children's Fire Trail *Kids*   This flat, undemanding stroll along a boardwalk presents an excellent opportunity to learn about the effects of the fire on the environment. Signposts encourage kids to get down and dirty to examine the indications of the forest's rejuvenation.

¾ mile (1.5km) RT. Easy. Access: The trailhead is on Tower Road, 6 miles (9.5km) east of Mammoth Hot Springs.

Osprey Falls Trail   The first 3 miles (5km) of this hike lead along an old, bike-friendly roadbed at the base of Bunsen Peak. From the Osprey Falls Trail turnoff, it's another 2 miles (3km) through a series of steep switchbacks in Sheepeater Canyon to a secluded waterfall on the Gardner River.

10 miles (16km) RT. Moderate. Access: Trailhead is at Bunsen Peak Trailhead 5 miles (8km) south of Mammoth Hot Spring on Mammoth–Norris Road.

Lower Terrace Interpretive Trail   This interpretive trail is one of the best ways to see this area. The boardwalk begins at 6,280 feet and climbs another 300 feet along marginally steep grades through a bare, rocky, thermal region to a flat alpine area and observation deck at the top, but it's not a difficult climb in exchange for some splendid views. A park guide says the 1½-mile round-trip (2.5km) walk to the Upper Terrace and back takes 2 hours, but it can be done in less.

1½ miles (2.5km) RT. Easy. Access: Trailhead is south of the village on the road to Norris.

Sepulcher Mountain Trail ✿✿   The Glen Creek Trailhead presents hikers with several alternative paths through the Sepulcher Mountain area. During the early summer, this plateau is a beautiful, wide-open area that follows the base of Terrace Mountain. Huge expanses of sagebrush and pines are interspersed with the brilliant yellows and blues of wildflowers, reaching to the horizon. This is an excellent place to escape the crowds. You will also get a feel for the real park in this wilderness area without making much of a physical commitment. Because the trail is in the Gallatin Bear Management Area, you'll want to make noise or tie a bell to a shoe while hiking here. You will notice very quickly that elk and other wildlife aren't nearly as tame as those that wander around the parking lots at the tourist centers; you'll see them, but they are likely to vanish quickly. Be sure to include a pair of binoculars in your backpack.

Three miles (5km) from the trailhead, you'll arrive at a fork in the trail. Now you have to make your choice: Continue another 2 miles (3km) up the steeper option to the mountain's summit, continue on to the east on the Terrace Mountain loop of the **Snow Pass Trail,** or retrace your steps to the trailhead. If you're continuing, I recommend the former. It's a moderate hike that climbs 2,300 feet as the trail winds through a diverse selection of wildlife and scenery.

6–12 miles (9.5–19km) RT. Easy to moderate. Access: Glen Creek Trailhead, 5 miles (8km) south of Mammoth on Mammoth–Norris Road.

Trout Lake Trail ✿   A short, somewhat steep hike through spruce and fir, this trail's destination is the small Trout Lake, which is encircled by a footpath. The lake, nestled between dramatic cliffs and Druid and Baronette peaks, is a favorite fishing hole and one of the best places in the park to witness the fascinating cutthroat spawn. Because of the density of the fish, the lake once served as a major source of food for Cooke City and continues to attract otters, beavers, and bears.

1¼ miles (2km) RT. Easy. Access: 10 miles (16km) west of the Northeast Entrance, at the trailhead 1 mile (1.5km) west of Pebble Creek campground.

GRAND CANYON OF THE YELLOWSTONE RIVER AREA

Clear Lake and Ribbon Lake Loop Trail 🐾 The hike to Clear Lake is 1½ miles (2.5km), a gradual climb across a high plateau, with Ribbon Lake less than 2 miles (3km) beyond it. Views of the plateau improve with each footstep until you find yourself surrounded by a panoramic view of the mountains surrounding the Canyon area. Clear Lake itself is intimately small and gives you the opportunity to see subsurface activity of the thermal areas below the lake. On a circumnavigation of the lake along a trail, you will see and smell vented gas making its way to the surface; in some spots, the lake looks like a small boiling pot. There is bear activity in this area early in the year, so check with rangers for current conditions before heading out.

6 miles (9.5km) RT. Moderate. Access: Wapiti Trailhead, across the street from the South Rim parking lot.

Howard Eaton Trail Both the Clear Lake and Ribbon Lake trails give access to the Howard Eaton Trail, the means to an arduously lengthy hike to Fishing Bridge and Yellowstone Lake. You'll see some riverside thermal features and waterfowl on the way, also passing a ford favored by bison crossing the Yellowstone River. There is bear activity in this area early in the year; check with rangers for current conditions before heading out.

15 miles (24km) one way. Moderate to difficult. Access: Trailhead across the street from the South Rim parking lot.

Mount Washburn Trail 🎯🎯🎯 This is a short hike to panoramic views, with wildflowers decorating the way and nonchalant bighorn sheep often browsing nearby. You might also see marmots and red fox; for a few years, two grizzly bears were regulars rooting in a meadow across from the Dunraven Pass trailhead. Trailheads are located at the summit at Dunraven Pass (elevation 8,895 ft.) and on Old Chittenden Road, where there's more parking available. Either hike is 6 miles (9.5km) round-trip with an increase in elevation of 1,400 feet. However, the climbs are fairly gradual and interspersed with long, level stretches, and you can reach the summit in an easy 90-minute walk if you keep a steady pace. From the summit, the park will lie before you like a map on a table: you'll see the Absaroka Mountains to the east, Yellowstone Lake to the south, and the Gallatin Mountains to the west and north. The summit is over 10,000 feet, so bring a wind shell and warm clothing to fend off the wind that often buffets the top. There's a warming hut in the base of the ranger lookout, with viewing telescopes and restrooms.

6 miles (9.5km) RT. Moderate. Access: Trailheads at the end of Old Chittenden Road and at Dunraven Pass.

North Rim Trail This trail, which is described more fully under "Canyon Village," in chapter 3, "Exploring Yellowstone," offers better views of the falls and the river than you'll get from the parking areas. It's a nice way to see a longer stretch of the canyon.

2 miles (3km) 1 way. Easy. Access: Trailhead at Inspiration Point.

South Rim Trail Like the North Rim Trail, there are more and better views of the canyon and river than you can see from a vehicle. It's easy and not long, and yet you'll have it mostly to yourself because most folks are in and out of the bus at the parking lots.

3¼ miles (5km) 1 way. Easy. Access: Trailhead at the parking lot just beyond South Rim Drive bridge.

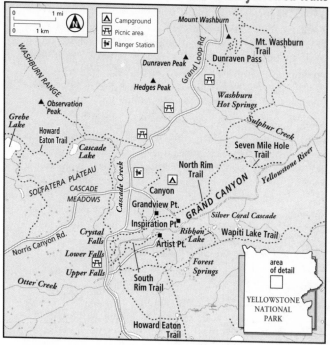

Seven-Mile Hole Trail You'll see the Silver Cord Cascade from the rim and then descend to the river after a couple of miles in an area where the canyon widens enough for trees. There are a few active hot springs along this hike, and it is popular with fisherman because of its river access. This is quite a drop (1,400 ft.), and novice hikers should remember that whatever goes down must come up.

5½ miles (9km) 1 way. Moderate to difficult. Access: Trailhead off North Rim Trail.

Uncle Tom's Trail The short trip is down 328 stairs and paved inclines that lead to an incredible perspective on Lower Falls. The staircase (shackled to the canyon's wall) and trails here are rather steep but can be negotiated in an hour, although it will be challenging for the neophyte hiker. Take your time, enjoy a break on the way back up, and watch for ice on cold mornings.

1 mile (1.5km) RT. Moderate. Access: Trailhead is located at the South Rim parking lot.

YELLOWSTONE LAKE AREA

Elephant Back Loop Trail   Here's an opportunity to look down on (literally!) the island-dotted expanse of Yellowstone Lake, the Absaroka Mountains, and the Pelican Valley. This is a great photo opportunity and a fairly easy hike for a novice.

4 miles (6.5km) RT. Easy. Access: From the east, the trailhead is on the right side of the road, just before the turnoff for the Lake Yellowstone Hotel.

Storm Point Trail 🐾🐾   The Storm Point Trail follows a level path that terminates at a point jutting into the lake, offering a rocky viewpoint of the lake, Stevenson Island, and the mountains beyond. (On a clear day, you'll see as far south as the Tetons.) It begins near Indian Pond, a favorite hangout for bison. During spring months, this is a popular spot with grizzlies, so the trail might be closed; however, even when it's open, check with rangers regarding bear activity.

2 miles (3km) RT. Easy. Access: Trailhead is 3½ miles (5.5km) east of Fishing Bridge, directly across from the Pelican Valley Trailhead (on the lake side of the road).

Pelican Valley Trail   Take this loop through a marsh- and meadow-dotted area north of the lake loaded with elk, bison, sandhill cranes, trout, eagles, grizzly, and the new kids on the block, wolves. You can take hikes of different length, up to a 16-mile (26km) loop, but a lot of folks, having had their fill of wildflowers and beasts, go no farther than Pelican Creek Bridge, about 3½ miles (5.5km) in. If you continue on, you'll pass through forest and "bear meadows," where you should be watchful and respectful of wildlife. This is a daytime-only hiking area, and it's closed in the early summer until July 4 because of bear activity.

7–16 miles (11–26km) RT. Moderate. Access: Trailhead is across from Lake Yellowstone's north shore.

OLD FAITHFUL AREA

Fairy Falls Trail   Though longer than the Mystic Falls Trail, the Fairy Falls Trail is popular because it leads to a taller waterfall, which drops 200 feet. The level hike begins at the Imperial Meadows Trailhead, 1 mile (1.5km) south of the Firehole River bridge on Fountain Flat Drive. After following an old roadbed that winds through an area populated by elk along Fairy Creek, you'll pass the Imperial Geyser. From here, the trail joins Fairy Creek Trail and travels east to the base of the falls. (You can also access the falls via this trail, which is ultimately a shorter trip but less scenic.) The total gain in elevation is only 100 feet.

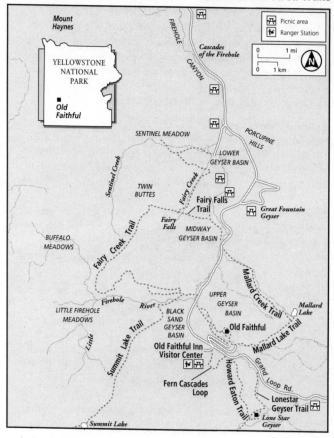

Old Faithful Area Trails

Mount Haynes

YELLOWSTONE NATIONAL PARK

■ Old Faithful

Picnic area
Ranger Station

0   1 mi
0   1 km

FIREHOLE CANYON

Cascades of the Firehole

PORCUPINE HILLS

SENTINEL MEADOW

LOWER GEYSER BASIN

Sentinel Creek

TWIN BUTTES

Fairy Creek

Fairy Falls Trail

Great Fountain Geyser

Fairy Falls

MIDWAY GEYSER BASIN

BUFFALO MEADOWS

Fairy Creek Trail

Firehole River

LITTLE FIREHOLE MEADOWS

Little

UPPER GEYSER BASIN

Mallard Lake

Mallard Creek Trail

BLACK SAND GEYSER BASIN

■ Old Faithful

Summit Lake Trail

Mallard Lake Trail

Old Faithful Inn Visitor Center

Howard Eaton Trail

Grand Loop Rd.

Fern Cascades Loop

Lonestar Geyser Trail

Summit Lake

Lone Star Geyser

7½ miles (12km) RT. Moderate. Access: Trailhead located at Imperial Meadows in Biscuit Basin.

Fountain Paint Pot Trail *(Kids)* This is a very accessible, popular area, so you might be forced to wait for a parking place. All types of thermal activity are on display, so as you stroll along the boardwalk, you'll be distracted at every turn by another bubbling pool or colorful mud pot.

½ mile (1km) RT. Easy. Access: Trailhead begins at Fountain Paint Pot parking lot.

Geyser Hill Loop One of the most interesting, and easiest, loops in the area, this trail winds among several thermal attractions.

Anemone Geyser puts on a good display of the various stages of a typical eruption as the pool fills and overflows, the Lion Group consists of four geysers interconnected beneath the surface, Doublet Pool is popular with photographers who are attracted by a complex series of ledges and deep blue waters, and Giantess Geyser is known for its violent eruptions.

1¼ miles (2km) RT. Easy. Access: Trailhead at Old Faithful Boardwalk.

Lonestar Geyser Trail 🐾 The popularity of this trail detracts from the pleasure of walking a fairly level, forested trail along the Firehole River, interrupted now and then by broad riverbank meadows. The geyser itself sits in a meadow pocked by steam vents and thermal features. About every 3 hours, it spouts water about 50 feet in the air from a vanilla- and chocolate-colored cone. The path is partially paved and open to bicycles as far as the geyser (hikers can go farther, over Grants Pass). In the winter, this is a popular route for cross-country skiers.

4½ miles (7.5km) RT. Easy. Access: Trailhead at the parking lot opposite Kepler Cascades.

Mystic Falls Trail This trail leads to a waterfall on the Little Firehole River that drops more than 100 feet, one of the steepest in the park. The trail starts at Biscuit Basin, crosses the river, and then disappears into the forest. The total distance to the base of the falls is only 1 mile (1.5km); there's a trail to take you to the top, and if you want to take a different way home, connect with the **Little Firehole Meadows Trail,** with long-distance views of Old Faithful, back to Biscuit Basin.

1 miles (1km) 1 way. Easy. Access: Trailhead located at Imperial Meadows in Biscuit Basin.

Observation Point Trail–Solitary Geyser 🐾🐾 *Moments* For a spectacular view of Old Faithful and the geyser basin from above, take this 2-mile (3km) loop. While it requires a bit more planning than watching Old Faithful from the bleachers, you'll have a totally different perspective from the masses below. The path up to the observation point is just half a mile (1km), and the elevation gain is only 200 feet, an easy 15-minute hike. From the top, you can see most of the major geysers, as well as inaccessible steam vents located in the middle of wooded areas. From the top of the boardwalk, continue to the Solitary Geyser on a downhill slope that leads past the geyser, through the basin, and back to the Old Faithful Inn, which completes the loop.

2 miles (3km) RT. Easy. Access: Trailhead at Old Faithful boardwalk.

2 Exploring the Backcountry

The backcountry of Yellowstone is the real thing: a domain of free-roaming wildlife and natural treasures predominately untouched by the hand of man. The National Park Service, through its system of permits, designated camping areas, and rules (for more on these, see below), has managed to preserve a true wilderness. Yellowstone has more than 1,200 miles (1931km) of trails (most of which are in the backcountry) and 300 backcountry campsites.

For **general information** on backpacking and safety, see chapter 2, "Planning Your Trip to Yellowstone & Grand Teton National Parks."

INFORMATION BEFORE YOU GO   Contact the **Yellowstone Backcountry Office,** P.O. Box 168, Yellowstone National Park, WY 82190 (✆ **307/344-2160**), and it will send you the useful *Backcountry Trip Planner* with a detailed map showing where the campsites are, how to make reservations, and how to prepare.

BACKCOUNTRY PERMITS   Backcountry permits are free, but you have to have one for any overnight trip, on foot, on horseback or by boat. Camping is allowed only in designated campsites, many of which are equipped with food storage poles to keep wildlife out of your stores. Some are also equipped with pit toilets. These sites are primitive and well situated, and you won't feel like you're in a campground.

Pick up your permit in the park within 48 hours of your departure at one of the following stations any day of the week during the summer: Bechler, west entrance, or south entrance ranger stations (no phone); or Canyon, Mammoth, Old Faithful, Tower, Grant Village, Lake, or Bridge Bay visitor centers (see "Essentials," in chapter 3, "Exploring Yellowstone," for phone numbers and information).

WHEN TO GO   Many of the trails into the park backcountry remain covered with snow and become muddy in the first weeks of melt, well into June. At the higher elevations, over 9,000 feet, summer doesn't truly begin until early July. Trail maintenance in the backcountry is much less thorough than on the more public trails near the roads: creeks and streams described as "intermittent" during summer months might be filled with snowmelt that converts them to impassable, swiftly running rivers, often drenching trails and converting them to mud. Look in the *Backcountry Trip Planner*

(Tips Planning Ahead

You can pick up a permit the day before beginning a trip, but if you'll be traveling during peak season, try to make a reservation in advance. If you don't, and someone else has reserved the campsites in the area you want to go, you're out of luck. It costs $20 to hold a site, and you can begin making reservations for the upcoming year on April 1.

Caution: The reservation is just that, a reservation; upon your arrival at the park, you'll need to secure the permit, which is valid only on the dates for which it is issued.

---

for approximate dates when specific campsites will be accessible and habitable.

MAPS   Park rangers suggest using the "Yellowstone Series" of maps produced by Trails Illustrated. Each of the four maps in the collection covers about nine of those produced by the U. S. Geologic Survey and is printed on durable plastic; the maps also show backcountry campsite locations. For more information, contact **Trails Illustrated** (© 800/962-1643; www.trailsillustrated. com) or the **Yellowstone Association,** P.O. Box 117, Yellowstone National Park, WY 82190 (© 307/344-2293; www.yellowstone association.org).

OUTFITTERS   An alternative to going on your own is to go with an outfitter. Outfitters provide most equipment, which can offset the cost of their services, which might include setting up tents and making meals.

In Gardiner, at the north entrance to the park, **Wilderness Connection Inc.** (© 406/848-7287; fax 406/848-2131) offers horseback trips in the park for groups of 4 to 10; rates begin at $200 per person, per day. **Yellowstone Guidelines** (© 800/314-4506 or 406/586-2876; www.yellowstoneadventures.com) offers customized, guided hikes and horseback trips with meals and lodging in tents or nearby hostelries. Plan on spending $250 per day or more, depending upon where you bed down. **Yellowstone Llamas** (© 406/586-6872; www.yellowstone-llamas.com) offers an excellent compromise: beasts of burden that carry the heavy gear, leaving you free to wander the trails. The trips typically cover 5 to 8 miles (8 to 13km) per day in the park, and gourmet meals are served at the end of the day along with stream-chilled bottles of wine. Cost is $195 a day per person, $145 for children 12 and under.

Also, many Jackson, Wyoming–based outfitters conduct trips into Yellowstone. Don't forget to check out chapter 6, "Hikes & Other Outdoor Pursuits in Grand Teton National Park," for more outfitters.

THE YELLOWSTONE BACKCOUNTRY

If you just can't get your fill of geysers, or if you've had your fill of people, several trails lead to more isolated backcountry. The **Shoshone Geyser Basin** and **Heart Lake Geyser Basin** contain active geysers, as do **Ponuntpa Springs** and the **Mudkettles** in the Pelican Valley Area, **Imperial Geyser** in the Firehole area, and the **Highland Hot Springs** on the Mary Mountain Trail. If you head in these directions, be careful about walking on unstable surfaces: A young man died in 1988 when he fell into a superheated pool.

SHOSHONE LAKE

Shoshone Lake is the largest backcountry lake in the Lower 48 and a popular spot for backcountry hikers. The shortest route to the lake is via the **Delacy Creek Trail,** which begins 8 miles (13km) east of Old Faithful on Old Faithful–West Thumb Road. From here, the trail winds 3 miles (5km) along Delacy Creek through moose country and the edge of the forest at the lake. At this point, it's a toss-up: You can head around the lake in either direction. Assuming that you take a clockwise track around the lake—a distance of 18 miles (29km)—you'll continue 4½ miles (7km) on the Delacy Creek Trail to its intersection with **Dogshead Trail,** and then head west on the **Shoshone Lake Trail** until it intersects with the **North Shoshone Trail** and returns to your starting point.

A detour: At the western end of the lake, you'll arrive at the 1-mile (1.5km) **Shoshone Geyser Basin Trail** 🐾🐾, which loops through a number of geysers, hot springs, and meadows that, during spring months, are ankle-deep in water and mud. Union Geyser, which erupts sporadically, is impressive because eruptions occur from three vents simultaneously. Because the crust of the earth is so thin here, your footsteps might sound like thumping on a hollow gourd.

As you travel the lake's loop trail along the **Delacy Creek Trail,** you'll have views of the lake at the top of a 100-foot rise. Then, on the **Shoshone Lake Trail,** you'll cross the Lewis Channel, which can have thigh-high water as late as July. Beyond that, the trail is a series of rises that are easily negotiable by the average hiker, passing across shallow Moose Creek and through meadows where you might spot deer or moose early in the morning or evening.

The 8½-mile (14km) **North Shoshone Trail** winds through a lodgepole-pine forest, over numerous ridges up to 200 feet high. The best views of the lake are from the high points on this trail. The loop trail is especially popular with overnighters because there are 26 campsites on the loop, the largest of which has space for 8 campers. (Some of the sites are accessible by paddlers only, however.)

THE BECHLER REGION

This area in the park's southwest section is often referred to as Cascade Corner because it contains a majority of the park's waterfalls. It escaped the fires of 1988 and offers great opportunities to view thermal features. Many backpacking routes cut through this region, including one that leads to Old Faithful on the **Bechler River Trail.**

To begin your hike, drive into the park from Ashton, Idaho, and check in at the Bechler Ranger Station. To reach the ranger station, drive east 17 miles (27km) from Ashton on the Cave Falls Road; 3 miles (5km) before reaching Cave Falls, you'll find the ranger station turnoff. The ranger station is 1½ miles (2.5km) down the gravel road.

The **Bechler Meadows Trail** takes you into this southwest corner, rich in waterfalls, cascades, and thermal areas that rarely have human visitors. About 6 miles (9.5km) into the journey, the trail fords the river several times as it enters Bechler Canyon, where it passes Collonade and Iris falls. There are places on this trail where you can view the Tetons in the distance and hot springs that warm the creeks. You can cover a good 30 miles (48km), depending on what turns you take. It's a camping trip best made late in the summer, to avoid high water during creek crossings. For a shorter trip, hike 3½ miles (5.5km) along the **Bechler River Trail** to the **Boundary Creek Trail,** and then return to the station via the **Bechler Meadows Trails,** a round-trip of 7 miles (11km).

The most adventurous and scenic route takes you 30 miles (48km) from the ranger station to the end of the trail at the **Lonestar Geyser Trailhead** near Old Faithful. Beyond Iris Falls and then Ragged Falls, you'll reach a patrol cabin at Three Rivers Junction at the 13-mile (21km) mark, a popular camping area with room for 12 people. There are a total of 10 campsites between the ranger station and Three Rivers. If you continue toward Old Faithful, you'll intersect the **Shoshone Lake Trail** at the 23½-mile (38km) mark and exit 6½ miles (10km) later.

THOROFARE AREA

When you enter this country in the park's southeast corner, you're venturing into the most remote, roadless area in the Lower 48. You can make a round-trip of around 70 miles (113km) deep into the wilderness, or you can take shorter hikes, such as a trip from the park's East Entrance Road to the Yellowstone River inlet on Yellowstone Lake's southeast arm. The remoteness of this country discourages many hikers, so you'll have it mostly to yourself. Along the way, teepee rings and lean-tos are reminders that Indians once used this trail as the main route between Jackson Hole and points north.

The **Thorofare Trail** ⚔ follows the eastern shore of Yellowstone Lake and then trails the Yellowstone River up into some of the most remote and beautiful backcountry in the Rockies. It's a lot of miles and climbing, but you'll be rewarded with spectacular views of the Upper Yellowstone Valley and Two Oceans Plateau, and there's a good chance of seeing some wildlife. You'll reach the Park Service's Thorofare Ranger Station at 32 miles (52km), and a few miles farther you'll come to Bridger Lake, outside the park, and a gorgeous alpine valley with a ranger station known as Hawk's Rest. Fishermen love this area, as do grizzly bears, especially during the cutthroat trout spawning season in early summer. You'll be a good 35 miles (56km) from the trailhead at the lake, and even the most capable hikers should consider riding with an outfitter. You can cut 9 miles (14km) off the trip by getting a boat shuttle (about $60 an hour) to the mouth of the lake's southwest arm (call the marina at ☏ **307/ 242-3876**), or you can come in through Bridger–Teton National Forest to the south (check with the forest's Blackrock Ranger Station in Moran, Wyoming; ☏ **307/543-2386**). Other than bears, the major obstacle to early season trips in the Thorofare is water; you'll encounter knee-deep water at **Beaverdam Creek** and at **Trapper Creek** as late as July.

THE SPORTSMAN LAKE TRAIL

This trail begins near Mammoth Hot Springs and extends west toward U.S. 191 to Sportsman Lake: a moderate, 14-mile (23km) trail that displays a diverse combination of flora and fauna. From the Glen Creek Trailhead 5 miles (8km) south of Mammoth Hot Springs, you'll spend 2 miles (3km) on the Glen Creek Trail as you traverse a mostly level, wide-open plateau covered with sagebrush that is the home of herds of elk and a bear-management area. At the **Sepulcher Mountain Trail** ⚔⚔ at the 3-mile (5km) mark, the terrain becomes steeper as you continue northwest on the **Sportsman Lake Trail**—the elevation gain is approximately 2,300 feet to the Sepulcher summit (although you don't go to it on this route). The trail eventually enters the forest and descends to a log that is used to cross Gardner River. Then it's uphill for another 4 miles (6.5km) to **Electric Divide,** another 2,000-foot gain in elevation. From there, the trail descends 2,100 feet in 3 miles (5km) to Sportsman Lake, which is located in an area burned by the 1988 conflagration. The lake, which sits in a meadow populated by moose and elk, is teeming with cutthroat trout. Two campsites provide overnight spaces for a total of 30 visitors.

THE SLOUGH CREEK TRAIL

Beginning in the Lamar Valley of the park's northeast corner, this trail takes hikers through some of the best wildlife habitat in the park. You can see elk, bison, trumpeter swans, and sometimes grizzly bears, and now wolves that have quite happily taken up residence among abundant prey. The presence of wolves has made this area much more popular, and the trail is also used by horse-packers. The trail starts from the road to Slough Creek campground, following the creek's valley north, and then crosses a ridge to a second valley. You can hike a few miles or take your camping gear and head for the park boundary, 11 miles (18km) to the north.

3 Other Activities

BIKING   Considering the vast expanse of real estate that the parks cover, the challenging terrain, and the miles of paved roads and trails, a cyclist might conclude that the parks are prime areas for biking, on or off the roads.

It looks good on paper, but the reality is more harrowing. The roads are narrow and twisty; there are no bike lanes, so bikers continually fight for elbow room with wide-bodied RVs and trailers, some of which have side-view mirrors designed to decapitate bicyclists. Off-road opportunities are limited because of the small number of trails on which bikes are allowed.

Nevertheless, plenty of bicyclists take the challenge. The following trails are available, but you'll be sharing the roads with hikers. The **Mount Washburn trail,** leaving from Old Chittenden Road, is a strenuous trail that climbs 1,400 feet. The **Lonestar Geyser trail,** accessed at Kepler Cascade near Old Faithful, is an easy 1-hour ride on a user-friendly, partly paved road. Near Mammoth Hot Springs, **Bunsen Peak Road** and **Osprey Falls trails** present a combination

Ⓚⁱᵈˢ Especially for Kids

You might find that several of the ranger programs will appeal to kids. And don't forget the **Children's Fire Trail,** an interpretive trail leading through a burned-out area of the park with signs to teach the young ones about forest fires. It's located on Tower Road, just east of Mammoth Hot Springs (described in more detail under "Day Hikes" above, in the Mammoth section).

Like many national parks, Yellowstone has a **Junior Ranger Program** for kids ages 5 to 12. For $3, you get a special activity paper, *Yellowstone's Nature.* (Sign up at any visitor center.) Kids get a Junior Ranger badge for completing certain activities.

There's also a unique education residential program for kids in fourth through sixth grades at Yellowstone called *Expedition: Yellowstone!* This residential program takes place at Lamar Buffalo Ranch in the spring and fall, with sessions lasting 4 to 5 days. Kids learn about the park, combining classroom work with a trip to Yellowstone. For more information, write: *Expedition: Yellowstone!* **Coordinator,** P.O. Box 168, Yellowstone National Park, WY 82190-0168.

ride/hike: The first 6 miles (9.5km) travel around Bunsen Peak; getting to the top requires a hike. A hike down to Osprey Falls adds another 3 miles (5km) to the journey.

Bike rentals are available in the gateway towns of West Yellowstone at **Yellowstone Bicycles** (☏ **406/646-7815**) and Jackson at **Hoback Sports,** (☏ **307/733-5335**). Rental fees for traditional bikes are about $25 to $30 a day; for a full suspension mountain bike, they're $25 to $50 a day.

BOATING   The best place to enjoy boating in Yellowstone is on **Yellowstone Lake,** which has easy access and beautiful, panoramic views. The lake is also one of the few areas where powerboats are allowed. Rowboats and outboard motorboats can be rented at **Bridge Bay Marina** (☏ **307/344-7381**). Cost for rowboats is about $32 per day or $6 per hour; an outboard with room for six rents for $30 per hour. Sea kayakers and canoeists should stay close to the shore on Yellowstone Lake because of high winds that can easily capsize a small craft. Motorboats, canoes, and kayaks can be used on Lewis Lake as well.

FISHING   Seven varieties of game fish live in the parks: native cutthroat, rainbow, brown, brook and lake trout, grayling, and mountain whitefish. Of the trout, only the cutthroats are native, and they are being pressured in the big lake by the larger lake trout. As a result, you can't keep any pink-meat cutthroat caught anywhere in Yellowstone, and you *must* keep every last lake trout. This catch-and-release policy has done little to discourage fly-fishing purists who are more interested in the sport than its spoils.

The Yellowstone season typically opens on the Saturday of Memorial Day weekend and ends on the first Sunday in November. Yellowstone Lake has a slightly shorter season, and the lake's tributaries are closed until July 15 to avoid conflicts between humans and grizzly bears, both of which are attracted to spawning trout.

Many fine anglers come to Yellowstone, and they are well informed about which seasons are best on which stretches of river. In June, try the **Yellowstone River** downstream of Yellowstone Lake, where the cutthroat trout spawn. In July, fish the **Madison River** near the west entrance, and fish again in late fall for rainbow and some brown trout. In late summer, you can try to hook the cutthroats that thin out by September on the **Lamar River** in the park's beautiful northeast corner.

Fishing on **Yellowstone Lake** has been popular until recent years, when regulations designed to bring back the waning population of cutthroat trout have sent some of the trolling powerboats elsewhere. The problem is the introduced lake trout, which compete with and eat the cutthroat. If you catch a lake trout, you *must* kill it, and if you catch a cutthroat, you *must* throw it back. Certain areas of the lake, such as the southeast arm, are closed to motorized boats—this makes the Yellowstone River inlet a wonderful area to canoe and camp and fish.

You can fish the **Yellowstone River** below the Grand Canyon by hiking down into **Seven-Mile Hole,** a great place to cast (not much vegetation to snag on) for cutthroat trout from July to September. You'll have the best luck around Sulphur Creek.

Other good fishing stretches include the **Gibbon** and **Firehole rivers,** which merge to form the Madison River on the park's west side, and the 3-mile (5km) **Lewis River Channel** between Shoshone and Lewis lakes during the fall spawning run of brown trout.

There is an access on the **Madison River** for anglers with disabilities, 3½ miles (5.5km) west of Madison Junction at the Haynes Overlook, where you'll find a wheelchair-accessible fishing platform overhanging the river's edge along 70 feet of the bank.

Suggested Reading   Two reference guides present excellent information about park fishing opportunities and requirements: *Fishing Yellowstone National Park,* by Richard Parks (Falcon Press), and *The Yellowstone Fly-Fishing Guide,* by Craig Mathews and Clayton Molinero (published by Lyons and Burford). Both can be purchased from the Yellowstone Association.

Permits   The required Yellowstone fishing permit is available at any ranger station, visitor center, or Hamilton Store in the park. Anyone older than 15 needs a fishing permit, which costs $10 for 10 days or $20 for the season. Kids ages 12 to 15 also need a permit, but it's free. Casters under 12 must be supervised by an adult. Season permits can be obtained by mail (**Visitors Services,** P.O. Box 168, Yellowstone National Park, WY 82190); 10-day licenses must be purchased at the park visitor centers, ranger stations, or Hamilton Stores.

Supplies & Fishing Guides   If you need supplies, in Gardiner, stop at **Parks' Fly Shop,** Highway 89 (© 406/848-7314). In West Yellowstone, check **Bud Lilly's,** 39 Madison Ave. (© 406/646-7801).

In **West Yellowstone,** the following tackle shops offer the full gamut of guided fishing trips and schools, from 1-day trips to weeklong excursions: **Arrick's Fishing Flies,** 37 Canyon St. (© 406/646-7290); **Bud Lilly's Trout Shop,** 39 Madison Ave. (© 406/646-7801); **Eagle's Tackle Shop,** 3 Canyon St. (© 406/646-7521); **Jacklin's,** 105 Yellowstone Ave. (© 406/646-7336); and **Madison River Outfitters,** 117 Canyon St. (© 406/646-9644).

Also, several Jackson, Wyoming–based fishing guides lead trips into Yellowstone. See "Fishing" in the "Other Activities" section in chapter 6, "Hikes & Other Outdoor Pursuits in Grand Teton National Park."

HORSEBACK RIDING   People who want to pack their gear on a horse, llama, or mule must either get permits to enter the Yellowstone backcountry or hire an outfitter with a permit (see below). Other visitors who want to get in the saddle but not disappear in the wilderness can put themselves in the hands of the concessionaire, **Yellowstone National Park Lodges** (© **307/344-7311;** www.travelyellowstone.com). Stables are located at Canyon Village, Roosevelt Lodge, and Mammoth Hot Springs. Roosevelt Lodge also offers **evening rides** from June into September. Choices are 1- and 2-hour guided trail rides daily aboard well-broken, tame animals. Wranglers refer to these as "nose-and-tail" tours, and an experienced rider is likely to find them awfully tame.

If you're looking for a longer, overnight horse-packing experience, contact the park and request a list of approved concessionaires that lead backcountry expeditions. Most offer customized, guided trips, with meals, horses, and camping and riding gear provided. Costs will run from $200 to $400 per day per person, depending on the length of the trip and number of people. In Gardiner, at the north entrance to the park, **Wilderness Connection Inc.** (© **406/848-7287**) offers horseback trips in the park for groups of 4 to 10; rates begin at $200 per day for customized, guided hikes and horseback trips, with meals and lodging in tents or nearby hostelries. On the south side of the park, try **Press Stephens, Outfitter** (© **307/455-2250**). While not a horse-packing excursion, per se, you might also try **Yellowstone Llamas** (© **406/586-6872;** www.yellowstone-llamas.com). This company offers an excellent compromise: Llamas carry the heavy gear, leaving you free to wander the trails. Tours typically cover 5 to 8 miles (8 to 13km) per day in the park and serve gourmet meals at the end of the day. Cost is $195 per day, per person.

4 Winter Sports & Activities

The average snowfall in a Yellowstone winter is nearly 50 inches, creating a beautiful setting for sightseers and a wonderful resource for outdoor winter recreation. The steaming hot pools and geysers generate little islands of warmth and clear ground, attracting not just tourists but wildlife as well. Nearby trees are transformed into "snow ghosts" by frozen thermal vapors. Bison become frosted, shaggy beasts, easily spotted as they take advantage of the more accessible vegetation on the thawed ground. Yellowstone Lake's surface freezes to an average thickness of 3 feet, creating a vast ice sheet that sings and moans as the huge plates of ice shift. But the ice is thinner where hot springs come up on the lake bottom, and you'll see otters surfacing at the breaks in the ice. Waterfalls become astounding pieces of frozen sculpture. Snow-white trumpeter swans glide through geyser-fed streams under clear-blue skies of clean, crisp mountain air.

Only two of the park's hostelries, **Mammoth Hot Springs** and the **Old Faithful Snow Lodge,** provide accommodations from December through March, as does **Flagg Ranch,** just outside the park's south entrance (see chapter 7, "Where to Stay & Dine in the Parks," for more information about all 3). The only road that's open for cars is **Mammoth Hot Springs–Cooke City Road.** Most visitors these days come into Yellowstone in winter from the west or south by snowcoach or snowmobile.

For additional information on all of the following winter activities and accommodations, as well as snowcoach reservations, contact **Yellowstone National Park Lodges** (© 307/344-7311). There are also many activities, outfitters, and rental shops in the park's gateway towns.

The **Yellowstone Association Institute** ☆☆☆ (© 307/344-2294) offers winter courses at the old Buffalo Ranch in Lamar Valley. Past offerings have included 3-day classes devoted to "Backcountry by Ski," "Yellowstone's Winter World," and "Tracking Yellowstone's Wolves."

CROSS-COUNTRY SKIING   There are 40 miles (64km) of cross-country trails in the Old Faithful area, including the popular **Lonestar Geyser Trail,** an 8-mile (13km) trail in a remote setting that starts at the Old Faithful Snow Lodge, and the **Fern Cascades trail,** which winds for 3 miles (5km) through a rolling woodland landscape on a short loop close to the Old Faithful area. In the Mammoth area, try the **Upper Geyser Basin and Biscuit Basin trail** (about 6 miles/9.5km), which some say is the best in Yellowstone, although it might take an entire day to negotiate.

Equipment rentals (about $12 per day), ski instruction, ski shuttles to various locations, and guided ski tours are all available at the **Old Faithful Snow Lodge** and the **Mammoth Hot Springs Hotel,** the park's two winter lodging options. Discounts are available for multiday rentals of skis or snowshoes. Ski instruction costs around $20 per person for a 2-hour group lesson. A half-day guided excursion costs around $34 per person; a full day costs $60 to $100 per person.

ICE SKATING   The **Mammoth Hot Springs ice rink** is located behind the Mammoth Hot Springs Recreation Center. On a crisp winter's night, you can rent a pair of skates ($1 per hour, $4 per day)

Winter Road Conditions

Due to the high elevation and the abundance of snow, most of the roads in Yellowstone are closed to all wheeled vehicles during winter. The only major park area that is accessible by car is Mammoth Hot Springs; cars are allowed to drive in the village at Mammoth Hot Springs. Signs will alert you as to how far south into the park you can actually go from here (usually to Tower Junction, 18 miles/29km away). From Tower Junction, it's another 29 miles (47km) to the northeast entrance. This entrance is open but not accessible from Red Lodge, Montana, and points east (because the Beartooth Highway is closed in winter). You can go only as far as Cooke City, Montana, and the roads are kept open specifically so that the folks in Cooke City aren't totally stranded during the long winters. **Snowcoaches, snowmobiles, and cross-country skiers,** however, use park roads regularly throughout the winter season. For up-to-the-minute information on weather and road conditions, call the **Visitor Information Center** at ✆ **307/344-7381.**

Basing Yourself in West Yellowstone From the West Yellowstone entrance, you're only 14 miles (22km) to the Madison Junction, which presents opportunities to head south to Old Faithful or north to the Grand Canyon and Mammoth Hot Springs. Because this is the most popular way to access the park, plan on making reservations early.

In West Yellowstone, contact **Alpine West,** 300 Hayden St. (✆ **800/858-9224** or 406/646-7633); **Hi Country Snowmobile**

and glide across the ice while seasonal melodies are broadcast over the PA system. It's cold out there, but there's a warming fire at the rink's edge. Call ✆ **307/344-7311** for more information.

SNOWMOBILING Roads that are jammed with cars during the summer fill up with bison and snowmobiles during the winter. In deference to the shaggier road warriors, moderate speed limits are strictly enforced, but this is still an excellent way to sightsee at your own pace. A driver's license is required for rental ($165 for a single rider, $175 per day for 2 at **Mammoth Hot Springs Hotel** or **Old Faithful Snow Lodge**), and a quick lesson will put even a first-timer at ease. A helmet is included with the snowmobile, and you can rent

Rental, U.S. 20 and Hayden St. (© **800/624-5291** or 406/646-7541); or **Old Faithful Snowmobile Rentals,** 215 Canyon St. (© **800/541-7354** or 406/646-9695), to arrange reservations. Expect to pay $100 to $150 per day for a machine and a helmet; however, unless you own winter gear that's adequate for temperatures in the teens, plan on spending another $25 for clothing.

Basing Yourself at Flagg Ranch   Accessing the Old Faithful area of Yellowstone from the south requires a greater commitment of time, money, and physical exertion.

After flying into Jackson, you can find lodging there or head north 51 miles (82km) on U.S. 89 to **Flagg Ranch,** where you'll find lodging, a restaurant, bar, and snowmobile and snowcoach rentals. Depending upon road conditions, the trip can take 2 hours by auto. For information about accommodations or snowmobile rentals, contact Flagg Ranch (© **800/443-2311** or 307/543-2861).

Flagg Ranch is within minutes—even by snowmobile—of the park's south entrance. From there, it's a 22-mile (35km) trip to the West Thumb Junction and 17 miles (27km) to the Old Faithful geyser basin and Old Faithful Snow Lodge. Depending upon weather and road conditions, the trip can be arduous, especially if winds are blowing snow across the roads and creating bone-chilling temperatures.

a clothing package for protection against the bitter cold. **Warming huts** are located at Mammoth, Indian Creek, Canyon, Madison, West Thumb, and Fishing Bridge. They offer snacks, a hot cup of coffee or chocolate, and an excellent opportunity to recover from a chill.

Keep an eye on snow conditions. While it's true that snowmobile trails are groomed for travel, when snow cover is scant, a normally smooth trip can become something akin to riding on a jackhammer.

Because of the resultant noise (and pollution), the park moved towards an outright ban on snowmobiles, but it remained mired in litigation at press time. While there has been a move toward cleaner, quieter machines, snowmobiles could be on their way out as soon as 2003. (See chapter 1, "Introducing Yellowstone & Grand Teton National Parks.")

Snowmobile rentals are also available from the outlets described in the sidebar "Winter Road Conditions," above, and in the **gateway communities** of Gardiner and West Yellowstone, Montana, and at Flagg Ranch. In West Yellowstone, try **Yellowstone Arctic/ Yamaha,** 208 Electric St. (© **406/646-9636**), or **Backcountry Adventure Snowmobile Rental,** 224 Electric St. (© **800/924- 7669**). In Gardiner, check out **Absaroka Lodge,** U.S. 89 (© **800/ 755-7414** or 406/848-7414), or the **Best Western at Mammoth Hot Springs,** U.S. 89 (© **406/848-7311**). In **Flagg Ranch,** snowmobiles are rented along John D. Rockefeller, Jr. Parkway just south of the park (© **800/443-2311** or 307/543-2861). Most rental shops accept reservations weeks in advance, so reserving at least a day or 2 weeks ahead of time is a good idea. Plan on making reservations for the week between Christmas and New Year's at least 6 months in advance.

SNOWCOACH TOURS   It is possible to enjoy the sights and sounds of Yellowstone without raising a finger, except to write a check or sign a credit card voucher, by taking one of the scenic snowcoach tours that originate at the south and west entrances, Mammoth, and Old Faithful. One-way trips range from $46 to $51, while round-trips cost $92 to $99.

If you've never seen a snowcoach, you're in for a treat. Don't be fooled into thinking that this distinctively Yellowstone mode of transportation is merely a fancy name for a bus that provides tours during winter. Imagine instead an Econoline van with tank treads for tires and water skis extending from its front, and you won't be surprised when you see this unusual-looking vehicle. The interiors are toasty-warm, with seating for a large group, and they usually allow each passenger two bags. They aren't the fastest, smoothest, or

---

Tips **Two Is a Crowd**

Because there's so much traffic on park roads and snowmobiles and snowcoaches make deep ruts in the snow, traveling two to a snowmobile can be especially uncomfortable for the person on the back, especially when you're covering long distances. It's cold, too.

most comfortable form of transportation, but they do allow large groups to travel together, and they're cheaper and warmer than snowmobiles. They're also available for hire by groups at many snowmobile locations. Guides provide interesting and entertaining facts and stories of the areas as you cruise the park trails, and they give you opportunities to photograph scenery and wildlife.

In West Yellowstone, contact **Three Bear Lodge** (© 800/221-1551), **Yellowstone Arctic** (© 800/646-9636), or **Yellowstone Alpen Guides** (© 800/858-3502 or 406/646-7242).

For Flagg Ranch or Jackson snowcoach information, contact **Flagg Ranch** (© 800/443-2311) or **Yellowstone National Park Lodges** (© 307/344-7311).

5

Exploring Grand Teton National Park

Although Grand Teton National Park is much smaller than Yellowstone, there is much more to it than just its peaks, a dozen of which climb to elevations greater than 12,000 feet. The park's size—54 miles (87km) long, from north to south—allows visitors to get a good look at the highlights in a day or two. But you'd be missing a great deal: the beautiful views from its trails, an exciting float on the Snake River, the watersports paradise that is Jackson Lake.

Whether your trip is half a day or 2 weeks, the park's proximity to the town of Jackson allows for an interesting trip that combines the outdoors with the urbane. You can descend Grand Teton and be living it up at the Million Dollar Cowboy Bar or dining in a fine restaurant that evening. The next day, you can return to the peace of the park without much effort at all.

1 Essentials

ACCESS/ENTRY POINTS Grand Teton National Park runs along a north-south axis, bordered on the west by the omnipresent Teton Range. Teton Park Road, the primary thoroughfare, skirts along the lakes at the mountains' base. From the **north,** you can enter the park from Yellowstone National Park, which is linked to Grand Teton by the **John D. Rockefeller Jr. Memorial Parkway** (U.S. Highways 89/191/287), an 8-mile (13km) stretch of highway, along which you might see wildlife through the trees, some still bare and blackened from the 1988 fires. If you enter this way, you will already have paid your entrance fee to both parks, but you can stop at a park information center at Flagg Ranch, just outside Yellowstone, to get Grand Teton information. From December through mid-March, Yellowstone's south entrance is open only to snowmobiles and snowcoaches, and there is a trail that connects to Grand Teton.

You can also approach the park from the **east,** via U.S. Highways 26/287. This route comes from Dubois, 55 miles (89km) east on the other side of the Absaroka and Wind River Mountains, and crosses **Togwotee Pass,** where you'll get your first (and one of the best) views of the Tetons towering over the valley. Travelers who come this way can continue south on U.S. 26/89/191 to Jackson without paying an entrance fee, although they are within the park boundaries, and enjoy spectacular mountain and Snake River views.

Finally, you can enter Grand Teton from Jackson in the **south,** driving about 12 miles (19km) north on U.S. Highways 26/89/191 to the Moose turnoff and the park's south entrance. Here you'll find the park headquarters and Moose Visitor Center, plus a small community that includes dining and shops.

VISITOR CENTERS & INFORMATION   There are three visitor centers in Grand Teton National Park. The **Moose Visitor Center** (✆ **307/739-3399**), mentioned above, is a half-mile (1km) west of Moose Junction at the southern end of the park; it's open 8am to 7pm daily from June through Labor Day, and 8am to 5pm the rest of the year. The **Colter Bay Visitor Center** (✆ **307/739-3594**), the northernmost of the park's visitor centers, is open 8am to 8pm from early June through Labor Day, and from 8am to 5pm from Labor Day through early October. There is also **Jenny Lake Visitor Center** (✆ **307/739-3392**), open 8am to 7pm daily from early June through Labor Day, and 8am to 5pm from Labor Day through early October. Maps and ranger assistance are available at all three, and there are bookstores and exhibits at Moose and Colter Bay. Finally, there is an information station at the **Flagg Ranch** complex (no phone), which is located approximately 5 miles (8km) north of the park's northern boundary.

To obtain park maps before your arrival, contact **Grand Teton National Park,** P.O. Drawer 170, Moose, WY 83012 (✆ **307/739-3600;** www.nps.gov/grte).

FEES   There are no park gates on U.S. Highways 26/89/191, so you can get a free ride through the park on that route; to get off the highway and explore, you'll pay $20 per automobile for a 7-day pass. If you expect to visit Yellowstone and Grand Teton (admission is good for both) more than once a year, buy a $40 annual permit. Better yet, if you visit parks elsewhere in the country, buy a $65 **Golden Eagle Passport,** good for all parks and national monuments for a year from the month of purchase, or a $50 **National Parks Pass,** good for a year's access to the parks but not the monuments.

Grand Teton National Park

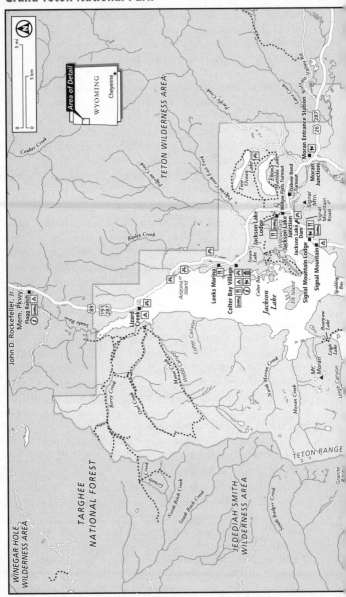

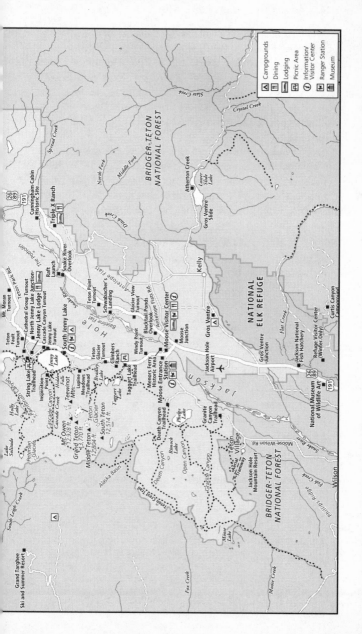

Legend

△	Campgrounds
∏	Dining
⌂	Lodging
木	Picnic Area
?	Information/Visitor Center
▢	Ranger Station
▦	Museum

Grand Targhee Ski and Summer Resort

Lake Solitude

South Leigh Creek

Peterson Glacier

Cascade Canyon
Cascade Creek

Mt. Owen
12,928 ft.
Grand Teton
13,770 ft.
Teton Glacier
Middle Teton
12,804 ft.
South Teton
12,514 ft.

Alaska Basin

Teton Crest Trail

Fox Creek

Moose Creek

Holly Lake

Paintbrush Canyon

Inspiration Point
String Lake Trailhead
Hidden Falls
Jenny Lake

Teewinot

Lupine Meadows Trailhead

Bradley Lake

Taggart Lake

Taggart Lake Trailhead

Death Canyon

Rimrock Lake

Open Canyon

Phelps Lake

Granite Canyon

Moose-Wilson Rd.

Aerial Tramway

Teton Village

Jackson Hole Mountain Resort

BRIDGER-TETON NATIONAL FOREST

Phillips Ridge

Fall Creek

Wilson

Snake River

Moose-Wilson Rd.

National Museum of Wildlife Art

Mt. Moran

Teton Park Rd.

The Potholes

String Lake Turnout

Teton Fault Turnout

Cathedral Group Turnout

North Jenny Lake Junction

Jenny Lake Lodge ∏

Cascade Canyon Turnout

Jenny Lake Turnout

South Jenny Lake

Jenny Lake

Teton Glacier Turnout

Climbers Ranch

Windy Point Turnout

Menors Ferry Historic Area

Moose Entrance Station

Death Canyon Trailhead

Granite Canyon Trailhead

JACKSON HOLE

Jackson Hole Airport

Raft Launch

Snake River Overlook

Teton Point Turnout

Schwabacher Landing

Baseline Flat

Glacier View Turnout

Blacktail Ponds Overlook

Antelope Flats Rd.

Moose Visitor Center

Moose Junction

Gros Ventre

Gros Ventre Junction

Cunningham Cabin Historic Site

Triple X Ranch ∏

Spread Creek

BRIDGER-TETON NATIONAL FOREST

Ditch Creek

North Fork

Middle Fork

Atherton Creek

Gros Ventre Slide

Lower Slide Lake

Crystal Creek

Slate Creek

Kelly

NATIONAL ELK REFUGE

Flat Creek

Jackson National Fish Hatchery

Refuge Visitor Center (Winter Only)

Curtis Canyon Campground

26 89 191

109

Senior citizens can get a **Golden Age Passport** for a one-time fee of $10, and blind or permanently disabled people can obtain a **Golden Access Passport,** which costs nothing. Most of the money from entrance fees goes back into the park where it was collected, so consider it a contribution worth making: In Grand Teton, this revenue has been spent on renovating the Jenny Lake Overlook, maintaining trails, and restoring the lakeshore at Jenny Lake, among other things.

Fees for **camping** are $12 per night at all the park campgrounds. For recorded information on campgrounds, call ✆ **307/739-3603.** For more information on camping, see "Where to Camp in Grand Teton," in chapter 7, "Where to Stay & Dine in the Parks." It is not possible to make advance reservations at campgrounds in Grand Teton.

SPECIAL REGULATIONS & WARNINGS See chapter 3, "Exploring Yellowstone," for a summary of the major park regulations, which are generally similar in both parks.

 FAST FACTS: Grand Teton

ATMs There are three ATMs in the park: at the Jackson Lake Lodge, at the Dornan's Store in Moose, and at the general store in Colter Bay Village.

Car Trouble/Towing Services There are no towing services inside the park; if you are not a member of an automobile club, try one of the services in nearby Jackson, Wyoming. The park's main information number is ✆ **307/739-3600.**

Emergencies Dial ✆ **911,** or dial 307/739-3300 and ask for park dispatch.

Gas Stations Gasoline is available at Flagg Ranch, Colter Bay Village, Jackson Lake Lodge, Signal Mountain Lodge, and Dornan's in Moose.

Laundry There are laundry facilities at the Colter Bay Village.

Medical Services There is a medical clinic at Jackson Lake Lodge (✆ **307/543-2514,** or 307/733-8002 before 10am or after 6pm), open mid-May to mid-October, and a hospital in Jackson, Wyoming (✆ **307/733-3636**).

Permits Boating permits and backcountry permits can be obtained at the Colter Bay and Moose visitor centers and at the Jenny Lake Ranger Station. For recorded information on climbing, call © **307/739-3604.**

Post Offices There are post offices in Moose (© **307/733-3336**) and Moran (© **307/543-2527**).

Supplies You'll find well-stocked general stores in the Dornan's complex at Moose Village and in Colter Bay Village; there are convenience stores at Flagg Ranch, Signal Mountain Lodge, and South Jenny Lake.

Weather Updates Call © **307/739-3611** for weather information.

2 The Highlights

No matter what you do in Grand Teton, you are nearly always in view of the big granite peaks dominating the western skyline. They define the park and, resultantly, deserve top billing of all of its highlights.

THE PEAKS The **Cathedral Group** ✸✸✸ is comprised of **Grand Teton** (elevation 13,770 ft.), **Mount Owen** (elevation 12,928 ft.), and **Teewinot** (elevation 12,325 ft.). Nearby, almost as impressive are **South Teton** (elevation 12,514 ft.) and **Middle Teton** (elevation 12,804 ft.). To the north, **Mount Moran,** at 12,605 feet, is the fourth largest of the Tetons (on a clear day, though, you can take a great photograph of this peak all the way from Colter Bay to North Jenny Lake Junction). If you come from the east, you will pass no toll booths on your way south on U.S. Highway 26/89/191, but there are frequent pullouts on the west side of the road that give you a panoramic overview of the Snake River and the Tetons. For that matter, you get a more distant but equally grand perspective of the mountains coming over **Togwotee Pass** on U.S. Highway 26-287. **Signal Mountain,** reached off Teton Park Road by Jackson Lake, is less a peak to look at than to look off—you can drive or hike to the top for a grand view.

COLTER BAY At the north end of the park, alongside Jackson Lake, Colter Bay offers a busy mix of information, services, activities on and off the water, and shopping. The **Visitor Center** (© **307/739-3594**) provides wildlife videos, slide programs, natural history hikes, and evening amphitheater programs. Most remarkable is the **Indian Arts Museum** ✸, which houses a collection of American Indian crafts, clothing, and beadwork, covering rooms on two floors.

JACKSON LAKE ✈   This biggest of park lakes was dammed to provide more water for potato farmers in Idaho, but that also makes it a good place to sail, fish, and ride around on powerboats. Several lodges dot its shores, but the one that bears its name, **Jackson Lake Lodge,** is set back from the lake, bordered by Willow Flats and marshlands—prime moose habitat. The views are striking, and some good hikes begin here.

SIGNAL MOUNTAIN AREA   The **Signal Mountain campground** is a favorite of park visitors, conveniently located on the lakeshore for folks with watercraft, and the **Signal Mountain Lodge** is a fine place to stop for a meal with a view or a room for the night. Across the road, you can climb the mountain, by foot or car, and get a panoramic view of the valley and mountains—the best way to get a perspective on the glacier-carved area known as Jackson Hole.

JENNY LAKE ✈✈   A loop off Teton Park Road takes you close to String and Jenny lakes and the exclusive **Jenny Lake Lodge** (home to what is probably the finest restaurant in any national park). Day visitors can go to the south end of the lake, the point of origin of both boat rides and the popular trail to **Inspiration Point and Hidden Falls** ✈, on the west side of the lake. There's also a small store. If you've got your wide-angle lens handy, stop at the **Cathedral Group Turnout,** a terrific spot for photographers.

MOOSE   You'll find plenty of services and shops here—even a fine wine store—and the **park headquarters** and a **visitor center.** It's been a service area since the days of Bill Menor, who ran a river ferry and a country store here a century ago. Half a mile (1km) from the park offices, the store and ferry have been re-created at the **Menor/Noble Historic District.** The nearby **Chapel of the Transfiguration** is a log church built in 1925. The altar window frames a view of the Grand Teton.

SNAKE RIVER   Below Jackson Lake Dam, the Snake River winds its way east and south, eventually turning west toward Idaho in the Snake River Canyon. There are beautiful stretches of river in the park, such as Oxbow Bend, where trumpeter swans and moose appear, which make it a destination for canoeists and kayakers. To the east and up on the flats, U.S. Highway 26/89/191 follows the river from Moran Junction to Jackson, with several pullouts and overlooks.

3 If You Have Only 1 Day

A 1-day trip around this park is not unreasonable, given its size, and you can do a loop where you see many major attractions without having to retrace your steps. For more complete information on what you'll see along the way, read the next section on touring the park. Although this 1-day itinerary assumes that you are entering Grand Teton from the north, after visiting Yellowstone, you could just as easily begin your itinerary in Jackson, which is 8 miles (13km) south of the Moose Entrance Station.

Begin at the south entrance of Yellowstone National Park, driving the **John D. Rockefeller Jr. Memorial Parkway** (U.S. 89/181/287) south past **Flagg Ranch** and to the park. As you drive south, you'll find yourself skirting the northern shore of Jackson Lake, with a view of **Mount Moran** to the west, and, farther south, the stunning **Cathedral Group.**

On the northeast shore, **Colter Bay Village** is one of the park's busiest spots. You can rent boats, take scenic cruises, embark on guided fishing trips, buy fishing licenses and supplies, rent a cabin, or camp. Several popular hiking trails start here. If you turn right at Colter Bay Junction, you'll be at the **Colter Bay Visitor Center** a half-mile later (1km); stop here to take in the **Indian Arts Museum** 🐾.

The **Lakeshore Trail** begins at the marina entrance and runs along the harbor for an easy 2-mile (3km) round-trip. It's level, paved, shady, and wheelchair-accessible, the best opportunity for a hike in this area if you don't have much time. Nearby, on the shore of the lake, is an amphitheater where ranger-naturalists conduct evening programs. The Douglas firs and pine trees here are greener and healthier than the lodgepole pines that you see at higher elevations in Yellowstone.

A few minutes' drive south of Colter Bay, you'll pass Jackson Lake Lodge (you might want to look in the lobby and out the big picture window) and then **Jackson Lake Junction,** where a right turn puts you on **Teton Park Road,** the beginning of a 43-mile (69km) loop tour. You'll be driving parallel to the mountain range, with Grand Teton as the 13,770-foot centerpiece. You'll see lakes created by glaciers thousands of years ago, bordering a sagebrush valley inhabited by pronghorn and elk.

Just 5 miles (8km) down the road along Jackson Lake, a left (east) turn will take you up **Signal Mountain,** where you'll have a 360° view of the valley. Then continue down Teton Park Road to

South Jenny Lake, where there is a huge parking area (which fills quickly in peak season) for the many people who stop to either hike around the lake or take a boat ride across. If you have time, get to the other side (it's a 2-mile/3km hike) and make the short climb to **Hidden Falls** *℟*. Another good day hike in this area is the **Moose Ponds Trail** (see chapter 6, "Hikes & Other Outdoor Pursuits in Grand Teton National Park").

When you leave South Jenny Lake, you'll drive along a flat, sagebrush-dotted stretch to Moose, the southernmost of the park's service centers. A half-mile (1km) before Moose Junction is the **Moose Visitor Center,** which features exhibits of the Greater Yellowstone area's rare and endangered species, a video room, and an excellent bookstore. While you're in Moose, you might want to visit the **Menor/Noble Historic District** and the **Chapel of the Transfiguration.**

Coming out of Moose, take a left (north) turn on **U.S. 26/89/ 191,** which crosses the open flats above the Snake River to Moran Junction. The best views along this road are the **Glacier View Turnout** and the **Snake River Overlook** *℟*, both of which are right off the road and well marked. At Moran Junction, turn left for a final 5-mile (8km) drive back to Jackson Lake Junction, past **Oxbow Bend,** a great spot for wildlife watching.

Worn out? Catch the dramatic sunset behind the Tetons and head for your campsite (if you're tenting, stake out a spot early) or room, either in the park or in Jackson, Wyoming.

4 Touring Grand Teton

A 1-day whirlwind tour of Grand Teton is far from ideal. Like Yellowstone, this park demands a visit of 2 days or more. An extended stay allows for some relaxed hiking, picnicking, and sightseeing—you'll gain a greater appreciation for the park and the area's culture and history. A day at the Jenny Lake area, for instance, will provide awe-inspiring views of the peaks and a chance to walk the trails around the lake, to Inspiration Point or beyond up Cascade Canyon. You could also easily spend a day in the Jackson Lake Lodge area, where there are several wildlife viewing spots, trails, and places for a secluded picnic.

As with the short tour in the previous section, I begin at the northern end of the park, but you could just as easily start exploring from the southern end near Jackson. From Jackson, it's 13 miles (21km) to the Moose Entrance Station, another 8 miles (13km) to

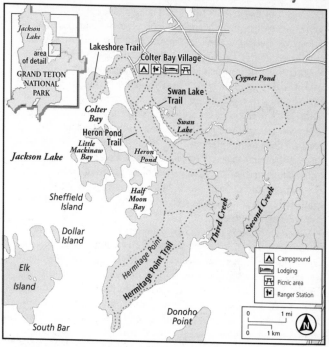

Jackson Lake: Colter Bay Area

the Jenny Lake Visitor Center, another 12 miles (19km) to the Jackson Lake Junction, and 5 more miles (8km) to Colter Bay.

JACKSON LAKE & THE NORTH END OF THE PARK

Many people enter Grand Teton National Park from the north end, emerging from Yellowstone's south entrance with a 7-day park pass that is good for admission to Grand Teton as well. Yellowstone is connected to Grand Teton by a wilderness corridor through which the **John D. Rockefeller Jr. Memorial Parkway** runs for 8 miles (13km), past meadows sometimes dotted with elk, over the Snake River above Jackson Lake, and through forests that in some places still show the mosaic burns of the 1988 fires.

Along the parkway, not far from Yellowstone, you'll come to the recently modernized **Flagg Ranch** (see chapter 7), with gas, restaurants, lodging, and other services. In the winter, this is a busy staging area for the snowcoach and snowmobile crowd.

Giant **Jackson Lake** ✾, a vast expanse of water filling a deep gouge left 10,000 years ago by retreating glaciers, dominates the north end of the park. While it is a natural lake, it was dammed nearly a century ago, encroaching the surrounding forest and dismaying conservationists. It empties east into the Snake River, curving around in the languid **Oxbow Bend**—a favorite wildlife-viewing float for canoeists. The water eventually turns south and then west through Snake River Canyon and into Idaho. Stream flow from the dam is regulated both for potato farmers downstream in Idaho and for rafters in the canyon. Elsewhere on the lake, things look quite natural, except when water gets low in the fall.

As the road follows the east shore of the lake from the north, the first development that travelers encounter is **Leeks Marina,** where boats launch, gas up, and moor from mid-May to mid-September. A casual restaurant here serves light fare and pizza during the summer, but there are also numerous scenic pullouts along the lake that are good picnic spots.

Just south of Leeks is **Colter Bay,** a busy outpost of park services where you can get groceries, postcards and stamps, T-shirts, and advice. At the **Colter Bay Visitor Center,** you can view park and wildlife videotapes and attend a park orientation slide program throughout the day. Ranger-led activities include museum tours, park orientation talks, natural history hikes, and evening amphitheater programs. Colter Bay has plenty of overnight options, from cabins and old-fashioned tent camps to a trailer park and campground (see chapter 7). There is also a general store, a laundry facility, two restaurants, a boat launch and boat rentals, and tours. You can take pleasant short hikes in this area, including a walk around the bay or out to **Hermitage Point** (see chapter 6).

The **Indian Arts Museum** ⋒ (✆ **307/739-3594**) at the Colter Bay Visitor Center is worth a visit, although it is not strictly about the Native American cultures of this area. The artifacts are mostly from Plains Indian tribes, but there are also some Navajo items from the Southwest. The collection was assembled by David T. Vernon and includes pipes, shields, dolls, and war clubs sometimes called "skull crackers." There are large historic photos in the exhibit area. Visiting Indian artists work in the museum all summer long and sell their wares onsite. Admission is free.

From Colter Bay, the road curves eastward and then south again, passing **Jackson Lake Lodge** (see chapter 7), a snazzy 1950s-style resort with a great view of the Tetons and brushy flats in the foreground where moose and coyotes often roam. Numerous trails emanate from here, both to the lakeshore and east to **Emma**

Jackson Lake: Signal Mountain Area

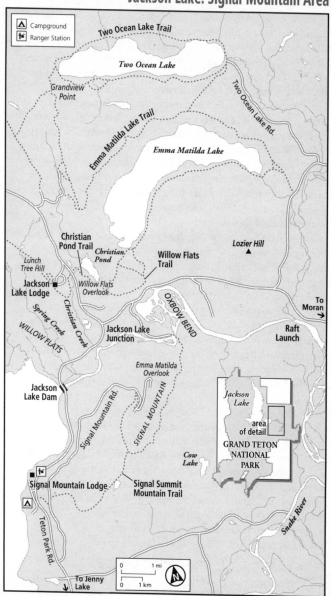

Campground

Ranger Station

Two Ocean Lake Trail

Two Ocean Lake

Grandview Point

Emma Matilda Lake Trail

Emma Matilda Lake

Two Ocean Lake Rd.

Christian Pond Trail

Christian Pond

Willow Flats Trail

Lozier Hill

Lunch Tree Hill

Jackson Lake Lodge

Willow Flats Overlook

OXBOW BEND

To Moran

Spring Creek

Christian Creek

Jackson Lake Junction

WILLOW FLATS

Raft Launch

Jackson Lake Dam

Emma Matilda Overlook

SIGNAL MOUNTAIN

Signal Mountain Rd.

Jackson Lake

area of detail

GRAND TETON NATIONAL PARK

Cow Lake

Signal Mountain Lodge

Signal Summit Mountain Trail

Snake River

Teton Park Rd.

To Jenny Lake

0   1 mi
0   1 km

N

Matilda Lake (see chapter 6). The road then comes to **Jackson Lake Junction,** where you can either continue west along the lakeshore or go east to the park's Moran entrance station. If you exit via the Moran entrance, you are still in the park, and can turn south on U.S. Highway 26/89/191 and drive along the Snake River to Jackson, making most of your journey within the park's borders. However, you're probably here to enjoy the park, so you should turn right (west) on **Teton Park Road** at Jackson Lake Junction. After only 5 miles (8km), you will arrive at **Signal Mountain.** Like its counterpart at Colter Bay, this developed recreation area, on Jackson Lake's southeast shore, offers camping sites, accommodations in cabins and multiplex units, two restaurants, and a lounge with one of the few live televisions in the park. If you need to stock up on gas or food, do so at the small convenience store here. Boat rentals and scenic cruises of the lake are also available.

If you turn east instead of west off Teton Park Road at Signal Mountain, you can drive up a narrow, twisty road to the top of the mountain, 700 feet above the valley, where you'll have a fine view of the ring of mountains—Absarokas, Gros Ventres, Tetons, and Yellowstone Plateau—that create Jackson Hole. Clearly visible are the "Kettles": potholes in the valley's hilly moraines that are the mark of long-gone glaciers. Below the summit, about 3 miles (5km) from the base of the hill, is **Jackson Point Overlook,** a paved path 100 yards long leading to the spot where legendary photographer William Henry Jackson shot his famous landscapes of Jackson Lake and the Tetons in the 1870s—proof to the world that such spectacular places really existed.

Looking for a hideaway? On the right (west) side of the road between Signal Mountain and North Jenny Lake Junction, approximately 2 miles (3km) south of the Mount Moran turnout, is an unmarked, unpaved road leading to **Spalding Bay.** It's a sheltered little campsite and boat launch area with a primitive restroom. There isn't much space if others have beaten you there, but it's a great place to be alone with great views of the lake and mountains. If you decide to camp, a park permit is required. An automobile or SUV will have no problem with this road, but speed will not be of the essence. Passing through brush and forest, you might just spot a moose.

JENNY LAKE & THE SOUTH END OF THE PARK

Continuing south along Teton Park Road, you move into the park's southern half, where the tallest peaks rise abruptly above a succession of small, crystalline lakes—**Leigh Lake,** the appropriately named

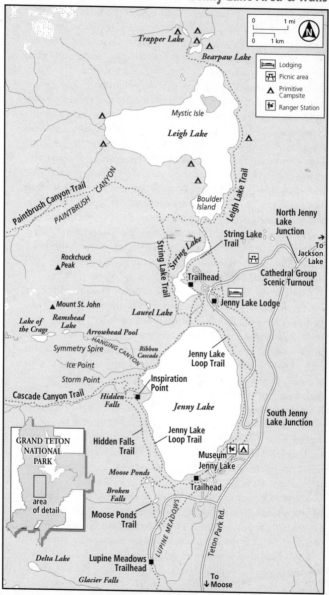

Jenny Lake Area & Trails

Trapper Lake

Bearpaw Lake

Mystic Isle

Leigh Lake

Boulder Island

Paintbrush Canyon Trail

PAINTBRUSH CANYON

Rockchuck Peak

String Lake Trail

String Lake

String Lake Trail

North Jenny Lake Junction

To Jackson Lake

Cathedral Group Scenic Turnout

Trailhead

Jenny Lake Lodge

Mount St. John

Lake of the Crags

Ramshead Lake

Arrowhead Pool

HANGING CANYON

Symmetry Spire

Ribbon Cascade

Laurel Lake

Ice Point

Storm Point

Cascade Canyon Trail

Hidden Falls

Inspiration Point

Jenny Lake Loop Trail

Jenny Lake

South Jenny Lake Junction

Hidden Falls Trail

Jenny Lake Loop Trail

Moose Ponds

Museum Jenny Lake

Broken Falls

Trailhead

Moose Ponds Trail

LUPINE MEADOWS

Teton Park Rd.

Delta Lake

Lupine Meadows Trailhead

Glacier Falls

To Moose

Lodging 🛏

Picnic area 🏕

Primitive Campsite ⛺

Ranger Station

0   1 mi
0   1 km

GRAND TETON NATIONAL PARK

area of detail

String Lake, and **Jenny Lake** ⚔⚔, beloved by many visitors. At North Jenny Lake Junction, you can take a turnoff west to **Jenny Lake Lodge** (see chapter 7). The road then continues as a one-way scenic loop along the lakeshore before rejoining Teton Park Road about 4 miles (6.5km) later.

Beautiful **Jenny Lake** attracts its share of crowds throughout the summer, both from hikers who circumnavigate the lake on a 6-mile (9.5km) trail and from more sedentary folks who pay for a boat ride across the lake to Hidden Falls and the short steep climb to Inspiration Point (see chapter 6). The parking lot at **South Jenny Lake** is often jammed, and there can be a long wait for the boat ride, so you might want to get there early in the day. Or, you can save your money by taking the 2-mile (3km) hike around the lake—it's level and easy. There is also a tents-only campground, a visitor center, and a general store stocked with a modest supply of prepackaged foods and even less fresh produce and vegetables. You'll have to buy a ticket and wait in line for the trip across the lake in a powerboat that holds about 30 people. Contact **Teton Boating Company** (© 307/733-2703); round-trips cost $6 for adults and $4 for children.

South of the lake, Teton Park Road ambles through wide-open sagebrush plains with immaculate views of the mountains. You'll pass the **Climbers' Ranch**—an inexpensive dormlike lodging alternative for climbers, run by the American Alpine Association—and some trailheads for enjoyable hikes to a handful of pristine alpine lakes. Look closely in the sagebrush for the shy pronghorn, more commonly (and incorrectly) labeled antelope. This handsome animal, with tan cheeks and black accent stripes, can spring up to 60 mph. Badgers also roam the brush here; you might encounter one of the shy but ornery creatures in the morning or at twilight.

The **Teton Glacier Turnout** presents a view of a glacier that grew for several hundred years until, pressured by the increasing summer temperatures of the past century, it reversed course and began retreating.

The road arrives at the park's south entrance and the sprawling **Moose Visitor Center,** which is also park headquarters. If you are approaching the park from the south rather than the north, this is where you'll get maps, advice, and some interpretive displays.

Just behind the visitor center is **Menors Ferry.** Bill Menor had a country store and operated a ferry across the Snake River at Moose back in the late 1800s. The ferry and store have been reconstructed, and you can buy items like those once sold here. Nearby is a historic cabin where a group of locals met in 1923 and planted the seed for the protection of the natural and scenic quality of the area, an idea that eventually led to the creation of the national park.

Also in this area is the **Chapel of the Transfiguration.** In 1925, this chapel was built in Moose so that settlers wouldn't have to make the long buckboard ride into Jackson. It's still in use for Episcopal services from spring to fall and is a popular place for weddings, with a view of the Tetons through a window behind the altar.

Dornan's is a small village area just south of the visitor center on a private holding of land owned by one of the area's earliest home-steading families. There are a few shops and a semi-gourmet grocery store, a post office, a bar with occasional live music, and, surprisingly, a first-rate wine shop.

THE EAST SIDE OF THE PARK

At Moose Junction, just east of the visitor center, drivers can rejoin the highway and either turn south to Jackson and the Gros Ventre turn or cruise north up U.S. Highway 89/26/191 to Moran Junction. This 18-mile (30km) trip is the fastest route through Grand Teton National Park and, being farther from the mountains, offers views of a broader mountain tableau.

The junction of U.S. 89 with **Antelope Flats Road** is 1¼ miles (2km) north of the Moose Junction. The 20-mile (32km) route beginning here is an acceptable biking route. It's all on level terrain, passing by the town of Kelly and the Gros Ventre campground before looping back to U.S. 26/89/191 at the Gros Ventre Junction to the south. (If you're interested in the area, you might also look at the end of the "Day Hikes" section in the next chapter, "Hikes & Other Outdoor Pursuits in Grand Teton National Park," where there's a short description of Kelly and the Gros Ventre Slide area, which can be viewed just beyond the park boundaries to the east.) If you continue straight on Antelope Flats Road, you'll reach the **Teton Science School** ⍟ at the road's end, about a 5-mile (8km) trip. The school offers interesting learning vacation programs, which are described more fully in chapter 2, "Planning Your Trip to Yellowstone & Grand Teton National Parks."

Less than a mile (1.5km) down U.S. 26/89/191, on the left, **Blacktail Ponds Overlook** offers an opportunity to see how beavers build dams and the effect these hard-working creatures have on the flow of the streams. The area is marshy early in summer, but it's still worth the ¼-mile hike down to the streams where the beaver activity can be viewed more closely.

Two miles (3km) farther along U.S. 89 brings you to the **Glacier View Turnout,** which offers views of an area that 140,000 to 160,000 years ago was filled with a 4,000-foot-thick glacier. The view of the gulch between the peaks offers vivid testimony of the power of the glaciers that carved this landscape. Lower **Schwabacher Landing** is at the end of a 1-mile (1.5km), fairly well maintained dirt road that leads down to the Snake River; you'll see the turnoff 4½ miles north of the Moose Junction. The road winds through an area filled with glacial moraine (the rocks, sand, and gravel are debris left behind as glaciers passed through the area), the remnants of the Ice Age. At the end of the road is a popular launch site for float trips and for fly-fishing. It's also an ideal place to retreat from the crowds. Don't be surprised to see bald eagles, osprey, moose, river otter, and beaver, all of which regularly patrol the area.

The **Snake River Overlook** ⟨⊛⟩, approximately 4 miles (6km) down the road beyond the Glacier View Turnout, is the most famous view of the Teton Range and the Snake River, immortalized by Ansel Adams. From this overlook, you'll also see at least three separate, distinctive 200-foot-high plateaus that roll from the riverbed to the valley floor, leaving a vivid example of the power of the glaciers and ice floes as they sculpted this area. In the early 1800s, this was a prime hunting ground for John Jacob Astor's Pacific Fur Company and a certain David E. Jackson, for whom the lake and valley are named. But by 1840, the popularity of the silk hat had put an end to fur trapping, and the hunters disappeared. Good thing—by the time they departed, the beaver population was almost decimated.

A half-mile (1km) north of the Snake River Overlook is the newly repaved road to **Deadman's Bar,** a peaceful clearing on the river-bank. Many float trips launch here (multiday trips also camp in the area), and there is a limited amount of fishing access.

Cunningham Cabin, 1¾ miles (3km) north of Deadman's Bar, is a nondescript historic site at which homesteaders Pierce and Margaret Cunningham built their ranch in 1890. By 1928, they had been defeated by the elements and sold out to Rockefeller's Snake River Land Co. You can visit it at any time for a peek into the rough life of early Jackson Hole ranchers.

If you head down the highway in the other direction (south) from Moose Junction, on U.S. Highway 26/89/191, you can turn east on the **Gros Ventre River Road** 5 miles (8km) before you reach Jackson and follow the river east into its steep canyon—a few miles past the little town of Kelly, you'll leave the park and be in **Bridger-Teton National Forest.** In 1925, a huge slab of mountain broke off the north end of the Gros Ventre Range on the east side of Jackson Hole, a reminder that nature still has an unpredictable and violent side.

The slide left a gaping open gash in the side of Sheep Mountain, sloughing off nearly 50 million cubic yards of rock and forming a natural dam across the Gros Ventre River half a mile (1km) wide. Two years later, the dam broke and a cascade of water rushed down the canyon and through the little town of Kelly, taking several lives. Today the town of **Kelly** is a quaint and eccentric community with a large number of yurts and, nearby, the **Teton Science School.** Up in the canyon formed by the Gros Ventre River, there is a roadside display with photographs of the slide area and a short nature walk from the road down to the residue of the slide and **Lower Slide Lake.** Here, signs identify the trees and plants that survived or grew in the slide's aftermath.

5 Organized Tours & Ranger Programs

The **Grand Teton Lodge Company** (© 307/543-2811; www.gtlc. com) runs half- and full-day bus tours of Grand Teton ($29 adults, $12 children) and Yellowstone ($50 adults, $29 children) from mid-May to mid-October, weather permitting.

The **Teton Science School** ⟨🖈, P.O. Box 68, Kelly, WY 83011 (© 307/733-4765; www.tetonscience.org), has an excellent curriculum for students of all ages, from integrated science programs for junior high kids to adult seminars covering everything from botany to astronomy. Classes take place at the newly renovated Stokes Family Learning Center in Kelly, and younger students can stay onsite in log cabins for some of the programs. The school's **Wildlife Expeditions** (© 307/773-2623; www.tetonscience.org/ wildlife) offers tours that bring visitors closer to the park's wildlife. These trips range from 2 days to a week, covering everything from bighorn sheep to the wolves of Yellowstone.

Within the park, there are several interesting ranger programs. These range from a ranger-led 3-mile (5km) hike from the Colter Bay Visitor Center to Swan Lake, to a relaxed evening chatting with a ranger on the back deck of the Jackson Lake Lodge, with the Tetons as a dramatic backdrop and spotting scope for watching moose and birds. There are numerous events during the summer at Colter Bay, South Jenny Lake, and the Moose Visitor Center. Check the daily schedules in the park's newspaper, *The Teewinot,* which you can pick up at any visitor center.

At the Taggart Lake trailhead, there are **wildflower walks** 🥾 led by rangers who can tell you the difference between lupine and larkspur, daily in June and July, and guided morning hikes to Hidden Falls from Jenny Lake (you take the boat across the lake), among other activities.

At Colter Bay, you can climb aboard a boat for an afternoon **fire and ice cruise,** during which a ranger will talk about volcanics, glaciers, and fires that have shaped, reshaped, and colored the landscape. There are programs on Indian art and culture, lakeshore strolls with rangers, and evening gatherings at the Colter Bay amphitheater in which rangers teach about park wildlife.

Youngsters 8 to 12 can join **Young Naturalist programs** at Colter Bay or Jenny Lake and learn about the natural world for 2 hours while hiking with a ranger. Signups are at the visitor centers (the fee is a mere $1), and the kids will need basic hiking gear.

There are also evening campfire gatherings at the Gros Ventre, Signal Mountain, Lizard Creek, and Colter Bay campground amphitheaters on a variety of park-related topics.

Hikes & Other Outdoor Pursuits in Grand Teton National Park

Beyond the watersports on its lakes and rivers, Grand Teton National Park is a hiker's dream. The varied trail system—more than 200 miles (322km) in all—offers both short, level trails around the valley floor and more demanding trails to the Teton Range that escape the crowds and challenge the body.

For a more extensive and detailed list of trails than what follows here, pick up *Teton Trails,* by Katy Duffy and Darwin Wile. It's available for $6.95 from the Grand Teton Natural History Association, P.O. Drawer 170, Moose, WY 83012 (*©* **307/739-3403;** www. grandtetonpark.org).

1 Day Hikes

The park's many trails vary greatly in length and level of difficulty, so you'll want to consult with rangers before tackling the trails. They can update you on everything from bear activity to trail damage (such as bridge outages) to weather concerns. Rangers might be able to suggest hikes suitable to your expectations and ability; they also conduct various guided walks.

Below is a fairly broad selection of hikes, ranging from easy to difficult. For those who have only a brief time at Grand Teton, here are two suggestions for the "if you can only do one hike" category: the **Signal Mountain Summit Trail** ⚡⚡ and the **Inspiration Point Trail** ⚡⚡ in the Jenny Lake area. You'll find that trails are generally very well marked. Turn to chapter 5, "Exploring Grand Teton National Park," for **maps** of the Colter Bay, Signal Mountain, Jackson Lake, and Jenny Lake areas that show the major trails described in this section.

And remember, if you are planning to hike for more than 30 minutes, be sure to carry a supply of water and some raingear.

COLTER BAY AREA

A map showing the trails in this area is found in chapter 5. "Exploring Grand Teton National Park."

Lakeshore Trail Originating in the Colter Bay area, this short jaunt starts at the marina and leads out to pebble beaches on the west side of Jackson Lake. The trail is wide and shady, and you can stop to look over the boats moored at the marina. Views of the entire Teton Range leap out at you from across Jackson Lake when you arrive at the end of the trail. The sounds of water lapping at the shore extend a peaceful atmosphere, as traffic and crowd noise are left well behind. The loop can be completed in about 1 hour of brisk walking.

2 miles (3km) RT. Easy. Access: Trailhead located at the Marina entrance.

TRAILS FROM THE HERMITAGE POINT TRAILHEAD

The **Hermitage Point Trailhead** near the marina is the starting point for an interesting variety of trips ranging from 1 to 9 miles (0.5 to 14.5km). With careful planning, it's possible to start the day with a hike beginning at Colter Bay that leads past **Cygnet Lake** across **Willow Flats** to **Jackson Lake Lodge,** where you can stop for lunch. Then, after a break, take the same path and return to Colter Bay in time for the evening outdoor barbecue. All told, that's 10 miles (16km) round-trip. The numerous trail options here can be confusing, so carry a map.

Hermitage Point Loop ⋒   From the trailhead, this footpath heads through a thickly forested area to the isolated Hermitage Point, a peninsula jutting into Jackson Lake. Beyond the timber, the terrain is comprised of gently rolling hills, passing ponds, streams, and meadows. If you're seeking solitude, this is an excellent place to find it, although you should check with rangers before leaving—this is bear country.

8¾ miles (14km) RT. Moderate. Access: There are directional signs near the Swan Lake/Heron Pond Trail Intersection.

Heron Pond Trail You journey through dense stands of lodgepole pine to this pond, inhabited by beavers most likely to be seen in the early morning. This is bear territory and a haven for Canada geese, trumpeter swans, and moose. Wildflowers are part of the show in the early summer: Look for lupine, gilia, heartleaf arnicas, and the Indian paintbrush. Don't be put off by the fact that the first 200 yards of the trail are steep; after reaching the top of a rise, it levels out and has only moderate elevation gains from that point

---

Tips **Photo Op**

Not far from the trailhead, the **Hermitage Point Loop** 𝄢 opens to a broad, sagebrush-carpeted meadow. In the summer, the area blooms with wildflowers to offer one of the most spectacular views of colossal **Mount Moran,** which is as impressive in its own way as the Grand Teton. To avoid retracing your steps past Heron Pond, bear right at the third creek intersection and continue straight ahead to the corrals at Colter Bay—this route adds no distance to the hike.

---

on. *Note:* Because three trails run through this area, the foliage and terrain for this, the Swan Lake Trail, and Hermitage Point Trail are virtually identical.

3 miles (5km) RT. Easy. Access: Trailhead located at Hermitage Point Trailhead, Colter Bay.

Swan Lake Trail   Finding swans at Swan Lake requires a trip to its southern shore, where a small island offers them isolation and shelter for nests. From Swan Lake, it's only ¼ mile (0.5km) through a densely forested area to the intersection with the trail to Heron Pond. Hermitage Point is 3 miles (5km) from this junction along a gentle path that winds through a wooded area that's popular with bears. If you circumnavigate the lake, expect to spend 2 hours on this hike.

3 miles (5km) RT. Easy. Access: Trailhead located at Hermitage Point Trailhead, Colter Bay.

Willow Flats Trail 𝄢   An alternative to the park's mountainous, forested trails, this trip from Colter Bay to Jackson Lake Lodge takes you across marshy flats where you'll have an idyllic view of the Tetons and a good chance of seeing a moose. Unfortunately, you begin by skirting the sewage ponds at Colter Bay, but it gets better. Pick up a trail east to Cygnet Lake and, instead of looping back to Colter Bay, you take a spur that crosses Pilgrim Creek going east across the flats. You can hike in either direction, but drop a car at each end if you don't want to double back on foot.

5 miles (8km) one-way. Easy. Access: Horse corrals at Colter Bay.

JACKSON LAKE LODGE AREA

A map showing the trails in this area is found in chapter 5.

Christian Pond Trail   Starting with a half-mile (1km) walk through a grassy, wet area to a pond with nesting trumpeter swans and other waterfowl, this is a short trail for all skill levels. If you're more ambitious, you can circumnavigate the pond, adding another 3 miles (5km) to the trip. In May and June, this is a great wildflower walk, but the area is also prime habitat for bears, so check with rangers before venturing onto the trail. The south end of the pond is covered with little grassy knolls upon which the birds build their nests and roost, and beavers have constructed a lodge here, too. It's a restful sanctuary, but one that's often infested by gnats and mosquitoes, so be sure to apply a coat of insect repellent.

1 mile (1.5km) RT. Easy. Access: The trailhead is some 200 yards south of the entrance to Jackson Lake Lodge, most easily accessed from the Jackson Lake Lodge corrals. It's unmarked, so look carefully.

Signal Mountain Summit Trail ★★ Venturing up this uneven trail will give you a few fine hours of quiet trail time with views of the mountains, wildflowers, and, at the pinnacle, a grand panorama of the glacially carved valley. After negotiating a steep climb at the beginning of the trail, you'll come upon a broad plateau covered with lodgepole pine, grass, and seasonal wildflowers. Cross a paved road to a lily-covered pond, and just beyond you'll choose two different trails up the mountain—take the right one up (ponds, maybe moose and bear) and the left one down (open ridges with views).

8 miles (13km) RT. Moderate. Access: The trailhead is near the entrance to the Signal Mountain Lodge, or you can drive 1 mile (1.5km) up Signal Mountain Road to a pond on the right and pick up the trail there.

TWO OCEAN & EMMA MATILDA LAKE TRAILS

You can arrive at these lakes from the east or west: from the west you'd begin at the Grand View Point Trailhead, 1 mile (1.5km) north of Jackson Lake Lodge, or at the Christian Pond Trailhead, just east of Jackson Lake Lodge. From the east, you'd go up Pacific Creek Road, 4 miles (6.5km) east of Jackson Lake Junction on the road to the Moran entrance. There is a pullout for Emma Matilda

---

Tips **Photo Op**

A wide-open meadow near the summit of Signal Mountain presents an excellent opportunity to look to the west for photos of both **Mount Moran** and the **Teton Range.** The best time to take those photos is before 11am, when the sun will be mostly at your back, or in the early evening, when the sun will be lower in the sky to the west.

Lake 2 miles (3km) up this road, or you can go a half-mile (1km) farther, take a left on Two Ocean Lake Road, and go to the Two Ocean Lake trailhead parking lot, with trails leading to both lakes.

Emma Matilda Lake Trail   Circumnavigating this lake involves a pleasant up-and-down trek with great views of the mountains and a good chance of seeing wildlife. Emma Matilda Lake was named after the wife of Billy Owen, reputedly the first climber to reach the peak of Grand Teton. The hike winds uphill for a half-mile (1km) from the parking area to a large meadow favored by mule deer. The trail follows the northern side of the lake through a pine forest 400 feet above the lake and then descends to an overlook where you'll have inspiring views of the Tetons, Christian Pond, and Jackson Lake. The trail on the south side of the lake goes through a densely forested area populated by Englemann spruce and subalpine fir. Be watchful and noisy because this is bear country. It's possible to branch off onto the Two Ocean Lake Trail along the northern shore of the lake.

11¾ miles (19km) RT. Easy to moderate. Access: Emma Matilda Lake Trailhead on Pacific Creek Road or trailhead off Two Ocean Lake Road north of Jackson Lake–Moran Road.

Two Ocean Lake Trail 🏃 *(Finds)*   Take your time and take a picnic on this delightful, underused trail around Two Ocean Lake. You can start at either end, but I recommend a side trip up Grand View Point, which will add about 2½ miles (4km) of hiking. You'll be rested for this climb because the walk around the lake is fairly level, and you'll be in a great mood if you've been watching ducks, swans, grebes, and loons on the water. The variety of habitat—marshes, lakes, woodlands, and meadows—means that you'll see birds, wildflowers, butterflies, and possibly bear, beaver, elk, deer, and moose. As usual, awesome views of the Tetons abound; for the best perspective, take the trip up to Grand View Point, a climb that will take you through lodgepole and fir en route to a hilltop covered with orange arrow-leaf balsamroot. You'll look down on lakes, meadows, and volcanic outcrops, and in the distance you'll gaze at the Tetons, the Mount Leidy Highlands, and Jackson Lake. It's possible to branch off onto the Emma Matilda Lake Trail at the east end of Two Ocean Lake.

5¾ miles (9km) RT. Easy. Access: Two Ocean Lake Trailhead on Two Ocean Lake Road, or Grand View Point Trailhead.

Youthful visitors (ages 8 to 14) to the park are encouraged to explore and experience Grand Teton as members of the **Young Naturalist** program. To participate, pick up a copy of the Young Naturalist activity brochure at any visitor center, and then complete projects outlined in the booklet during your stay. When you present the completed project (and $1) to a ranger at the Moose, Jenny Lake, or Colter Bay visitor center, you'll be awarded a Young Naturalist patch.

Two trails within Grand Teton are especially kid-friendly. The **Inspiration Point hike** 🐾🐾 is less strenuous if you take the boat shuttle across Jenny Lake. This reduces the hiking distance to less than a mile (1.5km); at 7 miles (11km) round-trip, the entire Jenny Lake Loop Trail is a bit too long for kids, but the terrain is fairly level if you stick to the portion along the eastern shore. Also, the **Christian Pond Trail,** a level, 1-mile (1.5km) round-trip from the corrals at Jackson Lake Lodge, is a nice diversion, offering great views and a chance to see a myriad of waterfowl.

JENNY LAKE AREA

A map showing the trails in this area is in chapter 5.

Amphitheater Lake Trail 🐾🐾   Here's a trail that can get you in and out of the high mountains in a day, presuming that you're in good shape and acclimated to the altitude—it's a 3,000-foot climb. You'll cross glacial moraines and meadows quilted with flowers and enter forests of fir and pine (including whitebark pine, a delicacy for bears—be alert!). Finally, you clear the trees and come into a ring of monstrous rock walls topped by Disappointment Peak, with Grand Teton and Teewinot in view. Surprise Lake and Amphitheater Lake sit in this dramatic setting, with a few gnarled trees struggling to survive on the slopes.

9½ miles (15.5km) RT. Difficult. Access: Use the Lupine Meadows Trailhead. From the Moose entrance station on Teton Park Road, drive 6½ miles (10.5km) to the Lupine Meadows Junction and follow signs to the trailhead; if you're coming from Jenny Lake, the trailhead is at the end of a road less than 1 mile (1.5km) south of South Jenny Lake.

Cascade Canyon Trail 🌟🌟🌟 *(Moments)* Cascade Canyon Trail is the most popular trail in the park for intermediate and expert hikers. You can begin the hike from South Jenny Lake, but you can also shave 2 miles (3km) off each way by riding the boat shuttle across the lake and beginning your hike at the boat dock. At this point, you're only a steep mile (1.5km) from Inspiration Point (see "Hidden Falls & Inspiration Point Trail," below), which is as far as most visitors ever get. From here, you make a brief climb up a sharp grade to the glacially rounded canyon. The trail flattens, allowing for a relaxing exploration of a true wonderland of nature: Wildflowers, waterfowl, and busy pikas abound. On a nice day, the warblers will be singing and you could see moose and bear.

If you want to go farther, you have two choices when you reach forks of North and South Cascade Canyon: Follow the South Fork to Hurricane Pass or the North Fork to Lake Solitude. At 23 (37km) and 18 miles (30km) , respectively, these are overnight trips for most mortals, so you'll need camping gear and a backcountry permit.

A less taxing alternative to the Cascade Canyon trip mentioned above is a detour to **Moose Ponds,** which begins on the Inspiration Point trail. The ponds, located 2 miles (3km) from either west or east boat docks, are near the south end of Jenny Lake and are alive with birds. The stretch near the base of Teewinot Mountain, which towers over the area, is populated with elk, mule deer, black bears, and moose. The trail is flat (at lake level), short, and easy to negotiate in 1 to 1.5 hours. The best times to venture forth are in early morning and evening.

4½ miles one-way. Moderate to difficult. Access: The trail into Cascade Canyon begins at Inspiration Point.

Hidden Falls & Inspiration Point Trail 🌟🌟 *(Kids)* Many people cross Jenny Lake, either by boat or on foot around the south end, and then make the short, forest-shaded uphill slog to **Hidden Falls** (less than 1 mile (1.5km) of hiking if you take the boat; 5 miles (8km) round-trip if you walk around), which tumbles down a broad cascade. Some think that's enough and don't go another steep half mile (1.5km) to **Inspiration Point.** Up there you get a great view of Jenny Lake below, and you can see the glacial moraine that formed it. If you're going to only these two overlooks, I recommend a relaxed and easy hike around the south end of the lake.

Whichever route you take to Inspiration Point, start early in the day to avoid the crowds. Then pace yourself. And once you've reached Inspiration Point, what's to stop you from proceeding on to Cascade Canyon?

1¾–5¾ miles (3–9.5km) RT. Moderate. Access: Trailheads at East Shore Boat Dock or at the West Shore Boat Dock of Jenny Lake (if you take the boat shuttle).

Jenny Lake Loop Trail 🐾🐾 This trail circumnavigates the lake, following the shore. You can cut it in half by taking the Jenny Lake Boat Shuttle from the East Shore Boat Dock to the West Shore Boat Dock. The unblemished lake, which is 2½ miles (4km) long, is in an idyllic setting at the foot of the mountain range, so it presents excellent views throughout the summer.

Warning: This is one of the most popular spots in the park; to avoid the crowds, travel early or late in the day. The trails to Hidden Falls, Inspiration Point, and the Moose Ponds branch off of this trail on the southwest shore of the lake. The trails to String and Leigh lakes branch off this trail on the northern shore of Jenny Lake.

6½ miles (10.5km) RT. Easy to moderate. Access: Trailhead at East Shore Boat Dock.

Leigh Lake Trail 🐾 This trail begins at String Lake, which is a small, finger-shape lagoon connecting Leigh and Jenny lakes. The trail for Leigh Lake is well marked and relatively flat, and it goes through a forested area that is always within sight of the lake. Picnickers willing to expend the energy necessary to hike roughly 1 mile (1.5km) from the String Lake picnic area to the end of the lake will find themselves eating in a less congested area with spectacular views of Mount Moran. The trail continues along the eastern shore of Leigh Lake to a meadow with typically wonderful views and then goes on to small Bearpaw Lake. A better option, if time allows, is to return to the picnic area, cross the String Lake inlet, and explore the western edge of Jenny Lake along the trail that circumnavigates its shoreline (see the "Jenny Lake Loop Trail," described above).

7½ miles (12km) RT. Easy. Access: The trailhead is located adjacent to the String Lake picnic area.

String Lake Trail This easy hike along the eastern shore of String Lake has two things going for it: It provides easy access to Leigh Lake, and it's in a forest that is a better alternative for a lunch break than the crowded picnic area. You'll wander in the shade of a pine forest along the shore with excellent views of Mount Moran above. However, because this is a heavily trafficked area, you should not count on seeing much wildlife, if any. This is also the starting point for a more ambitious trip up Paintbrush Canyon (see "Exploring the Backcountry," below).

3¼ miles (5km) RT. Easy. Access: Trailhead is located at the Leigh Lake Trailhead.

Taggart & Bradley Lakes Trail 🌣🌣   Want to get away from the crowds on Jenny Lake trails? Just down the road from South Jenny is the trailhead to Taggart and Bradley lakes, named for two members of the 1872 Hayden expedition. This hike winds through a burned-out area in the midst of recovery to Taggart Lake, which was created by glacial movements. The hike from the parking lot to the lake (where you can fish from the shore) is only 1½ miles (2.5km) along the southern (left) fork of the trail. Swimming in these cold waters is not recommended. From the lake, you can return by the same trail or continue north to **Bradley Lake** for a round-trip of 5 miles (8km). This route adds 1¾ miles (3km) to the trip, and the elevation gain is 467 feet, but the payoff is that, at its highest point, the trail overlooks all of Taggart Lake and the stream flowing from it. Like other hikes in Grand Teton, this one is best made during the early morning or early evening hours when it's cooler and there's less traffic.

5 miles (8km) RT. Moderate. Access: The trailhead is well marked and located west of Teton Park Road, approximately 6 miles (9.5km) south of Jenny Lake.

FARTHER AFIELD: SOUTHEAST OF MOOSE

Although it is situated near Kelly, outside the park boundaries, the **Gros Ventre Slide area** is an interesting hiking area and historical site. You can get to the slide area by traveling east from the Gros Ventre Junction on U.S. 89, 6 miles (9.5km) north of Jackson; alternately, 1 mile (1.5km) north of the Moose Junction on U.S. 89, take the Antelope Flats Road to the second right turn; then take the second left. There will be a sign.

It was at this spot in June 1925 that the side of Sheep Mountain broke loose and created one of the largest earth movements ever observed. Nearly 50 million cubic yards of sandstone formed a dam 225 feet high and ½ mile (1km) wide across the Gros Ventre River. Then, in 1927, the upper 60 feet of the dam gave way, creating a raging river that flooded the town of Kelly 3½ miles (5.5km) downstream.

Informational brochures and trail maps of the interpretive trail here, which is in the Bridger-Teton National Forest, are available from the U.S. Forest Service. You can stop in at the **Greater**

Yellowstone Visitor Center, at 532 N. Cache St. in downtown Jackson, where you can pick up all the information you'll need to hike in this area, or call the **Forest Service** at ℂ **307/739-5500.**

2 Exploring the Backcountry

Grand Teton might seem small compared to Yellowstone, but there are more than 200 miles (322km) of trails in the backcountry and plenty of opportunities for solitude and adventure. Like Yellowstone, a permit is required for camping in the backcountry— the permits are free and serve more to keep track of campers and to make sure that no one area is overused. Rather than receiving a specific site reservation, the permits allow you to establish camp in one of several camping "zones," where you'll have a choice of sites.

For **general information** on backpacking and safety, see chapter 2, "Planning Your Trip to Yellowstone & Grand Teton National Parks."

INFORMATION BEFORE YOU GO   For background information, write for the *Grand Teton Backcountry Camping* brochure, P.O. Drawer 170, Moose, WY 83012, or print it out from www.nps.gov/grte.

BACKCOUNTRY PERMITS   Backcountry permits from the Park Service are required to use an overnight campsite; the permits themselves are free, but an advance reservation entails a nonrefundable $15 fee. To avoid the fee, you may pick up a permit the day before you commence your trip. Reservations are accepted only from January 1 to May 15; it's wise to reserve a camp area if you're going in July or August. The permit is valid only on the dates for which it is issued.

Warning: The reservation is just that, a reservation; upon your arrival at the park, you'll need to secure the permit. Permits are issued at the Moose and Colter Bay visitor centers and the Jenny Lake Ranger station; reservations may be made by writing the **Permits Office,** Grand Teton National Park, P.O. Drawer 170, Moose, WY 83012, or faxing 307/739-3438.

WHEN TO GO   Remember that this region has a short summer and virtually no spring. While the valley floor of the park is open in May, some of the high country trails might not be clear of snow or high water before late June. Look in the *Backcountry Camping* brochure (see above) for approximate dates when specific campsites will be habitable.

MAPS   Topographic maps of Grand Teton are available from the U.S. Geological Survey and Trails Illustrated, as is the *Grand Teton Hiking and Climbing* map, which includes maps of Granite and Moran canyons and a trip planner; it is available from the **Grand Teton Natural History Association,** P.O. Drawer 170, Moose, WY 83012 (✆ **307/739-3403;** www.grandtetonpark.org).

THE BACKCOUNTRY IN GRAND TETON

The premier backcountry activity in Grand Teton is not hiking but rather **mountain climbing,** which you should not attempt alone unless you are an expert. For a complete discussion of mountaineering possibilities and outfitters in Grand Teton National Park, see "Climbing," below.

Perhaps the most popular backcountry trail in Grand Teton is the 19¼-mile (31km) **Cascade Canyon Loop** ★★★. The loop starts on the west side of Jenny Lake, winds northwest 9¼ miles (31km) on the **Cascade Canyon Trail** to Lake Solitude and the Paintbrush Divide, and then returns on the 10-mile-long (16km) **Paintbrush Trail** past Holly Lake, tucked into a cirque including Mount Woodring. While there are longer hikes, this is one of the most rigorous in either park because of gains in elevation—more than 2,600 feet—rocky trails, and switchbacks through loose gravel that can get slippery, especially in years when snow remains until the middle of summer on the north-facing side of Paintbrush Divide.

Rangers recommend the hike for several reasons, the most noteworthy of which is unsurpassed scenery. Moose and black bears call this part of the park home, so hikers are cautioned to be diligent about making noise (strap some bells on your pack). You might also see harlequin ducks, which nest near the trail in Cascade Creek. You'll see many other avians, a whole host of wildflowers, and large stands of whitebark pine trees.

Although it adds 5 miles (8km) to the trip (one way), a detour west from the Cascade Canyon Trail to **Hurricane Pass** will reward you with a view from the foot of **Schoolroom Glacier.** If it's an extended trip you're after, head west into the **Jedediah Smith Wilderness** on a trail that eventually crosses into Idaho. This trail doesn't stop anytime soon—you can actually continue trekking all the way to Alaska.

If you are looking to make a *long* day hike out of this, you can trek 7¼ miles (11.5km) on the Cascade Canyon Trail to **Lake Solitude** and return via the same trail. But you're better off planning for a multiday trip because camping zones are 6 miles (9.5km) west of the trailhead on the Cascade Canyon Trail and 8¾ miles (14km) northwest on the Paintbrush Canyon Trail at Holly Lake. Be sure to get a reservation.

Perhaps the quickest way to get up high in these mountains for a backcountry foray is to hitch a ride up **Rendezvous Mountain** 𝄢 on the Jackson Hole Ski Resort Tram. This puts you at 10,450 feet in **Bridger-Teton National Forest,** just south of the park, and ready to embark north toward the park's Middle Fork Cutoff. From here, you can head down into Granite Canyon to Phelps Lake, or go north along the **Teton Crest Trail** to Fox Creek Pass (over 8 difficult miles (13km) from the tram) and Death Canyon and beyond.

If you are hardy enough to make it to **Death Canyon Shelf,** a wildflower-strewn limestone ledge that runs above Death Canyon toward **Alaska Basin,** you'll have an extraordinary high-altitude view of the west side of the Tetons' biggest peaks. If you are on an extended backcountry trip, you can continue north to Hurricane Pass, where you can come back down to the valley floor by way of Cascade Canyon.

This kind of backcountry trip is truly an expedition and requires a certain level of skill and experience. Go over any such plans with park rangers, who can help you evaluate your ability to take on such a challenge.

3 Other Activities

In addition to the activities listed here, check out some of the other options in the Jackson area that are listed in chapter 8, "Gateways to Yellowstone & Grand Teton National Parks."

BIKING Bikes are banned from all hiking trails in the park, and, on the paved roads below, the problem is safety—there are huge RVs careening about, and some roads have only narrow shoulders. Construction has widened Teton Park Road a bit, but traffic is heavy on it. Instead, road bikers should try **Antelope Flats,** beginning at a trailhead a mile (1.5km) north of Moose Junction and going east. Sometimes called **Mormon Row,** this paved route crosses the flats below the Gros Ventre Mountains, past old ranch homesteads and the small town of Kelly. It connects to the unpaved **Shadow Mountain Road,** which actually leaves the park and continues into national forest, climbing through the trees to the summit. After a total distance of 7 miles (11km) and an elevation gain of 1,370 feet, you'll be looking at Mount Moran and the Tetons across the valley.

Mountain bikers have a few more options: Try **Two-Ocean Lake Road** (reached from the Pacific Creek Road just north of Moran Junction) or the **River Road,** a 15-mile (24km) dirt path along the Snake River's western bank. Ambitious mountain bikers might want to load their overnight gear and take the **Grassy Lake Road,** once used by Indians, west from Flagg Ranch on a 50-mile (80.5km) journey to Ashton, Idaho.

A map that shows bicycle routes, *Grand Teton Bicycling,* is available from the Park Service at visitor centers, or from **Adventure Sports,** at Dornan's in the village of Moose (© **307/733-3307**), which is inside the boundaries of Grand Teton National Park. You can also rent mountain bikes here, $25 for a full day and $18 for half a day.

BOATING   Boaters have more choices in Grand Teton than they do in Yellowstone. Motorboats are permitted on Jenny, Jackson, and Phelps lakes. Bigger boats, even a few yacht-size vessels, find room on Jackson Lake, where powerboats pull skiers, sailboats move noiselessly in summer breezes, and fishermen ply the waters. Those who venture on the big lake need to be aware that the weather can change suddenly, and late afternoon lightning is not uncommon; sailors should be particularly wary of the swirling winds that accompany thunderstorms. **Scenic cruises** of Jackson Lake, as well as breakfast and dinner cruises, are available daily at the **Colter Bay** marina from May through September, water level permitting.

If you bring your own boat, you must register it: For human-powered craft, it's $5 for 7 days, or $10 for a year permit; motorized skippers pay $10 for 7 days and $20 for an annual permit, which you can buy at the Colter Bay and Moose visitor centers. Boat and canoe rentals, tackle, and fishing licenses are available at Colter and **Signal Mountain** (rental fees of $19 per hour for motorboats include permits). For shuttles to the west side of Jenny Lake and for cruises, call **Teton Boating Company** (© **307/733-2703**).

Motorized boats are allowed on Phelps, Jackson, and Jenny Lakes, but on Jenny Lake the motor can't be over 8 horsepower. Only human-powered vessels are permitted on Emma Matilda, Two Ocean, Taggart, Bradley, Bearpaw, Leigh, and String lakes. Rafts, canoes, dories, and kayaks are allowed on the Snake River within the park. No boats at all are permitted on Pacific Creek or the Gros Ventre River.

Scenic cruises ⊛ of Jackson Lake are conducted daily, and breakfast and dinner cruises run twice weekly, both leaving from the

Colter Bay Marina from May through September. You'll travel to Elk Island, where they cook up a pretty good meal: trout and steak for dinner, and trout and eggs for breakfast. The scenic trips are 1.5 hours long and cost $15 for adults and $7 for kids; the meal cruises are twice that length and run $28 (breakfast) or $44 (dinner) for adults, and $16 or $26 for kids.

Additionally, you can rent kayaks and canoes at **Adventure Sports** at Dornan's in the town of Moose (© **307/733-3307**), which is in the boundaries of Grand Teton National Park. Rentals run around $30 per day and $20 for a half-day.

CLIMBING   Mountaineering in Grand Teton is wildly popular, but it's important to stay within the limits of your skill level. Every single year, there are rescues of climbers who fall or get trapped on Teton rock faces, and many years there are fatalities. Yet the peaks have a strong allure for climbers, even inexperienced ones, perhaps because you can reach the top of even the biggest ones in a single day, albeit not without a serious workout. The terrain is mixed, speckled with snow and ice even in midsummer—knowing how to self-arrest with an ice axe is a must—and the weather can change suddenly. The key is to get good advice, know your limitations, and, if you're not already skilled, take some lessons at the local climbing schools (see paragraph below). If you go without a professional guide, you should have experienced companions who know the mountain.

Climbers who go out for a day do not have to register or report to park officials, but they should be sure to tell friends where they're going and when they'll be back. Overnight climbers must pick up a free permit. Climbing rangers who can lead rescue efforts are on duty at the **Jenny Lake Ranger Station** (© **307/739-3343**) at South Jenny Lake from June until the middle of September. The American Alpine Club provides inexpensive dormitory beds for climbers at the **Grand Teton Climbers' Ranch** (P.O. Box 57, Moose, WY 83012; www.americanalpineclub.org). A pair of long-standing operations offers classes and guided climbs of Grand Teton: **Jackson Hole Mountain Guides** in Jackson (© **800/239-7642** or 307/733-4979; www.jhmg.com) and **Exum Mountain Guides** , in Moose (© **307/733-2297;** www.exumguides.com). Expect to pay around $500 for a guided climb or $100 for a class. Those who need to practice their moves on a rainy day should try the **Teton Rock Gym,** at 1116 Maple Way in Jackson (© **307/733-0707**).

The **Jenny Lake Ranger Station,** which is open only in summer, is the center for climbing information; climbers are encouraged to stop in and obtain information on routes, conditions, and regulations.

FISHING The lakes and streams of Grand Teton are popular fishing destinations, loaded with lively cutthroat trout, whitefish, and mackinaw (lake) trout in Jackson, Jenny, and Phelps Lake. Jackson has produced some monsters weighing as much as 50 pounds, but you're more likely to catch fish under 20 inches, fishing deep with trolling gear from a boat during hot summer months.

The Snake River runs for about 27 miles (43.5km) in the park and has cutthroat and whitefish up to about 18 inches. It's a popular drift boat river for fly-fishermen. If you'd like a guide who knows the holes, try **Jack Dennis Fishing Trips** (© 307/733-3270), **Triangle X-Osprey Float Trips** (© 307/733-5500), **Westbank Anglers** (© 307/733-6483), or **Fort Jackson River Trips** (© 800/735-8430). As an alternative, stake out a position on the banks below the dam at **Jackson Lake,** where you'll have plenty of company and just might snag something. While special fishing permits are issued by the Park Service in Yellowstone, a **Wyoming fishing license** is required of anglers in Grand Teton (nonresident $10 for 1 day, $65 for season; $15 for youngsters 14 to 18; no license for under 14), and you'll have to check the limits, which vary from year to year and place to place.

FLOAT TRIPS The upper end of the Snake River in the park can be deceptive—its smooth surface runs fast during the spring, and there are deadly snags of fallen trees and other debris. Without a local guide or past experience, you might want to think twice about dropping your personal raft in. Check in with rangers, and let them discourage you if they think your skills might not match the river. There are plenty of commercial-rafting outfitters that will help you get acquainted, listed below. If you want white water, there are a dozen commercial outfitters offering white-water trips down Snake River Canyon, outside the park (see "Jackson, Wyoming" in chapter 8, "Gateways to Yellowstone & Grand Teton National Parks").

The park's 27-mile (43.5km) stretch of river attracts all sorts of wildlife, with moose, eagles, and other animals coming to the water's edge. There are many commercial float operators in the park that generally run trips from mid-May to mid-September (depending on weather and river flow conditions). These companies offer

5- to 10-mile (8 to 16km) scenic floats, some with early-morning and evening wildlife trips. Try **Solitude Float Trips** (© 307/733-2871), **Barker-Ewing Float Trips** (© 800/365-1800), or **Grand Teton Lodge Company** (© 307/543-2811). You might also check out **Signal Mountain Lodge,** in Grand Teton National Park, P.O. Box 50, Moran, WY 83013 (© 307/543-2831); or **Flagg Ranch Float Trips** (© 307/543-2861). Scenic float trips cost about $40 for adults, with discounts for children under 12.

HORSEBACK RIDING Horseback riding is as popular in Grand Teton as it is in Yellowstone. The **Grand Teton Lodge Company** (© **307/543-2811**) offers tours from corrals at Colter Bay and Jackson Lake Lodge. Choices are 3- and 4-hour guided trail rides, including either breakfast or dinner, for about $40 per person. An experienced rider might find these tours too tame; wranglers refer to them as "nose-and-tail" tours. The names of several other companies that organize horseback trips are under "Jackson, Wyoming," in chapter 8."

4 Winter Sports & Activities

Park facilities pretty much shut down during the winter, except for a skeleton staff at the Moose Visitors Center, and the park shows no signs of becoming a winter magnet for snowmobilers or backcountry skiers, a la Yellowstone. That may be just as well—you can enjoy some quiet, fun times in the park without the crowds.

WINTER ROAD CONDITIONS **Teton Park Road** opens to conventional vehicles and RVs around May 1. The **Moose–Wilson Road** opens to vehicles about the same time. Park roads close on November 1 for the winter season. They are open to snowmobilers, snowshoers, and cross-country skiers after mid-December.

SPORTING GOODS & EQUIPMENT RENTALS Jackson has enough sporting equipment places to keep everyone in Wyoming outfitted. The **Jack Dennis Outdoor Shop** on the south side of Town Square (© 307/733-3270) has all the skis and outdoor clothing you can possibly need. **Teton Mountaineering,** 170 N. Cache St. (© **307/733-3595**), is the equipment shop of choice for the knowledgeable and advanced skier or ice climber; **Hoback Sports,** 40 S. Millward St. (© **307/733-5335**), is another good option. **Skinny Skis,** at 65 W. Deloney Ave. off the Town Square (© **307/733-6094**), is a year-round specialty sports shop focusing on Nordic skiing. For a great supply of seconds (same quality of material as "firsts"), stop at **Moosely Seconds** in Moose (☎ **307/733-1801**) or Jackson (☎ **307/733-7176**).

CROSS-COUNTRY SKIING   You can ski flat or steep in Grand Teton; the two things to watch out for are hypothermia and avalanches. As with climbing, know your limitations, and make sure you're properly equipped. Check with local rangers and guides for trails that match your ability. Among your options is the relatively easy **Jenny Lake Trail,** starting at the Taggart Lake Parking Area, about 8 miles (13km) of flat and scenic trail that follows Cottonwood Creek. A more difficult ski is the **Taggart Lake–Beaver Creek Loop,** a 3-mile (5km) route that has some steep and icy pitches coming back. About 4 miles (6.5km) of the **Moose-Wilson Road**—the back way to Teton Village from Moose—is unplowed in the winter and is an easy trip through the woods. You can climb the windy unplowed road to the top of **Signal Mountain**—you might encounter snowmobiles—and have some fun skiing down. There is an easy ski trail from the Colter Bay Ranger Station area to **Heron Pond**—about 2½ miles (4km), with a great view of the Tetons and Jackson Lake. Get a ski trail map from the visitor centers.

Skiers who come to Jackson Hole are usually after the hard, steep stuff at the Jackson Hole Mountain Resort, but there's a growing contingent of backcountry telemark skiers, who ski the Teton Pass area outside of the ski resort boundaries.

SNOWMOBILING   Snowmobiling is another popular winter option. The main roads in Grand Teton are groomed, providing access to trails in the nearby **Bridger-Teton National Forest,** the area to the immediate east of Grand Teton National Park, and to the **Continental Divide Trail,** which runs 320 miles (515km) through the Rockies.

For snowmobile rentals in Jackson, contact **Leisure Sports** (☎ **307/733-3040**) and **Wyoming Adventures** (☎ **800/637-7147**). Snowmobile rentals cost about $100 to $150 per day, with an extra charge for a second rider or a guided excursion. During winter, **Flagg Ranch Resort** (see chapter 7, "Where to Stay & Dine in the Parks") is a base for snowmobilers who explore the southern reaches of Yellowstone.

7

Where to Stay & Dine in the Parks

Before picking up the phone to make a reservation, take some time to study maps of the parks (see our maps in chapter 3, "Exploring Yellowstone," and in chapter 5, "Exploring Grand Teton National Park"). While the parks are small enough that you can drive practically anywhere in a day, you'll want to be acquainted with the locations of the park attractions that you most want to see and their proximity to accommodations. For instance, if you want to see Old Faithful at all different hours of the day and night, or if you want to bike the Lonestar Geyser Trail, try to get a room at the Old Faithful Inn or the Snow Lodge. If you find big bodies of water soothing, check in at the Lake Hotel or Colter Bay.

Also keep in mind that the characteristics of the lodgings vary considerably, and request specific information about the type of rooms available before making a reservation. If you are bedding down in one of the historic hotels or cabins in the parks, be aware that they offer fewer modern conveniences than your typical commercial motel.

One final bit of advice: Try to spend at least two nights within park boundaries, whether you prefer campgrounds or hotels. When the sun dips below the horizon, you'll see a summer sky that sparkles more brightly than in the gateway cities (weather permitting), and you might hear coyotes and other wildlife. And you will discover that the hours just after daybreak are an ideal time for exploring: The trails are empty, animals go about their early morning routines oblivious to visitors, and the silence is deafening.

1 Where to Stay in Yellowstone National Park

To book a room within Yellowstone, you need to contact **Yellowstone National Park Lodges**, P.O. Box 165, Yellowstone National Park, WY 82190 (© **307/344-7311;** www.travelyellowstone.com). Most Yellowstone accommodations are open from early May to mid-October. During Yellowstone's winter season, which begins in mid-December and runs through early March, accommodations and meals for snowmobilers and cross-country skiers can be found at either Mammoth Hot Springs Hotel or Old Faithful Snow Lodge. Because these dates are heavily dependent on weather conditions, it's best to call ahead to check the listed dates with the concessionaire.

It's easier to find a vacant room before June 15 and after September 15. The more popular lodges and campgrounds in the parks are typically fully booked during the peak season, so reservations should be made at least 6 months in advance. The rates often drop in October, to the tune of 30% to 40%, and those making reservations before April 1 can also get a significant discount. Both of these specials apply only to Old Faithful Inn and Snow Lodge, Lake Yellowstone Hotel, Grant Village, and Mammoth Hot Springs Hotel.

If you want television, air-conditioning, and other modern amenities typical of American hotels, stay in a gateway town rather than in the park. Some of the inns are close to a century old, and the park has encouraged the concessionaires to keep technology to a minimum. Although some of the park lounges now have televisions, and telephones have been added to many rooms, you won't find a single in-room TV in the park. Most of the accommodations do have heat, although, in some cases—the cabins at Roosevelt and the tent cabins at Colter Bay—it's a wood stove.

MAMMOTH HOT SPRINGS AREA

5 miles (8km) from the Gardiner (north) entrance to Yellowstone.

This area is open year-round and houses the park headquarters. It's a short drive from the park's north entrance, and you can often find a room here, even during the height of the peak season. Besides easy access, the area has quite a bit to offer: the park's best visitor center; colorful, travertine limestone terraces; a historic hotel with one of the park's better restaurants; and a campground.

Mammoth Hot Springs Hotel and Cabins   Below the steaming terraces of Mammoth Hot Springs, this is the only Yellowstone hotel open during both summer and winter seasons. The peaceful scene here, where elk often graze, is somewhat quickened by the flow of tourists stopping by the park headquarters and stores. Established in 1911, the hotel itself is less distinguished than the Lake Hotel or the Old Faithful Inn, but it manages to blend a wide range of rooms into a satisfying whole. Make sure you drift into the **Map Room**

(named for the massive inlaid map of the United States on one of the broad paneled walls), a great place to while away an evening reading or listening to a pianist.

The only truly high-end accommodations are the suites. Standard rooms and cabins are arranged around three grassy areas, offering minimal amenities with a fair amount of charm. Some rooms have tubs only, some rooms have showers only, and some share a bathroom down the hall. Personally, I prefer the cabins: cozy, cottage-style buildings, some with private hot tubs and sundecks.

At Mammoth Hot Springs (P.O. Box 165), Yellowstone National Park, WY 82190. 𝒞 307/344-7311. Fax 307/344-7456. www.travelyellowstone.com. 224 units, including 2 suites. $66–$93 double; $55–$88 cabin; $127 hot tub cabin; $274 suite. AE, DC, DISC, MC, V. **Amenities:** 2 restaurants, lounge; activities desk. *In room:* No phone (cabins).

CANYON VILLAGE AREA
40 miles (64km) from the West Yellowstone (west) entrance; 38 miles (61km) from the Gardiner (north) entrance.

This is one of the busiest areas in the park because the Grand Canyon of the Yellowstone is, like Old Faithful, on everyone's itinerary. Accommodations here are in modestly priced motel units or a large campground, and there are restaurants and coffee shops that fit most palates and pocketbooks, as well as a visitor center, general store, and post office. With the many amenities available here, it doesn't matter that it's 40 miles (64km) from the nearest gateway town.

Canyon Lodge and Cabins   This complex is one of the newer facilities in the park (the Cascade and Dunraven lodges here both were completed in the 1990s), but it can't escape the Disneyland-style atmosphere of the sprawling Canyon Village. However, the lodges are located a mere half-mile (1km) from the Grand Canyon of the Yellowstone and Inspiration Point, one of the most photographed spots in the park. Cascade offers simple rooms appointed with tasteful log furnishings in the three-story building; the newer Dunraven is similar, although it is more modern (with an elevator) and is located adjacent to a woodland setting. There are also clusters of cabins scattered throughout the village: clean, motel-style configurations. The cabins are single-story duplex and four-plex structures with private bathrooms that are among the largest in the park. They're much nicer than their more rustic counterparts in other centers, but, given the sheer number of units involved, this isn't the place to "get away from it all."

In Canyon Village (P.O. Box 165), Yellowstone National Park, WY 82190. ℂ 307/ 344-7311. www.travelyellowstone.com. 595 units. $127 double; $51–$101 cabin. AE, DC, DISC, MC, V. Closed Oct–late May. **Amenities:** Restaurant, lounge; activities desk; self-serve laundry. *In room:* No phone.

TOWER-ROOSEVELT AREA

23 miles (37km) from the Gardiner (north) entrance; 29 miles (47km) from the northeast entrance.

This is a throwback to the early days of Yellowstone: no big complex of shops and services, and a certain cowboy philosophy. Out of the way and far from the crowds, the lodge here offers easy access to the hiking trails and the beautiful corridor of the Lamar Valley. The basic cabins are an affordable (and apt) choice for families who want to "rough it" without pitching a tent.

Roosevelt Lodge Cabins ⚘ *(Kids)*   This is considered the park's family hideaway, a low-key operation with small, primitive cabins, horseback rides, and a lodge restaurant that's more like a big ranch house. The bare-bones cabins are called Roughriders, and they're furnished with two simple beds, clean linens, a writing table, and a wood stove. A step up, the Frontier cabins have their own bathrooms and showers. The lodge is a rugged but charming stone edifice with a large, inviting porch outfitted with rockers so that guests can take a load off and watch the world go by. Stagecoach rides, horseback trips, and Western trail cookouts give this place a cowboy flavor, and it's a less hectic scene than the other park villages.

P.O. Box 165, Yellowstone National Park, WY 82190. ℂ 307/344-7311 for reservations. 80 cabins (14 with private bathroom). $40–$77 cabin. AE, DC, DISC, MC, V. Closed early Sept–June. **Amenities:** Restaurant; activities desk. *In room:* No phone.

LAKE VILLAGE AREA

27 miles (43km) from the east entrance; 56 miles (90km) from the west Yellowstone (west) entrance; 43 miles (69km) from the south entrance.

More elegant than the Old Faithful Inn, this cluster of structures on the lake has the feel of a Victorian-era resort. There are accommodations in a historic hotel, motel and cabin units, and lakeside camping sites, all of which provide access to the lake's numerous recreational opportunities and the nearby hiking trails. The hotel's dining room is the finest in the park, although there are also low-priced alternatives in the neighborhood.

Lake Lodge Cabins   These cabins surrounding Lake Lodge stand near the lake, just around the corner north of the Lake Yellowstone Hotel. The old Western lodge's most attractive feature is a large porch with rockers that invite visitors to sit and gaze out across the waters. The accommodations are in well-preserved, clean, freestanding cabins near a trout stream that threads through a wooded area. There are nature walks around the lodge, but this is a trout spawning area, so access is usually restricted early in the summer when grizzlies emerge from hibernation. These cabins come in two grades: **Western** cabins provide electric heat, paneled walls, two double beds, and combination bathrooms, while **Frontier** cabins are smaller and sparsely furnished, with only one double bed each and small shower-only bathrooms. You'll need to head outdoors to enjoy the lake views; the only things you can see from your cabin are other cabins. Because the dining options here are a tad short on atmosphere, you might want to make the short trek to the Lake Yellowstone Hotel for a more sumptuous meal in a more appetizing setting.

On Lake Yellowstone (P.O. Box 165), Yellowstone National Park, WY 82190. (*) 307/ 344-7311. www.travelyellowstone.com. 186 cabins. $53 Frontier cabin; $116 Western cabin. AE, DC, DISC, MC, V. Closed mid-Sept to early June. **Amenities:** Restaurant, lounge; activities desk; self-serve laundry.

Lake Yellowstone Hotel and Cabins ✲✲

The ionic columns, dormer windows, and deep porticos on this classic yellow building faithfully recall the year it was built: 1891. It's an entirely different world from the rustic Western style of other park lodgings. The facility was restored in the early 1990s, and its better rooms are the most comfortable and roomy in the park, with soul-stirring views of the massive lake.

The three- and four-story wings house the hotel rooms, and there's also a motel-style annex and an assortment of cabins. The upper-end rooms here are especially lavish for Yellowstone, with stenciled walls and traditional spreads on one queen-size or two double beds. Smaller rooms in the annex are fitted with two double beds and bring to mind a typical motel chain, but I'd opt for one of the freestanding cabins instead. These are decorated with knotty-pine paneling, and furnished with double beds and a writing table—a desirable low-priced alternative. Request a single rather than a duplex because the thin walls are far from soundproof.

On the north side of the lake (P.O. Box 165), Yellowstone National Park, WY 82190. (*) 307/344-7311. www.travelyellowstone.com. 296 units, including 1 suite. $127–$167 double; $68 cabin; $411 suite. AE, DC, DISC, MC, V. Closed Oct 4–May 13. **Amenities:** 2 restaurants, lounge; activities desk; self-serve laundry. *In room:* No phone (cabins).

GRANT VILLAGE AREA
22 miles (35km) from the south entrance; 47 miles (76km) from the West Yellowstone (west) entrance.

This relatively modern addition doesn't have the romantic ambience that's exuded by the Old Faithful Inn or the Lake Hotel in spades. Nevertheless, it's reasonably priced and has a good location, near the south shores of beautiful Lake Yellowstone, with a good visitor center and access to various sights.

Grant Village   The southernmost of the major overnight accommodations in the park, Grant Village was completed in 1984 and is one of the more contemporary choices in Yellowstone. It's not as architecturally distinctive as the Old Faithful options, consisting of six motel-style chalets set back from the water's edge, but it's also less touristy and more isolated. Rooms are tastefully furnished, most outfitted with light wood furniture, track lighting, electric heat, and laminate counters. Nicer and more expensive rooms affording lake views have mullioned windows, one queen-size or one or two double beds, and full bathrooms.

On the West Thumb of Yellowstone Lake (P.O. Box 165), Yellowstone National Park, WY 82190. ⓒ 307/344-7311. www.travelyellowstone.com. 300 units. $93–$108 double. AE, DC, DISC, MC, V. Closed late Sept–late May. **Amenities:** Restaurant, lounge; activities desk.

OLD FAITHFUL AREA
30 miles (48km) from the West Yellowstone (west) entrance; 39 miles (63km) from the south entrance.

Despite the crowds, the Old Faithful area is probably the best spot to center a hotel-based visit to the park. First of all, you'll spend a night in the midst of the most famous geyser basin in the world. You'll also have more choices of rooms, restaurants, and services—including a visitor center, gas station, and Hamilton Store—than anywhere else in the park. And, from a logistical point of view, you'll have excellent access to attractions in every direction.

Old Faithful Inn ★★★   There are three hotels within viewing distance of the geyser, including a very nice new one, but this is undoubtedly the crown jewel of Yellowstone's manmade wonders. Seven stories tall with dormers peaking from a shingled, steep-sloping roof, it's an architectural wonder that was designed by Robert Reamer to blend into the natural environment—and it works. Inside, you can climb the stairs to its internal balconies, but seismic activity eventually closed the crow's nest, where, in the inn's early years, a chamber orchestra performed for the Victorian guests below. Only 30 miles (48km) from the west entrance and 40 miles (64km) from the south entrance, this is the first place visitors think of when they want a bed for the night, so make reservations far ahead during the busy summer months.

Guest rooms are in the main building and in wings that flank the main lodge. Original rooms are well appointed with conservative fabrics and park-theme art, but they might not have private bathrooms; the wing rooms offer better facilities and more privacy.

At Old Faithful (P.O. Box 165), Yellowstone National Park, WY 82190. ℂ **307/ 344-7311.** Fax 307/344-7456. www.travelyellowstone.com. 327 units, including 9 suites. $117–$167 double with private bathroom, $71–$126 double without bathroom; $263–$351 suite. AE, DC, DISC, MC, V. Closed mid-Oct to mid-May. **Amenities:** 2 restaurants, lounge; activities desk.

Old Faithful Lodge Cabins *Value*

These are the leftovers from the days when crude cabins littered the landscape around the world's most famous geyser. The ones closest to the geyser were hauled away years ago, but you still get a sense of what tourism was like in the park's early days, especially if you rent one of the **budget cabins,** which are just slightly less flimsy than tents and have basic beds and sinks, no more. Showers and restrooms are a short walk away. Next up the scale are the **economy cabins,** which have beds, sinks, and toilets, but no bathtubs. **Frontier cabins** are the best units, adding a private bathtub to other amenities. If amenities are irrelevant, these rustic, thin-walled cabins are an economical way to put a roof over your head in the park. The lodge is perhaps the busiest spot in the geyser area, featuring several snack shops and a huge cafeteria dishing up varied fast food.

At Old Faithful (P.O. Box 165), Yellowstone National Park, WY 82190. ℂ **307/ 344-7311.** www.travelyellowstone.com. 97 cabins (some without private bathroom). $44–$68 double. AE, DC, DISC, MC, V. Closed mid-Sept to mid-May. **Amenities:** 2 restaurants; activities desk. *In room:* No phone.

Old Faithful Snow Lodge and Cabins 🐾🐾

If your last visit to Yellowstone included a stay at the Old Faithful Snow Lodge, put the memory out of your mind. The old dormitory-style lodge was torn down in 1998, and this new, award-winning structure could aptly be called the New Faithful Snow Lodge. Its contemporary big-beam construction and high ceiling in the lobby echo the Old Faithful Inn, and a copper-lined balcony curves above the common area, where guests can relax in wicker furniture. Attention was paid to every last detail: The structure's wooden components were recycled from the actual mill that provided the lumber for the Old Faithful Inn in 1904, and wrought-iron bears abound on everything from lamps to fireplace grates. The modern rooms are spacious and comfortable, second only to the upper-end accommodations at the Lake Hotel. There's also the usual selection of surrounding cabins with motel-style furnishings.

At Old Faithful (P.O. Box 165), Yellowstone National Park, WY 82190. © **307/ 344-7311.** Fax 307/344-7456. www.travelyellowstone.com. 134 units. $137 double; $118 cabin. AE, DC, DISC, MC, V. **Amenities:** Restaurant, lounge; activities desk. *In room:* No phone (cabins).

2 Where to Camp in Yellowstone

Camping at Yellowstone's 12 developed campgrounds can be a happy affair, with the stars overhead, the scent of pine, and friendly neighbors from all over the world. The campgrounds are spaced throughout the park.

For those who carry their tents on their backs and want no neighbors other than their hiking buddies, there's plenty of room out there. Some areas in the Yellowstone backcountry are delicate habitat—the southeast arm of Yellowstone Lake is an example—and visitors must camp in designated areas for a limited time only. This in no way diminishes the sense of being in a true wilderness. Check with the **Yellowstone Backcountry Office** (© **307/344-2160**) for rules, reservations, and advice.

GETTING A CAMPSITE   The National Park Service has shifted management of five major campgrounds to Yellowstone National Park Lodges, which means, predictably, higher fees, but it thankfully allows you to make reservations ahead of arrival. The other seven campgrounds still managed by the park are available only on a first-come, first-served basis. These **lower-cost campgrounds** are at Indian Creek, Lewis Lake, Mammoth, Norris, Pebble Creek, Slough Creek, and Tower Fall. I happen to like the Norris, Slough Creek, and Lewis Lake sites, which tend to be available when others are full. Check with rangers about campsite availability when you enter the park; generally, you need to arrive early to get a site—some campgrounds fill up as early as 8am.

Yellowstone National Park Lodges operates the large campgrounds at Bridge Bay, Canyon, Grant Village, Madison, and Fishing Bridge. Some are rather barren of trees unless you get a site on the fringes. Reservations can be made by calling © **307/ 344-7311;** by writing Yellowstone National Park Lodges, P.O. Box

165, Yellowstone National Park, WY 82190; or online at www.travelyellowstone.com.

REGULATIONS You can set up your tent only in designated areas, and stays are limited to 14 days between June 15 and Labor Day, and to 30 days the rest of the year, except at Fishing Bridge, where there is no limit. Checkout time at all campgrounds is 10am. Quiet hours are enforced between the hours of 8pm and 8am. No generators or loud music are allowed during these hours.

THE CAMPGROUNDS For exact information on prices, opening dates, and amenities, refer to the chart "Amenities for Each Campground: Yellowstone National Park," in this section.

These are campgrounds, not motels, so the amenities are sparse, but some have laundry facilities, showers, bathrooms, and potable water, which are luxuries to campers who've experienced the world's more primitive campgrounds.

In the northeast area of the park, the **Tower Fall campground** is near a convenience store, restaurant, and gas station at Tower Lodge, 19 miles (31km) north of Canyon Village and 18 miles (30km) east of Mammoth. **Slough Creek campground** 🅕 is in a remote section of the Lamar Valley near the northeast entrance; the good news is that there are fewer people, good fishing, and the possibility of wolf sightings; the bad news is that restroom facilities are pit toilets.

Canyon campground is the busiest in the park. Sites are in a heavily wooded area; the store, restaurants, visitor center, and laundry at Canyon Center are all nearby.

Because it's in an area of spring bear activity, attempts have been made over the years to close the RV park at **Fishing Bridge.** It's still open, but only hard-sided camping vehicles are allowed here.

Bridge Bay is located near the shores of Yellowstone Lake, so you get tremendous views, especially at sunrise and sunset. Unfortunately, though surrounded by the forest, much of the area has been clear-cut, so there's not a whole lot of privacy. It's close to the marina (where fishing charters originate) and the boat rental operation.

Madison 🅕 is in a wooded area just south of the river, a popular spot with good access to fishing and hiking. **Norris** 🅕 is one of the park's better camping areas, with attractive, wooded locations in the heart of the park, close to wildlife activity and the Gibbon River. These camp areas seem less like outdoor motels than the big campgrounds on the park's east side.

Amenities for Each Campground: Yellowstone National Park

Campground	Total Sites	RV Hookups	Dump Station	Toilets	Drinking Water	Showers	Fire Pits/ Grills	Laundry	Public Phone	Reserve	Fees	Open
Inside the Park												
Bridge Bay*	430	No	Yes	Yes	Yes	No	Yes	No	Yes	Yes	$15	Late May–mid-Sept
Canyon*	272	No	Yes	Yes	Yes	Yes	Yes	Yes	Yes	Yes	$15	June–mid-Sept
Fishing Bridge*	344	Yes	Yes	Yes	Yes	Yes	Yes	Yes	Yes	Yes	$28	Mid-May–mid-Sept
Grant Village*	425	No	Yes	Yes	Yes	Yes	Yes	Yes	Yes	Yes	$15	Mid-June–Sept
Indian Creek	75	No	No	Yes	Yes	No	Yes	No	No	Yes	$10	June–Sept
Lewis Lake	85	No	No	Yes	Yes	No	Yes	No	No	No	$10	Mid-June–Nov
Madison*	280	No	Yes	Yes	Yes	No	Yes	No	Yes	Yes	$15	Early May–mid-Oct
Mammoth	85	No	No	Yes	Yes	No	Yes	No	Yes	No	$12	Year-round
Norris	116	No	No	Yes	Yes	No	Yes	No	Yes	No	$12	Mid-May–Sept
Pebble Creek	36	No	No	Yes	Yes	No	Yes	No	No	No	$10	Mid-June–Sept
Slough Creek	29	No	No	Yes	Yes	No	Yes	No	No	No	$10	Late May–Oct
Tower Fall	32	No	No	Yes	Yes	No	Yes	No	No	No	$10	Mid-May–Late Sept
Near the Park												
Bakers Hole	72	No	No	Yes	Yes	No	Yes	No	Yes	Yes	$12	Late May–mid-Sept
Lonesomehurst	26	No	No	Yes	Yes	No	Yes	No	No	Yes	$12	Late May–mid-Sept
Rainbow Point	85	No	No	Yes	Yes	No	Yes	No	Yes	Yes	$12	Late May–mid-Sept

*Reserve through Yellowstone National Park Lodges.

Fishing Bridge accepts hard-sided vehicles only.

3 Where to Camp Near Yellowstone

There are three National Forest Service campgrounds in the **West Yellowstone** area, all located in the Gallatin National Forest (see "Amenities for Each Campground: Yellowstone National Park," above, for amenities, prices, and opening dates). They accommodate both RVs and tents, but during some periods in late summer they accept hard-sided vehicles only. All three are first-come, first serve, so it's best to stake out a spot early. The heavily forested **Bakers Hole,** just 3 miles (5km) north of West Yellowstone on U.S. 191, is popular because of its fishing access. Both tents and RVs are accepted, but there are no hookups. **Lonesomehurst,** 8 miles (13km) west of the park on U.S. 20 and then 4 miles (6.5km) north on Hebgen Lake Road, is only one-third the size of Bakers Hole and fills up quickly in summer. It has tent and RV sites, some of them right on the shore of Hebgen Lake. **Rainbow Point** is reached by driving 5 miles (8km) north of West Yellowstone on U.S. 191, then 3 miles (5km) west on Forest Service Road 610, and then north for 2 miles (3km) on Forest Service Road 6954. Tucked away in the forest near Hebgen Lake, it accommodates both tents and RVs (no hookups) and has boating and fishing access. For further information on these campgrounds, call the **Hebgen Lake Ranger District** (© **406/823-6961**). You can find a wealth of information on the Forest Service website at www.fs.fed.us/gallatin.

In addition, there are a few RV parks in or near West Yellowstone. While these parks have full utility hookups and are generally designed for hard-sided vehicles, if there's space left over and you're willing to pay the price for a utility hookup that you won't be able to fully utilize, an owner of an RV park might allow you to pitch your tent. The shady **Hide-Away RV Campground,** 320 Electric St. (© **406/646-9049**), has cable TV hookups and showers, open May through October. The **Madison Arm Resort** on the south shore of Hebgen Lake (© **406/646-9328**) has both RV and tent sites, a marina, and a peaceful setting.

4 Where to Dine in Yellowstone

While they're not world-class establishments, Yellowstone's restaurants are well suited to their location and the appetites of their patrons: The portions definitely won't leave anyone going hungry. Most of the menus include a selection of unadventurous, all-American meat-and-potatoes grub alongside several more creative entrees with a splash of zest. While nitpickers might decry a lack of variety or exotic cuisine, the park's eateries, like its accommodations, are quite democratic and offer something for all but the most finicky of tastes.

If you're not up for restaurant dining but you don't want to cook over your camp stove the whole time, there is counter-style fast food service at the **Hamilton General Stores,** as well as snacks shops and cafeterias at Canyon, Mammoth, Grant Village, Lake Lodge, and Old Faithful.

MAMMOTH HOT SPRINGS

You'll find the **Terrace Grille** at the opposite end of the building in which the **Mammoth Hot Springs Dining Room** is located. Here the typical restaurant fare is served in a less formal and less pricey dining room, but no reservations can be made.

Mammoth Hot Springs Dining Room ✦ STEAKS/SEAFOOD

At Mammoth, there's a good balance between casual and formal because the dining room is reminiscent of an above-average neighborhood restaurant: comfortable and pleasant without too much of the hotel's Victorian past. The view of the Old Fort Yellowstone buildings and surrounding slopes is also quite enjoyable. The breakfast buffet is quite similar to what you'll find here at other locations, featuring eggs, French toast, and the like. The lunch menu focuses on an array of sandwiches, including teriyaki chicken breast, a grilled vegetarian sandwich, and grilled German bratwurst. The dinner menu is more substantial, and the house-smoked entrees are quite good.

At Mammoth Hot Springs. ☎ **307/344-7901.** Dinner reservations required. Breakfast $4–$8; lunch $6–$11; dinner $9–$23. AE, DC, DISC, MC, V. Summer daily 6:30–10am, 11:30am–2:30pm, and 5–10pm.

CANYON VILLAGE AREA

Like restaurants in the other park centers, the eating options at Canyon Village consist of three choices: a casual, soda fountain–style restaurant, a fast-food cafeteria, and a conventional dining room.

The **Canyon Glacier Pit Snack Bar,** which is operated by Hamilton Stores, is in the same building as the convenience store and souvenir shop. Seating is on stools in the fashion of a 1950s soda fountain; expect a wait of up to 30 minutes during peak hours. Breakfast consists of egg dishes, lunch is soup and sandwiches, and dinner is traditional Western food. Hours are daily 6:30am to 10pm from May 18 to September 24.

The **Canyon Lodge Cafeteria** (☎ **307/344-7901**) is a fast-food alternative managed by Yellowstone National Park Lodges and is across the parking lot in the Canyon Lodge area. Hours are the same as at the snack bar, and the menu bears some striking similarities— but you might get through the cafeteria line faster than you would get a stool at the soda fountain. The cafeteria is open from June 1 to September 15.

Canyon Lodge Dining Room *(Kids* STEAKS/SEAFOOD This is a spacious dining area, a tad sterile perhaps, and when it fills up, it's noisy. The salad bar is long and loaded, but otherwise the dinner fare is largely geared toward the carnivore, with a wide selection of steaks alongside some seafood and pasta selections. The breakfast buffet is a good way to start your day, with all the standard American fixings. The crowds can be large at Canyon Village, but there is a relaxed and unhurried feel to this place that you don't find at some of the park's other busy points. Families, in particular, might appreciate the ability to take their time with their meals.

At Canyon Lodge. ✆ 307/344-7901. Reservations required. Breakfast $3–$8; lunch $5–$10; dinner $12–$20. June to mid-Sept daily 7–10:30am, 11:30am–2:30pm, and 5–10pm.

TOWER-ROOSEVELT AREA

Roosevelt Lodge STEAKS/SEAFOOD This is supposed to be the cowboy alternative to the fancier cuisine served at the bigger Yellowstone hotels, but the unadventurous menu will win over only the most naïve city slickers. For breakfast, it's eggs and flapjacks; lunch is burgers and sandwiches. Come suppertime, the Roosevelt beans are the standout because the short menu is dominated by middle-of-the-road American specialties, such as ribs and steaks. A better idea: Join Roosevelt's Old West Dinner Cookout, and ride by horse or wagon thorough the Pleasant Valley to a chuck wagon din- ner that includes cornbread, steak, watermelon, those famous beans, and apple crisp. It's a daily summer event (reservations required) that costs $42 to $52 for an adult, depending on the route of your horseback ride, or $32 if you go by wagon. Children pay $10 less.

At Tower Junction. ✆ 307/344-7901. Breakfast $4–$8; lunch $6–$13; dinner $9–$22. AE, DC, DISC, MC, V. Summer daily 7–10:30am, 11:30am–3pm, and 5–9pm.

YELLOWSTONE LAKE

For the eat-on-the-run traveler, a **deli** in the Lake Yellowstone Hotel serves lighter fare in an area that is slightly larger than a broom closet from 11am to 9pm. Just down the road, the **Hamilton store** offers three meals in a section of the store that is shared with tourist items; the best bet here is breakfast or a burger. It's open from 7am to 9pm. Inexpensive meals are served cafeteria-style at the **Lake Lodge and Cabins** (✆ **307/344-7901**) from 7am to 8pm. All hours listed here are from mid-May to early October.

Lake Yellowstone Hotel ⭐⭐ CONTINENTAL This represents the finest dining Yellowstone has to offer, with a view of the lake stretching south from a vast dining room that doesn't feel crowded even when it's full. One of the best ways to start your day is with a generous breakfast buffet, but the huevos rancheros and pan-fried trout and eggs are also quite good. There's also a wide selection of fresh fruit, juices, pastries, and cereals. The dinner menu is even more inviting. Appetizers include duck quesadillas and *spanakopitas* (a tasty Greek pastry stuffed with spinach and cheese), while entrees include lovingly prepared sea scallops, pan-seared yellowfin tuna, and, of course, several beef dishes. The food here is of the quality one expects at a grand hotel.

On the north side of the lake. ✆ **307/344-7901**. Dinner reservations required. Breakfast $4–$8; lunch $5–$13; dinner $10–$25. AE, DC, DISC, MC, V. Mid-May to early Oct daily 6:30–10:30am, 11:30am–2:30pm, and 5–10pm.

GRANT VILLAGE

The casual choice here is the **Lake House** (✆ **307/344-7901**), footsteps away from the Grant Village restaurant. It specializes in less expensive fish entrees, as well as burgers and beer. Meals are served from 5:30 to 9pm late May to early October. No reservations are accepted.

Grant Village ⭐ AMERICAN Breakfast and lunch at the Grant Village restaurant are much like those at the other restaurants in the park, although the chef often surprises diners with interesting dinner items that stray from the norm. Lunch might include pan-fried trout covered with toasted pecans and lemon butter, huge burgers, and a top-notch taco salad. The dinner menu ranges from huckleberry chicken to swordfish with lemon dill beurre to blackened prime rib, but the specialty is trout, prepared in a variety of creative ways. Quality and ambience here are comparable to those of the better dining rooms at the major park hotels.

At Grant Village. ✆ **307/344-7901**. Dinner reservations required. Breakfast $4–$8; lunch $6–$10; dinner $10–$23. AE, DISC, MC, V. June–Sept daily 6:30–10am, 11:30am–2:30pm, and 5:30–10pm.

OLD FAITHFUL AREA

Choices abound here. For quick and inexpensive, the **Old Faithful Inn** cafeteria serves lunch and dinner in a fast-food environment that fits the mood of a crowd on the move; an ice cream stand in the lobby is your best choice for dessert. The **Hamilton Store** also has a lunch counter.

Old Faithful Inn 𝄞𝄞 STEAKS/SEAFOOD There's nothing wrong with the food here, but the real highlight is the gnarled log architecture of this distinguished historic inn. Breakfast is buffet or a la carte, and there's a lot to choose from. There's another buffet at lunchtime (headlined by barbecue beef and chicken), as well as a generous assortment of salads and sandwiches. The dinner menu is extensive, with four cuts of prime rib, several fish dishes, meatloaf, and pastas. The fare has gotten more distinguished in recent years, with such creative options as roasted pork loin with jalapeno cream sauce and shrimp scampi making regular appearances on the menu. I recommend that you have at least one dinner here while you're visiting the park to at least take in the ambience of the inn—and top it off with a decadent Yellowstone Sundae.

At the Old Faithful Inn. ℭ **307/545-4999.** Dinner reservations required. Breakfast $7–$9; lunch $5–$11; dinner $9–$24. AE, DC, DISC, MC, V. May to mid-Oct daily 6:30–10:30am, 11:30am–2:30pm, and 5–10pm.

Obsidian Dining Room 𝄞 STEAKS/SEAFOOD In the snazzy new Snow Lodge, a spacious restaurant provides a comparatively contemporary alternative to the dining room at the Old Faithful Inn. It's a little quieter, a little less expensive, and a little less formal, which is reflected in a menu heavy on burgers and salads. It still has some flash on the menu—teriyaki salmon and huge porterhouse pork chops—and there is a breakfast gem in the Southwestern eggs. All things considered, it's a huge improvement over the cramped restaurant of the old Snow Lodge.

At the Old Faithful Snow Lodge. ℭ **307/344-7901.** Breakfast $4–$8; lunch $5–$12; dinner $9–$18. AE, DC, DISC, MC, V. May to mid-Oct and mid-Dec to mid-May, daily 6:30–10am, 11:30am–2:30pm, and 5–10pm.

5 Where to Stay in Grand Teton National Park

The three concessionaires that operate lodgings within Grand Teton provide a range of accommodations that can suit any wallet or taste, but not every schedule. I say fairly often in this guide that fall and spring are the best times to have the parks to yourself, but these are not the easiest times to find a room. If you come in early May, you'll find padlocks on the doors everywhere but at Flagg Ranch, which technically isn't in Grand Teton anyway, but on the John D. Rockefeller Jr. Memorial Parkway. Likewise, by mid-October, you'll be bunking in Jackson.

You can get information about or make reservations for Jackson Lake Lodge, Jenny Lake Lodge, and Colter Bay Village through the **Grand Teton Lodge Company,** Box 240, Moran, WY 83013 (© **800/628-9988** or 307/543-3100; www.gtlc.com). For **Signal Mountain Lodge,** contact P.O. Box 50, Moran, WY 83013 (© **307/543-2831;** www.signalmtnlodge.com). Reservations at **Flagg Ranch** can be made by contacting P.O. Box 187, Moran, WY 83013 (© **800/443-2311;** www.flaggranch.com).

Rooms in Grand Teton National Park properties have telephones but no televisions or air-conditioning. You'll find televisions in the lounge areas at the Jackson Lodge, Signal Mountain Resort, and Flagg Ranch.

FLAGG RANCH VILLAGE AREA

2 miles (3km) from the south entrance to Yellowstone; 5 miles (8km) from the northern boundary of Grand Teton.

Like Grant Village in Yellowstone, Flagg Ranch offers travelers the full gamut of services: cabins, tent and RV sites, an above-average restaurant, and a gas station. It's also a popular jumping-off spot for snowmobilers during winter months. However, because it's situated in a stand of pines in the middle of nowhere, there's not much to do in the immediate vicinity except watch the Snake River roll by.

Flagg Ranch Resort ☆ A few years ago this resort just outside Yellowstone National Park was showing its age—the sort of place where a hunter would rent a drafty room to collapse in after a few days in the woods. Not anymore: It's all fixed up, transformed into an all-seasons resort on the Snake River with log-and-luxury ambience. The newest accommodations are duplex and four-plex log cabins constructed in 1994 that feature king-size beds, spacious sitting areas with writing desks and chests of drawers, wall-to-wall carpeting, and bathrooms with tub-shower combinations and separate vanities.

The only livestock on the ranch these days are the herds of snowmobiles that gather here in the winter to warm up before entering Yellowstone. In the summer, there are float trips, horseback rides, and excellent fishing in Polecat Creek or the Snake River. The new lodge is a locus of activity, with its double-sided fireplace, fancy dining room, gift shop, espresso bar and pub with large-screen television, convenience store, and gas station. A campground and RV facility are situated on the grounds amid a stand of pine trees.

P.O. Box 187, Moran, WY 83013. © 800/443-2311 or 307/543-2861. www.flagg ranch.com. 92 cabins, 171 RV sites. Spring and fall $100 cabin double; winter, $110 cabin double; summer $135 cabin double. AE, DISC, MC, V. **Amenities:** Restaurant, lounge; activities desk.

COLTER BAY VILLAGE AREA

11 miles (18km) from the park's northern boundary; 10 miles (16km) from the Moran (east) entrance.

The village provides an excellent base of operations for visitors who want to hike or enjoy the lake. It encompasses two restaurants, a visitor center, an amphitheater, a museum, a general store, a post office, a sporting-goods shop, and laundry facilities. Scenic cruises, fishing charters, and boat rentals of all kinds can be arranged at the marina. The village operates from mid-May to late September.

Colter Bay Village *⛰ (Kids)* You might call this the people's resort of Grand Teton, with simpler lodgings, lower prices, and a lively, friendlier atmosphere that seems particularly suited to families. Situated on the eastern shore of Jackson Lake, Colter Bay Village is a full-fledged recreation center. Guest accommodations are in rough log cabins perched on a wooded hillside; they are clean and simply furnished with area rugs on tile floors and reproductions of pioneer furnishings—chests, oval mirrors, and extra-long bedsteads with painted headboards.

If you want to take a trip back to the early days of American auto travel, when car camping involved unwieldy canvas tents on slabs by the roadside, you can spend an inexpensive night in "tent cabins." (Bring your own sleeping bags.) The shower and bathroom are communal. Overall, the village provides an excellent base of operations for visitors because it has the most facilities of any area in the park.

P.O. Box 240, Moran, WY 83013. © **800/628-9988** or 307/543-3100. www.gtlc. com. 166 units. $33–$125 log cabin; $33 tent cabin. AE, DC, MC, V. Closed late Sept–late May. **Amenities:** 2 restaurants; activities desk; shopping arcade; self-serve laundry. *In room:* No phone.

Jackson Lake Lodge *⛰* Much the way that Old Faithful Inn or the Lake Hotel captures historic eras of Yellowstone tourism, Jackson Lake Lodge epitomizes the architectural milieu of the period when Grand Teton became a park. That era was the 1950s, however, an age of right angles, flat roofs, and big windows. Still, the lodge is popular, particularly for its wonderful setting overlooking Willow Flats, the lake in the distance, and, towering over it, without so much as a stick in the way, the Tetons and Mount Moran. You don't even have to go outside to see this impressive view—the lobby has 60-foot-tall windows. Guest rooms are in the three-story main lodge and in cottages scattered about the property, some of which have large balconies and mountain views. Lodge rooms are spacious and cheery, and most offer double beds, electric heat, and newly tiled bathrooms. Both the lodge and cottage rooms are comparable to an upper-tier chain hotel, with an American Indian motif. For a premium, the view rooms provide guests with a private picture window facing the Tetons.

P.O. Box 240, Moran, WY 83013. © **800/628-9988** or 307/543-3100. www.gtlc. com. 385 units. $120–$210 double; $146–$210 cottage; $385–$550 suite. AE, DC, MC, V. Closed mid-Oct to mid-May. **Amenities:** 2 restaurants, lounge; heated outdoor pool; airport shuttle; activities desk.

SIGNAL MOUNTAIN AREA
15 miles (24km) from the north entrance; 9 miles (14.5km) from the Moran (east) entrance.

Signal Mountain Lodge 🐾 *(Finds)*   Signal Mountain has a different feel—and different owners—from the other lodgings in Grand Teton, adding to the sense that any place you choose to stay in this park is going to give you a fairly unique atmosphere. What they all have in common is the Teton view, and this lodge, located right on the banks of Jackson Lake, might have the best. To top it off, it's got lakefront retreats, which you can really inhabit, with stoves and refrigerators and foldout sofa beds for the kids. Other accommodations, mostly rustic log cabins, come in a variety of flavors, from motel-style rooms in four-unit buildings set amid the trees to family bungalows with decks, some enjoying beach frontage. The carpeted cabins feature handmade pine furniture, electric heat, covered porches, and tiled bathrooms; some have fireplaces. Recreational options include cycling, rafting, water-skiing, and fishing, but note that boat rentals are expensive here. A convenience store and gas station are on the property.

P.O. Box 50, Moran, WY 83013. © **307/543-2831**. www.signalmtnlodge.com. 80 units. $95–$225 double. AE, DISC, MC, V. Closed Nov–Apr. **Amenities:** 2 restaurants; activities desk. *In room:* Kitchenettes.

JENNY LAKE AREA
28 miles (45km) from the northern boundary; 17 miles (27km) from the Moran (east) entrance; 16 miles (26km) from the Moose entrance.

Jenny Lake Lodge 🐾🐾🐾   This lodge justifiably prides itself on seclusion, award-winning food, and the individual attentions that come with a cabin resort kept intentionally small. The property is a hybrid of mountain lake resort and dude ranch, with various extras included in its prices, such as horseback rides, meals, and bicycles. The cabins, each named for a resident flower, are rustic on the outside and luxurious within. Inside are bright braided rugs, dark wood floors, beamed ceilings, log furniture with cowhide upholstery, and tiled combination bathrooms. Rooms have one queen-size, one king-size, or two double beds. No televisions, of course.

Catering to an older, affluent clientele, the style here is an odd mixture of peaceful rusticity and occasional reminders of class and formality (dinner jackets are "appreciated"). Generally, though, if you aren't sweating the prices, Jenny Lake Lodge offers a wonderful chance to unwind in a fairly isolated, feet-up-on-the-rail atmosphere with scenery that can't be matched.

Box 240, Moran, WY 83013. Ⓒ **800/628-9988** or 307/543-3100. www.gtlc.com. 37 units. $418 double; $565–$590 suite. Rates include MAP (modified American plan). AE, DC, MC, V. Closed mid-Oct to May. **Amenities:** Restaurant, lounge; activities desk. *In room:* No phone.

6 Where to Camp in Grand Teton

Because Grand Teton is so much smaller than its counterpart to the north, distances between campgrounds are reduced substantially. As a consequence, selecting a site in one of the five National Park Service campgrounds within the park becomes a matter of preference (rather than geography) and availability. Five campgrounds in Grand Teton are operated by the National Park Service: Gros Ventre, Jenny Lake, Signal Mountain, Colter Bay, and Lizard Creek. Two other campgrounds, the Colter Bay Trailer Village and the Flagg Ranch campground, are operated by park concessionaires and are the only campgrounds with RV hookups (Flagg Ranch has sites suitable for RVs as well as tents, while the Colter Bay Trailer Village is for RVs only). The only sites in the park where RVs are not allowed are those at Jenny Lake, which has a tent-only campground.

GETTING A CAMPSITE Campgrounds operate on a first-come, first-served basis, but reservations are available to groups of 10 or more by writing **Campground Reservations,** Grand Teton National Park, Moose, WY 83012. You can get recorded information on site availability by calling (Ⓒ **307/739-3603**). Reservations for **trailer sites** at Colter Bay campground may be made by contacting the **Grand Teton Lodge Co.,** P.O. Box 240, Moran, WY 83013 (Ⓒ **307/543-2855**). Additionally, **Grand Teton Campground** is a concessionaire-operated campground located in the Flagg Ranch complex on the John D. Rockefeller Jr., Memorial Parkway. The area has 93 sites with utility hookups, 74 tent sites, showers, and a launderette. For reservations, contact **Flagg Ranch,** P.O. Box 187, Moran, WY 83013 (Ⓒ **800/443-2311**).

Amenities for Each Campground: Grand Teton National Park

Campground	Total Sites	RV Hookups	Dump Station	Toilets	Drinking Water	Showers	Fire Pits/ Grills	Laundry	Public Phone	Reserve	Fees	Open
Inside the Park												
Colter Bay	350	No	Yes	Yes	Yes	Yes	Yes	Yes	Yes	No	$12	Mid-May–Late Sept
Colter Bay Trailer Village	112	Yes	Yes	Yes	Yes	No	Yes	Yes	Yes	Yes	$29	Mid-May–Late Sept
Gros Ventre	360	No	Yes	Yes	Yes	No	Yes	No	Yes	No	$12	Early May–Oct
Jenny Lake*	49	No	No	Yes	Yes	No	Yes	No	Yes	No	$12	Late May–Late Sept
Lizard Creek	60	No	No	Yes	Yes	No	Yes	No	Yes	No	$12	Early Jun–Early Sept
Signal Mountain	86	No	Yes	Yes	Yes	No	Yes	No	Yes	No	$12	Mid-May–Oct
Near the Park												
Flagg Ranch	165	Yes	Yes	Yes	Yes	Yes	Yes	Yes	Yes	Yes	$20/$35	Mid-May–Late Sept
Snake River Park KOA	80	Yes	Yes	Yes	Yes	Yes	Yes	Yes	Yes	Yes	$28/$36	Mid-Apr–Mid-Oct
Teton Village KOA	148	Yes	Yes	Yes	Yes	Yes	Yes	Yes	Yes	Yes	$27/$35	May–Mid-Oct
Wagon Wheel	12	Yes	Yes	Yes	Yes	Yes	Yes	Yes	Yes	Yes	$30	Mar–Oct

*Tents only are allowed here

THE CAMPGROUNDS For exact information on prices, opening dates, and amenities, refer to the chart, "Amenities for Each Campground: Grand Teton National Park," in this section. Note that where campgrounds accommodate RVs, they are not given a separate section from tent campers.

All the park-run campgrounds but Jenny Lake can accommodate tents, RVs, and trailers, but there are no utility hookups at any of them. **Jenny Lake Campground,** a tents-only area, is situated in a quiet, wooded area near the lake. You have to be here first thing in the morning to get a site.

The largest campground, **Gros Ventre,** is the last to fill, if it fills at all—probably because it's located on the east side of the park, a few miles from Kelly on the Gros Ventre River Road. If you arrive late in the day and you have no place to stay, go here first.

Signal Mountain Campground *☞*, with views of the lake and access to the beach, is another popular spot that fills first thing in the morning. It overlooks Jackson Lake and Mount Moran, as well as a pleasant picnic area and boat launch. There's a store and service station nearby.

Colter Bay Campground and Trailer Village has access to the lake but is far enough from the hubbub of the village to offer a modicum of solitude; spaces are usually gone by noon.

Lizard Creek Campground, at the north end of Grand Teton National Park near Jackson Lake, offers an aesthetically pleasing wooded area near the lake with views of the Tetons, bird-watching, and fishing (and mosquitoes—bring your repellent). It's only 8 miles (13km) from facilities at Colter Bay, and its sites fill by 2pm.

7 Where to Camp Near Grand Teton

There are several places to park the RV or pitch a tent around Jackson Hole, and a few of them are reasonably priced and not too far away from the park. Most charge around $30 per night, although prices seem to change at the drop of a hat, just like local motel prices. Your best bets are outside of city limits, away from the crowds and the constant buzz of traffic. See the chart, "Amenities for Each Campground: Grand Teton National Park," above, for amenities, prices, and opening dates.

In Jackson, the **Wagon Wheel Campground** (© 307/733-4588) is about 5 blocks north of Town Square at the Wagon Wheel Motel. The **Teton Village KOA** (© 307/733-5354) is 12 miles (19km) northwest of Jackson. Also away from the crowds, the **Snake River**

Park KOA Campground is on U.S. 89, 10 miles (16km) south of town (© **307/733-7078**).

8 Where to Dine in Grand Teton

Just as in Yellowstone, there are not enough places at the table to serve all the travelers in Grand Teton during the busiest meal times of July and August, but the higher-end options are the best restaurants in any of the national parks. Because there is more than one concessionaire operating the full-service dining rooms, there is no central number for making reservations.

NEAR THE NORTHERN BOUNDARY

In addition to Flagg Ranch, fast food is available at **Leeks Marina** (© **307/543-2494**), which is located inside the park, a few miles north of Colter Bay.

Flagg Ranch (Kids) AMERICAN   The food at this oasis is better than what's typically found in what most refer to as a "family restaurant," and servings are generous. The dinner menu includes fish, chicken, and beef dishes, as well as home-style entrees such as ranch beef stew and chicken pot pie. The ambiance is also pleasant during both winter and summer months; wooden chairs and tables with colorful upholstery liven up this newly constructed log building.

At Flagg Ranch, John D. Rockefeller Jr. Pkwy. © 800/443-2311. Breakfast $2–$6; lunch $4–$9; dinner $10–$25. AE, DISC, MC, V. Summer 7am–1:30pm and 5–9:30pm.

COLTER BAY

John Colter Cafe Court DELI/FAST FOOD   Here you find the two sit-down restaurants in the village (although there's also a snack shop in the grocery store). Three meals are served daily during the summer months. The **deli** serves sandwiches, chicken, pizzas, salads, and soup, with prices that range from $4.50 for an individual pizza to $12.99 for a chicken dinner. The **Chuckwagon Steak and Pasta House's** breakfast menu dishes up everything from plain eggs to a chuck wagon omelet, with a vast, scrumptious all-you-can-eat buffet available. Lunch is soup, salad, and hot sandwiches; dinner is a buffet with a nightly special each evening. Among the dinner entrees are trout, lasagna, pork chops, beef stew, and New York strip steaks. The ambience is very casual and straightforward because these restaurants cater mostly to families.

Across from the visitor center and marina in Colter Bay Village. © 307/543-2811. Breakfast $3–$6; lunch $5–$8; dinner $6–$14. DISC, MC, V. Daily 6am–10pm. Closed Oct–Apr.

JACKSON LAKE JUNCTION

The **Blue Heron** cocktail lounge at the Jackson Lake Lodge is one of the nicest spots in either park to enjoy a cocktail. The lounge here offers the same views as at The Mural Room (see below), as well as live entertainment.

The Mural Room 🎯🎯 BEEF/WILD GAME Jackson Lake's main dining room is quiet and fairly formal, catering to a more sedate crowd as well as corporate groups; it's also more expensive than other park restaurants. The floor-to-ceiling windows provide stellar views across a meadow that is moose habitat, to the lake and the Cathedral Group. Walls are adorned with hand-painted Western murals (what else?). Three meals are served daily in summer. Breakfast items include a continental breakfast, Belgian waffles, and vegetarian eggs Benedict. Dinner might be a grand, five-course event that includes a shrimp cocktail, French onion soup, and Caesar salad, followed by an entree of Idaho trout, buffalo strip loin, vegetable lasagna, or rack of lamb. Aside from the dining room at Jenny Lake Lodge, this is the most romantic and upscale eatery in the park

At Jackson Lake Lodge. ✆ **800/628-9988** or 307/543-2811, ext. 1911. Breakfast buffet $10.25; lunch $6–$9; dinner $16–$22. AE, MC, V. Summer daily 7–9:30am, noon–1:30pm, and 6–9:30pm.

Pioneer Grill *(Kids)* AMERICAN Bedecked with regional home-steading antiques and photos, this 1950s-style luncheonette, with its curling counter and old-fashioned soda fountain, offers hearty meals and a casual, friendly atmosphere. Breakfasts are basic but ideal for hiking appetites—bagels, eggs, flapjacks, and the like. For lunch, try the Moran chicken sandwich, smothered in melted cheese and pro-sciutto ham or the ever-popular buffalo burger. Dinner is similarly laid-back and traditional—you can't miss with the pan-fried local rainbow trout. When a tour bus stops at the lodge, the restaurant is often overrun with business, so you might want to head next door to the Mural Rooms if you're looking for peace or romance. If you're looking for convenience, good service, and a relatively quick meal, though, this is the spot. It's the only restaurant in the area to offer a kids' menu.

At Jackson Lake Lodge. ✆ **800/628-9988** or 307/543-2811, ext. 1911. Breakfast $4–$8; lunch and dinner $6–$11. AE, MC, V. Summer daily 6am–10:30pm.

Signal Mountain Resort *(Value)* SANDWICHES/MEXICAN/ ECLECTIC There are actually two restaurants here, serving deli-cious food in the friendliest style in the park. The fine dining room and lounge are called **The Peaks** and **Deadman's Bar,** respectively, and the **Trapper Grill** supplements that top-notch fare with Mexican entrees and plump sandwiches. You eat up the scenery, too, with a view of Jackson Lake.

Bargain-hunting locals flock to the bar for the decadent nachos supreme. Because the bar has one of three televisions in the park and is equipped with cable for sports nuts, the crowd tends to be young and noisy. As an alternative, full meals are served in the proper dining room. Entrees include chicken pot pie, Mediterranean pasta, and veal saltimbocca, the most expensive entree.

At Signal Mountain Resort. ⟨ᵗ⟩ **307/543-2831.** Breakfast $4–$8; lunch $6–$8; dinner $8–$30. AE, DISC, MC, V. Summer daily 7–10am and 11:30am–10pm.

JENNY LAKE

Jenny Lake Lodge Dining Room ⟨★★★⟩ CONTINENTAL
The finest meals in either park are served here, where a cordon bleu chef creates culinary delights for guests and, occasionally, a president of the United States. Only breakfast and dinner are served here, and both are spectacular. The five-course dinner is the bell-ringer though; guests choose from appetizers that might include chilled lobster salad or smoked sturgeon ravioli, buffalo mozzarella and plum tomato salads, and entrees that might include grilled salmon, rack of lamb, or prime rib of buffalo. Desserts are equally decadent. Price is no object, at least for guests, because meals are included in the room charge; nonguests should expect a hefty bill; if you're wearing shorts and hiking boots, your first and only course could be a plateful of chilly snobbery.

At Jenny Lake Lodge. ⟨ᵗ⟩ **307/733-4647.** Prix-fixe breakfast $14; prix-fixe dinner $45.50, not including alcoholic beverages. AE, MC, V. Summer daily 7:30–9am, noon–1:30pm, and 6–9pm.

8

Gateways to Yellowstone & Grand Teton National Parks

Yellowstone and Grand Teton National Parks are accessible from all four points of the compass. One of the biggest decisions facing you will be where to commence your journey and base yourself while you're in the area, if you choose not to stay in one of the parks themselves.

1 West Yellowstone, Montana

At the west entrance of Yellowstone National Park.

Yellowstone's west entrance is a bastion for tourism, chock full of accommodations, restaurants, souvenir shops, and outfitters. The personality of the town has changed since the popularity of snowmobile excursions increased winter traffic on Yellowstone's roads; it now offers more, and better, year-round facilities. Likewise, as a potential ban has arisen, the town has staunchly opposed any restrictions on the rumbling snow machines.

Originally called Riverside and then Yellowstone, the name was officially changed to West Yellowstone in 1920 when Gardiner residents grudgingly complained that people would assume that the town was the park. Regardless of its name, this place is about shopping, not nature, and its biggest attraction is a zoolike look at wildlife in the Grizzly Discovery Center.

ESSENTIALS

GETTING THERE For information on air service and car rentals, see "Getting There," in chapter 2, "Planning Your Trip to Yellowstone & Grand Teton National Parks." To drive to West Yellowstone from Bozeman (91 miles/147km), take U.S. Highway 191 south to its junction with U.S. 287 and head straight into town. From Idaho Falls, take Interstate 15 north to U.S. Highway 20, which takes you directly into West Yellowstone, a 53-mile (85km) drive.

VISITOR INFORMATION   Contact the **West Yellowstone Chamber of Commerce,** 30 Yellowstone Ave. (P.O. Box 458), West Yellowstone, MT 59758 (🕾 **406/646-7701;** www.westyellowstone chamber.com).

GETTING OUTSIDE

Yellowstone is obviously the big draw here, but there is plenty of wilderness west of the park in the Targhee and Gallatin national forests. The area around West Yellowstone ranks among the best **fishing** locales in the country. Come winter, **snowmobiling** and **snowcoach tours** are huge draws for West Yellowstone, and the town has steadfastly opposed any regulations on the former pursuit. Every major hotel and motel in town offers snowmobile packages that include a room and a sled rental; just be sure to book well in advance. For more information on all of these activities, see chapter 4, "Hikes & Other Outdoor Pursuits in Yellowstone National Park."

SEEING THE SIGHTS

Grizzly Discovery Center   Those who haven't the patience to search out and observe the free-ranging wildlife of Yellowstone might want to try this not-for-profit educational center—although it seems a pity to come all this way to see caged animals, even if they receive top-notch care. Now that wolves are back in the park, they have joined the grizzlies here. The interpretive center gives a detailed explanation of these animals' history in this country, along with the difficult and controversial efforts to revive them in the wild. This is a closer look than you'll likely get with animals in the wild, but did you really come to Yellowstone to look at grizzlies imported from Alaska in an enclosure?

201 Canyon St. in Grizzly Park. 🕾 800/257-2570 or 406/646-7001. www.grizzly discoveryctr.org. $8.50 adults, $4 children 5–12, free for children under 5. Daily 8am–dusk.

Museum of the Yellowstone 🖈   Located in the historic 1909 Union Pacific depot, this is the only museum that focuses on the park's cultural history and provides an interesting snapshot into the ways of the park's first tourists, with scads of memorabilia, postcards, and concessionaire ephemera. There are also displays on the Yellowstone ecosystem, covering epochal events such as the 1959 earthquake that created Quake Lake and the 1988 fires, along with a mounted grizzly bear known in his animate days as "Old Snaggletooth."

Canyon St. and Yellowstone Ave. ℂ **406/646-1100**. www.yellowstonehistoric
center.org. $20 family, $7 adults, $5 seniors and children, free for children under 5.
Mid-May to mid-Oct daily 9am–9pm.

Yellowstone IMAX Theater　This theater is next door to the
Grizzly Discovery Center and, together, they form the centerpieces
of a real estate development on the edge of the park, which includes
several new hotels. Regardless, the IMAX concept works pretty well
here—there are things an airborne camera can show you on a six-
story-tall screen that you'll never see on your own two feet. Six chan-
nels of stereo surround-sound add to the sense of "being there." A
film called *Yellowstone* plays fairly often, with swooping views of the
canyon and falls and other sights.

101 Canyon St., West Yellowstone, MT 59758. ℂ **888/854-5862** or 406/646-4100.
www.yellowstoneimax.com. $8 adults, $6 children 3–12, free for children under 3.
Call for show times.

WHERE TO STAY

Make your reservations early if you want to visit in July or August,
or if you're going to spend Christmas to New Year's here. If you're
smart, you'll come in the fall, when there are plenty of empty rooms
and better rates, and spend your days fishing the Henry's Fork or
one of the other great streams in the vicinity. Rates for rooms often
reflect the seasonal traffic, and prices fluctuate. Unless noted, all
these establishments are open year-round.

　West Yellowstone Central Reservations handles booking for
many of the hotels (ℂ **888/646-7077**). Among the new ones, you'll
find chains like the **Marriott Fairfield Inn** (ℂ **800/565-6803**), at
105 S. Electric St., with summertime doubles for $129; and the
Days Inn (ℂ **800/548-9551**), at 301 Madison Ave., around $85 a
night for a double. There are three **Best Western** affiliates, ranging
from $80 to $120 a night during the summer. Call ℂ **800/
528-1234** for information and reservations. The **Stage Coach Inn,**
at 209 Madison Ave. (ℂ **800/842-2882** or 406/646-7381), is
another good choice, with doubles for $69 to $139, with three different levels of rooms.

　Less expensive options (doubles run $67 to $99) include the
Brandin' Iron Inn, 201 Canyon St. (ℂ **800/217-4613** or 406/
646-9411), with 84 rooms; and the 1912 **Madison Hotel,** 139
Yellowstone Ave. (ℂ **800/838-7745** or 406/646-7745), where historic rooms go for $36 to $42 for two and newer motel rooms cost
$45 to $60.

Firehole Ranch 🌟🌟   Visitors can take a boat ride to this lodge's location on a mile of private shore along Hebgen Lake, only 16 miles (26km) from Yellowstone National Park. The resort is surrounded by thousands of acres of national forest in which guests can ride horses, hike, canoe, and make use of the ranch's supply of mountain bikes. The focus is squarely set on angling, however, with guided fishing trips on Hebgen Lake and in six different streams near the park, and there's a full-service fly shop on the premises. Lodging is in 10 cabins, each suitable for 2 to 4 guests. The nicest units have separate living quarters, complete with wood-burning stoves, bedrooms furnished with king-size beds, and private bathrooms with tub-shower combinations. Cocktails are served in a cozy nook before the arrival of exquisite meals prepared by a French chef. Breakfast is made to order, and there are box lunches at midday.

11500 Hebgen Lake Rd., West Yellowstone, MT 59758. ☎ **406/646-7294.** Fax 406/646-4728. www.fireholeranch.com. 10 cabins, each sleeps up to 4. $270–$300 per person per night. Rate includes all meals. 4-day minimum stay required. No credit cards. Kids under 12 allowed only with prior approval. **Amenities:** Restaurant; airport shuttle; bike rental; self-serve laundry. *In room:* No phone.

The Hibernation Station 🌟🌟   The Grizzly Discovery Center re-creates a natural environment, but it's surrounded by something entirely unnatural—a real-estate development that includes these cozy accommodations. These luxury cabins, each named after a local river or stream, are furnished Western-style with hand-hewn log beds draped in down comforters, wall tapestries, fireplaces, and enormous bathrooms with jetted tubs. They can fit from two to eight people, and some have kitchenettes. Every year a few more cabins go up, and the owners' plan also includes a big central lodge. The outdoor sculptures on some of the roofs are eye-catching if not gallery-quality, and this place is not exempt from the winter obsession of West Yellowstone—you can rent a snowmobile and all the requisite gear with your cabin.

212 Gray Wolf Ave., West Yellowstone, MT 59758. ☎ **800/580-3557** or 406/646-4200. www.hibernationstation.com. 40 cabins. $99–$269 per cabin. AE, DISC, MC, V. **Amenities:** Jacuzzi. *In room:* TV, kitchenette.

Three Bear Lodge 🄺ⁱᵈˢ   The cozy, pine-furnished rooms of this family-style inn are located less than 3 blocks from the park entrance. The motel-style rooms are of above average quality, reliable and clean, and there are some in-room hot tubs and a few large family rooms for those traveling with kids. Like every other lodging in West Yellowstone, the Three Bear offers park tour and snow-mobile packages with or without licensed guides—but, unlike else-where, it also offers some inexpensive cycling tour packages.

217 Yellowstone Ave., West Yellowstone, MT 59758. © 800/646-7353 or 406/646-7353. www.three-bear-lodge.com. 74 units. $73–$108 double. DISC, MC, V. **Amenities:** Restaurant, lounge; outdoor heated pool (seasonal); 4 indoor Jacuzzis; children's activities; self-serve laundry. *In room:* TV.

Holiday Inn SunSpree Resort ⚘ From its individual rooms to its restaurant to its conference facilities, this big new resort is first-rate. The rooms are sizeable and comfortable, a notch above that of the typical chain, and, if you've been hiking or snowmobiling around all day, the Jacuzzis in the King Spa suites are indispensable. At the activities desk, you can arrange fishing and rafting trips, bike and ATV rentals, and chuck wagon cookouts. The Iron Horse Saloon serves regional microbrews, and the Oregon Short Line Restaurant serves Western cuisine including buffalo, elk, and seafood dishes. At the center of the restaurant sits the restored railroad club car that brought Victorian gents to Yellowstone a century ago.

315 Yellowstone Ave., West Yellowstone, MT 59758. © 800/HOLIDAY or 406/646-7365. www.yellowstone-conf-hotel.com. 123 units. $79–$144 double; $90–$200 suite. AE, DISC, MC, V. **Amenities:** Restaurant, lounge; large indoor pool; exercise room; Jacuzzi; sauna; bike rental; children's program; activities desk; self-serve laundry. *In room:* A/C, TV, microwave, fridge, coffeemaker, hair dryer, iron.

WHERE TO DINE

Just as the chain motels have arrived, so have garden-variety fast-food joints; West Yellowstone is a good place to stop for a quick bite on your way into the park. Apart from the choices listed below, **Jocee's Baking Company,** 29 Canyon St. (© **406/646-9737**), is a small but excellent alternative to steak 'n' eggs breakfast joints. The bakery combines fresh morning pastries with coffee and espresso, and offers deli sandwiches and pizza in the afternoon. For the best variety of coffee drinks and baked goods, visit **the espresso bar** at the excellent Book Peddler in Canyon Square (© **406/646-9358**). At **Pete's Rocky Mountain Pizza Company,** 104 Canyon St. (© **406/646-7820**), you can design your own pizza. The **Texas Rose,** 335 Firehole Ave. (© **406/646-0095**), is one of the few 24-hour joints in town, serving respectable Tex-Mex all summer long.

Bullwinkle's Saloon, Gambling and Eatery AMERICAN Boisterous and noisy crowds, families and fishermen, and gamblers and goof-offs fill this restaurant frequently, and they don't leave hungry. Both luncheon and dinner menus are packed with traditional entrees: burgers and salads for lunch, and ribs, steaks, pastas, and seafood at dinner. Try the inexpensive and plentiful Bullwinkle's salad (shrimp included) or the house specialty, the hazelnut-crusted scallops, and check the updated fishing conditions charted on the wall. You can try small-stakes gambling on video poker machines, featured in many Montana bars.

19 Madison Ave. ℂ **406/646-7974.** Lunch $5–$8; dinner $9–$24. MC, V. Summer daily 11am–2am.

The Canyon Street Grill *(Value* AMERICAN   It's hard not to like an establishment whose slogan is, "We are not a fast food restaurant. We are a cafe reminiscent of a bygone era when the quality of the food meant more than how fast it could be served." This delightful 1950s-style spot serves hearty food for breakfast, lunch, and dinner. Hamburgers and chicken sandwiches are popular, accompanied by milk shakes made with hard ice cream. A combo of steak, mashed potatoes, and veggies goes for around $12.

22 Canyon St. ℂ **406/646-7548.** Most dishes $6–$13. MC, V. Daily Apr or May–early Nov 7am–7pm.

Eino's Tavern *(* *Finds* AMERICAN   Locals snowmobile out from West Yellowstone to Eino's (there's a trail that follows U.S. Highway 191) to become their own chefs at the grill here. It's a novel concept and one that keeps people coming back for more to a restaurant with a fine view of Hebgen Lake. If you want to blend in with the locals, go up to the counter and place your order for a steak, teriyaki chicken, hamburger, or hot dog, and keep a straight face when you're handed an uncooked piece of meat. Go to the grill, slap it on, and stand around, drink in hand, shooting the breeze with other patrons until your food is exactly the way you like it. Steaks and chicken come with your choice of a salad (or twice-baked potatoes in winter), and hamburgers come with chips.

8955 Gallatin Rd. (6 miles (9.5km) north of West Yellowstone on U.S. 191). ℂ **406/646-9344.** Reservations not accepted. Main courses $5–$16. No credit cards. Winter daily 9am–9pm, rest of year daily noon–9pm. Closed Thanksgiving to mid-Dec.

The Outpost Restaurant *(Kids* AMERICAN   Tucked away in a downtown mall, this restaurant serves old-fashioned home-style fare, such as its hearty beef stew. There's also salmon, steaks, trout, liver, and an excellent salad bar. For breakfast, if you're really hungry, you can't beat the Campfire Omelette, smothered in homemade chili, cheese, and onions. The menu isn't all that adventurous, and there's none of the vices you'll find in the local taverns (no video poker, beer, wine, liquor, or smoking), but it offers solid fare in a quiet, family-friendly atmosphere.

115 Yellowstone Ave. (in the Montana Outpost Mall). © 406/646-7303. Main courses $6–$18. AE, DISC, MC, V. Daily 6am–11pm. Closed Oct 15–Apr 15.

2 Gardiner, Montana ⟨★

At the north entrance to Yellowstone National Park.

At the other end of the spectrum from West Yellowstone is Gardiner, which provides the only year-round access to Yellowstone on the north. Although this tiny town (population 1,000) booms and busts with the tourist season, full-time residents manage to lead regular lives that include soccer practice, a day on the river, and a night on the town. For these folks, deer, elk, and bison meandering through the streets are no big deal. If you need additional information, contact the **Gardiner Chamber of Commerce,** 222 Park St., P.O. Box 81, Gardiner, MT 59030 (© **406/848-7971;** www. gardinerchamber.com).

WHERE TO STAY

Gardiner has long had funky, friendly lodging—thin-walled motels where, if you show up late, they've gone to bed and left a key in the door. These days it also has some newer, chain-affiliated properties, built to accommodate the ever-increasing traffic to the park. As with all the gateway towns, make your reservations early if you're coming during the peak season. The steep off-season decline in traffic results in discounts that can be considerably less expensive than the high-season rates quoted below, so be sure to ask.

Motels with numbers in their names are moving in and filling up during the summer months: **Motel 6** (109 Hellroaring Dr.; © **877/ 266-8356** or 406/848-7520) and **Super 8** (on U.S. 89 South; © **800/800-8000** or 406/848-7401) are open year-round with rates during the high season between $80 and $100 for a double. The **Best Western by Mammoth Hot Springs,** on U.S. 89 (© **800/828-9080** or 406/848-7311) is another solid option, with doubles for $89 to $109 in the summer.

Absaroka Lodge ★★   Every room in this lodge has its own furnished balcony, many with jaw-dropping views of the Yellowstone River and the mountain scenery beyond it. The lodge's riverbank location—with a nice slope of lawn overlooking the river gorge—is just a few blocks from the village center, and the rooms are well-appointed with queen-size beds. Suites with kitchenettes cost a little more. Like most other properties in town, the lodge has staff ready and able to assist in arrangements with outfitters for fly-fishing, rafting, and, in the fall, hunting.

U.S. 89 at the Yellowstone River Bridge. (C) 800/755-7414 or 406/848-7414. www. yellowstonemotel.com. 41 units. $40–$100 double. AE, DC, DISC, MC, V. *In room:* A/C, TV, kitchenette.

Yellowstone Suites Bed and Breakfast   *Finds*   This quiet B&B on the south bank of the Gardner River is a good alternative to the motels that line U.S. 89. Originally built in 1904, legend has it that the second story's quarried stone exterior is actually a leftover from the Roosevelt Arch. The rooms are frilly and cozy, with a teddy bear motif in the Roosevelt Room and a Victorian theme in the Jackson Room; the Yellowstone Suite has a television and a kitchenette. The real perks here are the impeccably gardened backyard and the breakfasts, which might feature French toast stuffed with cream cheese or ham-and-cheese quiche.

506 4th St., P.O. Box 277, Gardiner, MT 59030. (C) 800/948-7937 or 406/848-7937. www.wolftracker.com. 4 units. Summer $80–$110 double; winter $47–$69 double. Rates include complimentary full breakfast. AE, MC, V. **Amenities:** Outdoor Jacuzzi. *In room:* Kitchenette, no phone.

Comfort Inn   This log cabin–style hotel looks like it belongs here, unlike a lot of chain operations. The centerpiece is a 3,000-square-foot rustic lobby decorated with wild game trophies, and a large second-floor balcony that offers views of Yellowstone scenery and passing wildlife. Family suites that sleep six and luxurious Jacuzzi suites are also available.

107 Hellroaring Dr., Gardiner, MT 59030. (C) 800/228-5150 or 406/848-7536. Fax 406/848-7062. www.yellowstonecomfortinn.com. 80 units. Summer $65–$150 double; winter $50–$80 double. Rates include complimentary continental breakfast. AE, DC, DISC, MC, V. **Amenities:** 3 indoor Jacuzzis; self-serve laundry. *In room:* A/C, TV.

WHERE TO DINE

An indication that Gardiner has kept in touch with its mining town roots is the relative dearth of fancy restaurants— you'll find mostly steakhouse fare, hearty breakfasts, and travelers' food. A few upscale eateries have shown up in recent years, but the dish-clattering local color of the park-side coffee shops is hard to beat. For more local color and "the best pizza in the West," try the **K Bar,** Main Street and U.S. 89 ((C) **406/848-9995**).

Park Street Grill and Cafe   **   ITALIAN/STEAKS   Adding a dash of zest to Gardiner's staid meat-and-potatoes dining scene, this

eatery opened in 1999 to rave reviews. Served in a room with an exposed pine interior, the menu here is a refreshing mix of gourmet Italian entrees, fresh seafood, and good old American chicken, pork, and beef dishes. The Crazy Mountain Alfredo is a good choice from the pasta menu: Reputedly served in Italy's insane asylums, the delectable sauce is spiced with sweet and hot peppers, julienne chicken breast, and Italian sausage. Hearty appetites won't mind the huge racks of barbecue pork ribs (served with a fresh-fruit salsa) or the slow-roasted prime rib, and there's a decent selection of lighter fare as well.

204 Park St. *C* 406/848-7989. Reservations are recommended. Main courses $14–$21. MC, V. Daily 5:30–10pm. Closed mid-Oct to May.

The Chico Inn *R* CONTINENTAL   It's 30 miles (48km) north of Gardiner, but if you're in the area, stop here for some of the best food in the Rockies and a quick soak in this resort's hot springs. The carnivorous traveler will enjoy the selection of top-drawer beef, and the pine nut–crusted Alaskan halibut is a seafood aficionado's dream. Many of the incredibly fresh veggies originate in the resort's garden and greenhouse, and the menu always includes a vegetarian selection. You'll want to linger over the food, so consider a night's stay.

Old Chico Rd., Pray, MT. *C* 800/HOT-WADA. Reservations recommended. Main courses $20–$30. AE, DISC, MC, V. Summer daily 5:30–10pm; winter Sun–Thurs 6–9pm, Fri–Sat 5:30–10pm.

Sawtooth Deli DELI/ECLECTIC   This restaurant can fit the needs of almost any appetite that passes through Gardiner, with a casual delicatessen atmosphere during lunch hours and a decidedly more upscale dinner atmosphere. On warm summer nights, the breezy garden patio is the best place in town to take in a meal. The deli menu includes sandwiches both traditional (BLT, pastrami, and Swiss) and unexpected (vegetarian, chicken parmesan), but the dinners, especially the mesquite-smoked chicken and the seafood specials, and the indulgent homemade desserts are the real standouts. Pasta, steaks, salads, and a respectable wine list round out the offerings.

270 W. Park St. *C* 406/848-7600. Reservations not accepted. Lunch $4–$6.50; dinner $9–$15. Credit cards not accepted. Mon–Sat 9am–10pm. Closed Sun and Nov–Apr.

3 Cooke City, Montana *R*

Near the northeast entrance to Yellowstone National Park.

Mining gold and platinum and other precious metals pumped intermittent life into Cooke City for 100 years, but now there is only

> ## *Tips* Timing Your Visit
>
> In the winter, when the cloud-scraping **Beartooth Pass** closes to the north, supplies for Cooke City and Silver Gate have to come through the park. *My advice:* Visit in summer and take the breathtaking drive north over the pass (U.S. 212 toward Red Lodge) or south along the scenic Chief Joseph Highway (Wyo. 296).

park tourism. Fewer than 100 residents live year-round in the town today, and Silver Gate, right next to the park entrance, is even smaller.

Contact the **Colter Pass/Cooke City/Silver Gate Chamber of Commerce** at Box 1071, Cooke City, MT 59020-1071 (© **406/ 838-2495;** www.cookecity.com) for information.

A room for the night will be less expensive than in other gateway towns, anywhere from $60 to $80 a night. The **Soda Butte Lodge,** 209 Main St. (© **800/527-6462** or 406/838-2251), is the biggest, newest, and poshest motel in Cooke City, and it includes the good **Prospector Restaurant** and a small casino; or, you can go to the cheaper, bare-bones **Alpine Motel,** 105 Main Street (© **406/ 838-2262**). For a bite to eat and a great selection of beers, try the funky **Beartooth Cafe** (© **406/838-2475**), also on Main Street.

4 Jackson, Wyoming ★★

Near the south entrance of Grand Teton National Park.

Of all the gateway towns to Yellowstone and Grand Teton, Jackson has managed best to reap the fruits of tourism while retaining some semblance of its original ranch-town character. There's no denying that the heart of Jackson is thick with shops and motels and tourists, but what's admirable about the town is the way it has used some of its prosperity to preserve open space and enhance the arts and cultural agenda of the community.

Jackson has a wealth of outdoor recreation to occupy hordes of visitors. In summer, you can play golf at world-class courses, chase trout in pristine streams or lakes, drift a river in a raft or kayak, or ride horses at one of the area's dude ranches. Come winter, you can carom down the mountain slopes, cross-country ski on the seemingly endless trails, or ride a snowmobile into the forest.

And if you're tired of the great outdoors, well, you can go shopping. Jackson has national brand-name fashion outlets, tourist curio shops, some excellent art galleries, clothing stores, antiques shops, and outdoor equipment suppliers. The retail frenzy concentrates around the town's delightful central square, a grassy park with entryways arched by tangles of elk antlers.

Oh, yeah, there are a couple of nice parks up the road, too.

ESSENTIALS

Information on air service to Jackson and rental car agencies is discussed under "Getting There," in chapter 2, "Planning Your Trip to Yellowstone & Grand Teton National Parks."

GETTING THERE   If you're driving, come north from I-80 at Rock Springs on U.S. Highway 191/189, or east from I-15 at Idaho Falls on U.S. Highway 26, and either travel via Snake River Canyon on that highway or veer north over Teton Pass on Wyoming Highway 32. If you are driving south from Yellowstone National Park, stay on U.S. Highway 89, which runs north-south through both parks and into town. Likewise, from I-80, take U.S. 189 or 191 north to the park, or U.S. 89 from I-15 in Ogden, Utah. For up-to-date weather information and road conditions, contact the **Chamber of Commerce** (see below) or call © **888/WYO-ROAD** (in-state).

VISITOR INFORMATION   The **Jackson Hole Chamber of Commerce** is a source of information concerning just about everything in and around Jackson. Along with the U.S. Forest Service and National Park Service, representatives of the chamber can be found at the **Greater Yellowstone Visitor Center** (no phone), 532 N. Cache. For information on lodging, events, and activities, contact the Chamber at P.O. Box E, Jackson, WY 83001 (© **307/ 733-3316**; www.jacksonholechamber.com). For lodging information and reservations, call **Jackson Hole Central Reservations** (© **800/443-6931**; www.jhsnow.com).

GETTING AROUND   Taxi service is available from **Buckboard Cab** (© 307/733-1112). **Alltrans, Inc.** (© **800/443-6133** or 307/ 733-4325) offers shuttle service from the airport and national park tours. Before you call a cab, remember that many of the hotels and car-rental agencies in the Jackson area offer free shuttle service to and from the airport.

The **Southern Teton Area Rapid Transit (START)** offers bus transport from Teton Village to Jackson daily for $2 (students up to

Fun Fact **Jackson or Jackson Hole?**

You'll see every kind of merchandise imaginable fashioned with an image of the Tetons and the words JACKSON HOLE, WYOMING scrawled over it. You *might* notice that on the map, the town just south of Grand Teton National Park is called Jackson. But your plane ticket says "Jackson Hole, Wyoming." But wait a minute—the postmark just says "Jackson." The names seem to be used interchangeably, and the reason is actually pretty simple.

Three mountain men ran a fur trapping company in these parts in the 1800s: one named David Jackson, another named Jedediah Smith, and a third named William Sublette. Mountain men in those days referred to a valley as a hole. As the story goes, Sublette (for whom the county southeast of Teton County is named) called the valley Jackson's Hole because his friend and partner David Jackson spent a great deal of time in it. That name was shortened, and when the town materialized, it was also named for David Jackson. So, the city itself is Jackson, Wyoming, and it lies in the great valley that runs the length of the Tetons on the east side, Jackson Hole.

high school age ride free). Service includes 60 trips a day between downtown and Teton Village in the winter, and 10 in the summer; it shuts down around 11pm year-round. For specific schedule information, contact START at © **307/733-4521** or browse www.startbus.com.

GETTING OUTSIDE

Whether you're a raw beginner, a seasoned pro, or an adrenaline addict, Jackson can make you feel at home. There's mountain biking, hiking, fishing, kayaking, and river-running in the summer, and skiing, snowmobiling, and snowboarding in the winter.

SPORTING GOODS & EQUIPMENT RENTALS Serious climbers with serious wallets will appreciate the gear at **Teton Mountaineering** ⋆, at 170 N. Cache St. (© **800/850-3595** or 307/733-3595), a block from the square, where you can get killer Nordic skis and high-grade fleece jackets. **Adventure Sports,** at Dornan's in the town of Moose (© **307/733-3307**), has a small selection of mountain bike, kayak, and canoe rentals, and advice on where to go with the gear. When snowboards are put away for the summer, the **Boardroom** switches to BMX bikes and skateboards, at 225 W. Broadway (© 307/733-8327). The competition in Teton Village is the winter-only **Jackson Hole Sports** (© 307/ 739-2687). **Hoback Sports,** 40 S. Millward (© 307/733-5335), has a large selection of skis, boards, and summer mountain bikes for rent and sale. **Skinny Skis,** at 65 W. Deloney off Town Square (© 307/733-6094), is a year-round specialty sports shop and has an excellent selection of equipment and clothing. For serviceable factory seconds at steeply discounted prices, head north to the little town of Moose near the entrance to Grand Teton National Park and shop **Moosely Seconds** ✿ (© 307/733-1801).

SUMMER SPORTS & ACTIVITIES

FISHING   Yellowstone and Grand Teton national parks have incredible fishing in their lakes and streams; see the park sections for details.

The Snake River emerges from Jackson Lake Dam as a broad, strong river, with decent fishing from its banks in certain spots— such as right below the dam—and better fishing if you float the river. Fly-fishers should ask advice at local stores on recent insect hatches and good stretches of river, or hire a guide to keep them company. Outdoor gear stores will provide all the tackle you need and more information on fishing conditions in the area than you can likely process. **High Country Flies** ✿, 185 N. Center St. (© 307/733-7210; www.highcountryflies.com), has a vast selection of high-quality fishing gear, flies, and fly-tying supplies, along with lessons and guided trips ($350 for a full day, 1 or 2 people), as well as free advice if you just want to gab about where to cast. The **Jack Dennis Outdoor Shop** on the Town Square at 50 E. Broadway (© 307/733-3270; www.jackdennis.com) is a much bigger store with room to display some big boats, and it also offers lessons and guides. There's a smaller edition of the Dennis store in Teton Village (© 307/733-6838).

GOLF   The **Jackson Hole Golf and Tennis Club** (© 307/ 733-3111), north of Jackson off U.S. 89, has an 18-hole course that's one of the best in the country. Green fees run $135 for 18 holes, with cart and range balls included. The **Teton Pines Resort,** 3450 N. Clubhouse Dr. (© 800/238-2223 or 307/733-1005), designed by Arnold Palmer and Ed Seay, is a challenging course;

green fees range from $16 to $180, depending on the season. Both are open to the public.

HIKING In addition to the myriad trails in Grand Teton National Park (see chapter 6, "Hikes & Other Outdoor Pursuits in Grand Teton National Park"), there are trails in the surrounding forest—they might be less well maintained, but they also get less use, which means more solitude for hikers. Adjacent to Grand Teton on the east and south is **Bridger-Teton National Forest;** go east and over the Continental Divide, and you're in **Shoshone National Forest.** Together, these forests encompass a huge piece of mountain real estate, including glaciers, 13,000-foot peaks, and some of the best alpine fishing lakes in the world. Among the mountain ranges included in these forests are the **Absarokas,** the **Gros Ventre,** the **Wyoming,** and the **Wind River Range.** The **visitor center** located in the sod-roofed A-frame at 532 N. Cache St. provides all of the hiking and access information you'll need for Bridger-Teton, including the Gros Ventre and Teton wilderness areas. If you need detailed information in advance, call the Forest Service's district office (© 307/739-5500).

HORSEBACK RIDING Trail rides are a staple of the Western vacation experience, and there are several companies in the area that will put you in the saddle. Some hotels, including those in Grand Teton National Park, have stables and operate trail rides for their guests. For details, contact **Jackson Hole Trail Rides** (© 307/733-6992), **Snow King Stables** (© 307/733-5781), **Spring Creek Ranch Riding Stables** (© 800/443-6139), or the **Mill Iron Ranch** (© 307/733-6390). Rides cost around $40 for 2 hours.

KAYAKING, CANOEING & SAILING Several operators in Jackson run schools and guide paddlers of all skill levels. The two major outfits are the **Snake River Kayak and Canoe School,** 365 N. Cache St., Jackson 83001 (© **800/KAYAK-01;** www.snakeriver kayak.com), and **Rendezvous River Sports,** 225 N. Cache St. (P.O. Box 9201), Jackson, WY 83002 (© **307/733-2471;** www.jhkayak school.com).

RAFTING There are two parts to the Snake River—the smooth water, much of it running through Grand Teton Park north of Jackson, and the white water of the canyon, to the south and west. A rafting trip down the upper Snake, usually from Jackson Lake Dam or Pacific Creek to Moose, is not about wild water but about wildlife: Moose, bald eagles, osprey, and other creatures come to the water just like we do. Several operators provide scenic float trips in the park; see chapter 6, "Hikes & Other Outdoor Pursuits in Grand Teton National Park," for a list.

For the more adventurous, the most popular way to experience the Snake River is white-water rafting; these are wet, wild, white-knuckle tours. Several companies offer adrenaline-pumping day trips down the Snake, but don't plan on just being a passenger—this is a participatory sport. Contact **Barker-Ewing** (© **800/448-4202**), **Charlie Sands Wildwater** (© **800/358-8184** or 307/733-4410), **Dave Hansen Whitewater** (© **800/732-6295**), **Jackson Hole Whitewater** (© **800/648-2602**), **Lewis and Clark Expeditions** (© **800/824-5375**), or **Mad River Boat Trips** (© **800/458-7238** or 307/733-6203). Generally, a full-day trip runs around $70, with lunch included, and a half-day trip costs about $40.

WINTER SPORTS & ACTIVITIES
CROSS-COUNTRY SKIING   With five Nordic centers and a couple of national parks at your feet, plus the 3.5-million-acre Bridger-Teton National Forest, cross-country skiers have plenty of choices. If you're new to cross-country skiing on any level, you might choose to start on the groomed, level trails at one of the Nordic centers. If, however, you have experience in the steep, deep powder of untracked wilderness, visit or call the National Park Service in **Grand Teton National Park** (© **307/739-3300**) or the **Bridger-Teton National Forest** in downtown Jackson at 340 N. Cache (© **307/739-5500**), and check in before you go.

The local ski shops are excellent sources of unofficial advice about the area's backcountry. Keep in mind that many of the trails used by cross-country skiers are also used by snowmobiles. For those seeking instruction, lessons are available at the Nordic centers, or you can check the schedule of **Teton Parks and Recreation** (© **307/ 733-5056**).

The **Jackson Hole Nordic Center,** 7658 Teewinot, Teton Village (© **307/733-2629**), on the flats just east of Teton Village, is a small part of the giant facility that includes some of the best downhill skiing around (see below).

Teton Pines Cross Country Skiing Center (© **307/733-1005**) has 7¾ miles (13km) of groomed trails that wind over the resort's golf course. **Spring Creek Ranch Touring Center,** 1800 N. Spirit Dance Rd., Jackson (© **800/443-6139**), maintains 8½ miles (14km) of groomed trails, and you don't have to be a guest to enjoy them. For more information on both, see "Where to Stay," below.

At **Grand Targhee** (© 307/353-2304), you can rent or buy anything you need in the way of equipment and take off on the resort's 8 miles (13km) of groomed trails.

DOGSLEDDING   If your idea of mushing is not oatmeal but a pack of yipping dogs, you might want to try your hand at dogsledding, an enjoyable open-air way to tour the high country during the winter. **Jackson Hole Iditarod,** P.O. Box 1940, Jackson, WY 83001 (© 800/554-7388 or 307/733-7388; www.jhsleddog.com), associated with Iditarod racer Frank Teasley, offers both half- and full-day trips in five-person sleds (the fifth companion is your guide), and you can take a turn in the driver's stand. The half-day ride costs $135 per person, gives the dogs an 11-mile (18km) workout, and includes a lunch of hot soup and cocoa before you head back to the kennels. For $225 a head, you can take the full-day excursion out to Granite Hot Springs, a 22-mile (35km) trip total. You get a hot lunch, plus your choice of barbecued trout or steak for dinner. Another Iditarod veteran, Bill Snodgrass, leads trips in the national forests around Togwotee Pass with his **Washakie Outfitting** (© 800/249-0662; www.dogsledwashakie.com). These trips book up quickly, so call 3 to 4 days in advance to reserve a spot.

DOWNHILL SKIING   This is one of the premier destinations for skiers in the entire country. Despite a relatively remote location, chilly temperatures, and a high percentage of black diamond trails (although still plenty of intermediate trails), skiers flock here in droves. The two largest ski resorts in the area have been putting in faster chairs in recent years, eliminating long waits in lift lines.

Jackson Hole Mountain Resort 🐾🐾, 7658 Teewinot, Teton Village, WY 83025 (© 307/733-2292 or 307/733-4005; www.jacksonhole.com), is making improvements to move into the elite international ranks; incidentally, prices are moving up, too. Take the tram to the top of **Rendezvous Mountain** and plunge down Tensleep Bowl if you want to get a taste of skiing on the edge, or try the gentler, intermediate runs down the sides of **Apres Vous Mountain.**

Grand Targhee Resort 🐾🐾, Ski Hill Rd., Box SKI, Alta, WY 83422 (© 800/TARGHEE or 307/353-2300; www.grandtarghee.com), has the best snow in the universe: deep, forgiving powder from November through spring (over 500 in. annually), and a more peaceful, less crowded village that provides a worthy alternative to Teton Village.

Snow King Resort, 100 E. Snow King, Jackson, WY 83001 (© 800/522-5464 or 307/733-5200; www.snowking.com), lights up its hill above Jackson at night; it's the smallest of the valley's resorts, with fairly steep and unvaried terrain, but it's within walking distance of downtown Jackson.

SNOWMOBILING Although West Yellowstone is the most popular base for snowmobiling in the Yellowstone area, Jackson has a growing contingent of snowmobile aficionados and outfitters. You don't really need a guide to tour Yellowstone, where snowmobiles are required to stay on groomed roads—if they avoid an all-out ban, that is. You can also handle Togwotee Pass and the Granite Hot Springs area if you stick to groomed trails. Snowmobilers also head for the rugged Gros Ventre Mountains and the Grey's River area, 45 miles (72km) west of Jackson.

The operators who rent snowmobiles (including the necessary clothing and helmets) also have guides to take you on 1-day and multiday tours of Jackson Hole and the surrounding area. **High Country Snowmobile Tours,** at 3510 S. Hwy. 89 in Jackson (© **800/524-0130**), offers touring service for Jackson Hole, Yellowstone, and the Gros Ventre Mountains. **Jackson Hole Snowmobile Tours,** 1000 S. Hwy. 59 (© **800/633-1733**), offers 1-day trips in Yellowstone and multiday trips along the Continental Divide. In addition to renting snowmobiles, **Wyoming Adventures,** 1050 S. Hwy. 89 (© **800/637-7147**), takes trips along the Continental Divide as well as Grey's River. A typical 1-day outing costs from $150 to $200, with pickup and drop-off service, equipment, fuel, a continental breakfast, and lunch at Old Faithful included. Also in Jackson, snowmobiles can be rented at **Leisure Sports,** 1075 S. Hwy. 89 (© **307/733-3040**).

A BIRD'S-EYE VIEW

AERIAL TOURING For a much quicker climb to the tops of the mountains, call **Jackson Hole Aviation** (© **307/733-4767**; www.jhaviation.com), at the Jackson Hole Airport, or **Teton Aviation,** Driggs Airport, Driggs, ID 83422 (© **800/472-6382** or 208/354-3100). You'll actually be looking down at the summits that climbers strain to top, and you'll get a new perspective on the immensity of the Grand Teton (although you won't get too close—the park has some air-space restrictions). Take your pick: Jackson Hole Aviation offers airplane trips for $75 an hour, and Teton has the Super Teton Ride ($158) in a glider that takes you to 11,800 feet on the west side of the Grand.

BALLOONING The folks at the **Wyoming Balloon Company** ✪, P.O. Box 2578, Jackson, WY 83001 (© **307/739-0900**;

www.wyomingballoon.com), like to fire up early, in the still air that cloaks the Teton Valley around 6am. Their "float trips" stay aloft for a little more than an hour, cruising over a 3,000-acre ranch with a full frontal view of the Tetons. The journey concludes with a champagne breakfast at the landing site. Prices are $195 adults and $125 for kids.

WILDLIFE WATCHING

National Elk Refuge ⊛ It's not exactly nature's way, but the U.S. Fish & Wildlife Service makes sure that the elk in this area eat well during the winter by feeding them alfalfa pellets. It keeps them out of the haystacks of area ranchers and creates a beautiful tableau on the peaceful flats along the Gros Ventre River: thousands of elk, some with huge antler wracks, dotting the snow for miles. Drivers along Highway 89 might also see trumpeter swans, coyotes, moose, bighorn sheep, and, lately, wolves. As autumn begins to chill the air in September, you'll hear the shrill whistles of the bull elk in the mountains; as snow begins to stick on the ground, they make their way down to the refuge. Although the cultivated meadows and pellets help the elk survive the winter, some biologists say this approach results in overpopulation and the spread of diseases such as brucellosis.

Regardless, this is a great opportunity to see these magnificent wapiti up close. Each winter from mid-December until March, the Fish and Wildlife Service offers **horse-drawn sleigh rides** that weave among the refuge elk. Rides early in the winter will find young, energetic bulls playing and banging heads, while late-winter visits (when the Fish and Wildlife Service begins feeding the animals) wander through a more placid scene. Rides embark from the museum between 10am and 4pm on a first-come, first-served basis. Tickets for the 45-minute rides cost $12 for adults and $6 for children 6 to 12, and can be purchased at the National Museum of Wildlife Art. Ask about a combination pass ($15) for the sleigh ride and the museum.

Located 3 miles (5km) north of Jackson on U.S. 26/89, P.O. Box 510, Jackson, WY 83001. © **307/733-9212.** www.nationalelkrefuge.fs.gov. Free admission. Visitor center: summer daily 8am–7pm; winter daily 8am–5pm.

AREA ATTRACTIONS

Beyond its role as a staging area for explorations of Grand Teton and Yellowstone national parks, Jackson is a place to relax, shop, play some golf, or kick up your heels at an authentic Western saloon. There is also a good deal of attractions, running the gamut from history and art to pure entertainment.

Jackson Hole Aerial Tram Rides ✹ Here you can see the Tetons from an elevation above 10,000 feet, but don't expect a private tour. During busy summer days, the tram carries 45 passengers, packed in like the skiers that take the lift in the winter. The top of Rendezvous Mountain offers an incredible view, but it can get pretty chilly, even in the middle of summer, so bring a light coat.

At Jackson Hole Ski Resort, 7658 Teewinot, Teton Village. ✆ **307/739-2753**. Tickets $15 adults, $13 seniors, $5 children, free for children 5 and under. Late May–Sept daily 9am–5pm; mid-June to Aug daily 9am–7pm. Tram runs approximately every half-hour.

National Museum of Wildlife Art ✹✹ If you don't spot this museum on your way into Jackson from the north, consider that a triumph of design: Its jagged, red-sandstone facade is meant to blend into the steep hillside facing the elk refuge. Within this 50,000-square-foot castle is some of the best wildlife art in the country, as well as exhibits on the elk refuge wildlife and a 200-seat auditorium where there are regular slide shows and lectures on a wide range of subjects. There are 14 exhibit galleries that display traveling shows and collections dating from the 19th century to the present, including galleries on John James Audubon and local great Carl Rungius. The museum houses a repository of internationally acclaimed wildlife films, and in the winter it's the take-off point for sled tours of the elk refuge (you can also view the wildlife through spotting scopes on the balcony). There's a good little cafe, too.

2820 Rungius Rd. (3 miles (5km) north of town on U.S. Hwy. 89, across from the National Elk Refuge). ✆ **307/733-5771**. www.wildlifeart.org. Admission $6 adults, $5 students and seniors, free for children under 6. Summer daily 8am–5pm; winter daily 9am–5pm.

Jackson Hole Museum Dedicated local volunteers maintain this repository of early photographs, artifacts, and other items of historical significance, and they'll carefully guide you through the collections. You can browse the exhibits or go down the street to the Historical Society at Glenwood and Mercil to do some research. At the museum, you'll find collections of trade beads, antique pole furniture, pistols, and Indian artifacts, spread out in 3,000 square feet of floor space.

105 N. Glenwood (at the corner of Deloney). ✆ **307/733-2414**. www.jackson holehistory.org. Admission $6 families, $3 adults, $2 seniors, $1 students and children. Mon–Sat 9:30am–6pm, Sun 10am–5pm. Closed Oct–May.

Jackson

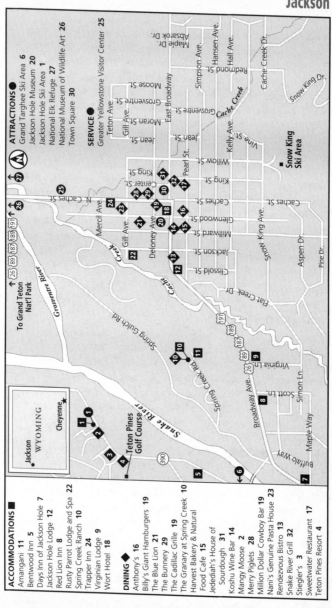

ATTRACTIONS ●

Grand Targhee Ski Area **6**
Jackson Hole Museum **20**
Jackson Hole Ski Area **1**
National Elk Refuge **27**
National Museum of Wildlife Art **26**
Town Square **30**

SERVICE ●

Greater Yellowstone Visitor Center **25**

ACCOMMODATIONS ■

Amangani **11**
Bentwood Inn **5**
Days Inn of Jackson Hole **7**
Jackson Hole Lodge **12**
Red Lion Inn **8**
Rusty Parrot Lodge and Spa **22**
Spring Creek Ranch **10**
Trapper Inn **24**
Virginian Lodge **9**
Wort Hotel **18**

DINING ◆

Anthony's **16**
Billy's Giant Hamburgers **19**
The Blue Lion **21**
The Bunnery **29**
The Cadillac Grille **19**
The Granary at Spring Creek **10**
Harvest Bakery & Natural
   Food Cafe **15**
Jedediah's House of
   Sourdough **31**
Koshu Wine Bar **14**
Mangy Moose **2**
Merry Piglets **28**
Million Dollar Cowboy Bar **19**
Nani's Genuine Pasta House **23**
Rendezvous Bistro **13**
Snake River Grill **32**
Stiegler's **3**
Sweetwater Restaurant **17**
Teton Pines Resort **4**

185

ART GALLERIES

Collectors, tired of bighorn sheep on the crags and weather-beaten cowboys on their horses, often dismiss Western art. But while Jackson has plenty of that genre in stock, some of its two dozen galleries are more adventurous and sophisticated.

The **Martin-Harris Gallery,** at 60 E. Broadway (© **307/ 733-0350**), looks down its nose (well, it's located upstairs) at the less sophisticated Western art in neighboring galleries, but it backs up its snobbery with beautifully displayed art, original and contemporary, while still sticking largely to Western themes. Prices are second-story as well. The beauty of Tom Mangelsen's wildlife photography has been somewhat diluted by its display in airports and malls, but Jackson is where he started, and at the **Images of Nature Gallery,** 170 N. Cache St. (© **307/733-9752**), you'll find some of his work signed and numbered. The **Center Street Gallery,** 110 Center St. (© **307/733-1115**), has the lock on abstract Western art in Jackson. A mile (1.5km) north of town, at 1975 U.S. 89 (toward the park), is the **Wilcox Gallery** (© **307/733-6450**), which showcases more than 20 painters and sculptors from across the nation.

WHERE TO STAY

The thin-walled, dimly lit motels of the past are just memories now—Jackson lodgings these days come with palatial trappings and, in some cases, prices that start at $500 a night. Prices are generally discounted in off-season (spring/fall), but not during ski season.

Clustered together near the junction west of downtown where Hwy. 22 leaves U.S. Hwy. 26/89 and heads north to Teton Village is a colony of chain franchises: **Motel 6** (600 S. Hwy. 89; © **307/ 733-1620**) and the not-just-numerically superior **Super 8** (750 S. Hwy. 89; © **800/800-8000** or 307/733-6833). Also in the vicinity are the more upscale and expensive **Days Inn** (350 S. Hwy. 89; © **800/329-7466** or 307/733-0033), with private hot tubs and fireplaces in suites; and the **Red Lion Inn** (930 W. Broadway; © **800/844-0035** or 307/734-0035). High-season prices for the motels range from $85 to $160. Rooms at the Red Lion during high season run from $100 to $289 a night.

IN JACKSON

Jackson Hole Lodge   Although it sits near one of the busiest intersections in Jackson and it's packed into a small space, this lodge is quiet and well designed, so its location in the heart of town becomes a plus. The pool is not just for splashing—you can lap its

40-foot length, sit in one of the whirlpools, take a sauna, or sit out on your own sundeck. The rooms are more comfortable and complete than what you'll find at a chain property, blending Western ambiance with scads of in-room options. Best of all are the condo lodgings, with two upstairs bedrooms, a full kitchen, and a living room with foldout couch. This gives families a little space, and it's also affordable.

420 W. Broadway, Jackson, WY 83001. © **800/604-9404** or 307/733-2992. www. jacksonholelodge.com. 59 units. $109–$134 double; $184–$304 condo. AE, DC, DISC, MC, V. **Amenities:** Outdoor pool; 2 Jacuzzis; sauna; game room. *In room:* A/C, TV, kitchen.

Rusty Parrot Lodge and Spa ⟨★★★⟩

The name sounds like an out-of-tune jungle bird, but since 1990 the Rusty Parrot has shown excellent pitch, cultivating a country lodge and spa right in the heart of busy Jackson. Located across from Miller Park, the Parrot is decorated in the nouveau Western style of peeled log, with an interior appointed with elegant furnishings and river rock fireplaces. One very attractive lure is The Body Sage spa, where you can get yourself treated to all sorts of scrubs, wraps, massages, and facials. The breakfast that comes with your room includes omelets, fresh pastries, fruits, cereals, and freshly ground coffee; food also appears later in the day, but the lodge likes to make that a surprise (sorry). Rooms are gigantic, and several have private balconies.

175 N. Jackson, Jackson, WY 83001. © **800/458-2004** or 307/733-2000. www. rustyparrot.com. 31 units. $108–$275 double; $500 suite. Rates include full breakfast. AE, DC, DISC, MC, V. **Amenities:** Restaurant, lounge; spa. *In room:* TV.

Trapper Inn

The employees here are some of the most helpful you'll find in Jackson, and they'll tip you off on the best deals in the valley. Just 2 short blocks from the town square, the Trapper is hard to miss if you're walking north on Cache from the town square. On the west side of Cache, you'll notice the crazy Trapper guy on the sign. You can walk anywhere downtown within minutes. The rooms are spacious, featuring cozy quilts and stately lodgepole pine furnishings. There are two structures here: Fittingly, the newest building, erected in 1991, features rooms with a more modern feel.

235 N. Cache, Jackson, WY 83001. © **800/341-8000** or 307/733-2648 for reservations. www.trapperinn.com. 54 units, including 4 suites. $98–$178 double; $170–224 suite. AE, DC, DISC, MC, V. **Amenities:** Jacuzzi; self-serve laundry. *In room:* A/C, TV, microwave, fridge, coffeemaker.

Virginian Lodge ⟨★⟩

It's not brand-new. It's not a resort, it doesn't have a golf course, and the highway is right outside the door. Since its overhaul in 1995, however, the Virginian is attempting to earn its spurs as one of the better motels in Jackson. Given its location on the busy Broadway strip, that's not likely to happen, but the prices remain reasonable, and it's a busy, cheerful place to stay. You can get a room with a private Jacuzzi or a kitchenette, and many have "dry" bars and sofa sleepers.

750 W. Broadway, Jackson, WY 83001. ✆ **800/262-4999** or 307/733-2792. Fax 307/733-4063. www.virginianlodge.com. 181 units. $95–$109 double; $125–$185 suite. AE, DC, DISC, MC, V. **Amenities:** Restaurant, lounge; outdoor pool; Jacuzzi; game room; self-serve laundry. *In room:* A/C, TV, kitchenette.

Wort Hotel 🐾🐾 Located on Broadway just off the town square—an area constantly in flux with new buildings and new shops—the Wort stands like an old tree, although its Tudor-style two-story building was largely rebuilt after a 1980 fire. Opened in the early 1940s by the sons of Charles Wort, an early-20th-century homesteader, it has an old-fashioned style to it, both in the noisy and relaxed **Silver Dollar Bar** (distinctively graced with 2,032 silver dollars) and the quiet, formal dining room (there's also a new Starbucks Coffee outlet onsite). In the manner of an old cattle-baron hotel, the lobby is graced by a warm, romantic fireplace; another fireplace and a huge, hand-carved mural accents a mezzanine sitting area, providing a second hideaway. The rooms aren't Tudor at all—the Wort labels them "New West" and have totally renovated each of them since New Year's 2000. Brass number plates and doorknobs welcome you into comfortable, air-conditioned guest rooms with modern decor, thick carpeting, and armoires.

50 N. Glenwood, Jackson, WY 83001. ✆ **307/733-2190.** www.worthotel.com. 60 units. $140–$245 double; $275–$485 suite. AE, DISC, MC, V. **Amenities:** Restaurant, lounge; exercise room; Jacuzzi. *In room:* A/C, TV.

NEAR JACKSON

Amangani 🐾🐾🐾 Cut into the side of East Gros Ventre Butte, Amangani's rough rock exterior blends incredibly well so that the lights from its windows and pool appear at night to glow from within the mountain. The style is understated and rustic, but every detail is done with expensive style. Walking through the high-ceilinged corridors or lounging by the outdoor pool, you know not to strike up a casual conversation with your neighbor—this place is all about class and privacy. Owner Adrian Zecha has resorts like this around the world, from Bali to Bora Bora, and while the designs are tailored to the landscape, the approach is the same: personal service, luxury, and all the little touches. To name a few of the latter, there are CDs in every bedroom, cashmere throws on the day beds, and stunning slate and redwood interiors.

1535 NE Butte Rd., Jackson, WY 83002 (on top of East Gros Ventre Butte). © 877/734-7333 or 307/734-7333. www.amangani.com. 40 units. $625–$900 double. AE, DC, DISC, MC, V. **Amenities:** Restaurant, lounge; outdoor pool; spa; Jacuzzi. *In room:* A/C, TV/VCR, minibar.

Bentwood Inn *★★ (Finds* This B&B is an architectural marvel. Built from 200-year-old timber cleared from Yellowstone to make room for a rest area, the inn is a 6,000-square-foot log mansion with 43 corners. The parlor, centered about a three-story river rock fireplace, is an ideal place to while away a thunderstorm, but the real beauty here is outside, situated just east of the Snake River on 3 acres of cottonwood and pine forest with a breezy deck and back lawn. The rooms themselves, all with remote-controlled gas fireplaces, private balconies, and Jacuzzi tubs, are extensions of the innovative design, with touches equally urban and rural, from ornate tilework to longhorn skulls above the bed. Innkeepers Bill and Nell Fay (the former designed the inn himself) pay a great deal of attention to detail and it shows. The breakfasts are simultaneously hearty and gourmet, and the fridge is always stocked with a wide range of soft drinks and libations. One room is pet-friendly,

4 miles (6.5km) west of Jackson on Teton Village Rd., P.O. Box 561, WY 83001. © 307/739-1411. Fax 307/739-2453. www.bentwoodinn.com. 5 units, including 1 suite. $165–$295 double; $245–$325 suite. Rates include complimentary full breakfast and evening cocktails. AE, DISC, MC, V. **Amenities:** Game room. *In room:* TV.

Spring Creek Ranch *★★* Perched atop East Gros Ventre Butte, 1,000 feet above the Snake River and minutes from both the airport and downtown Jackson, this resort commands a panoramic view of the Grand Tetons and 1,500 acres of land populated by deer, moose, and the horses at its riding facility in the valley below. It seems a little less exclusive now that Amangani has opened next door. But Spring Creek still has much going for it: The rooms, divided among nine buildings with cabinlike exteriors, all have fireplaces, Native American floor and wall coverings, and balconies with views of the Tetons. Most rooms have a king- or two queen-size beds, and the studio units boast kitchenettes. In addition to its own rooms, the resort arranges accommodations in the privately owned condominiums that dot the butte—large, lavishly furnished, and featuring completely equipped kitchens and sleeping accommodations.

1800 Spirit Dance Rd. (on top of the East Gros Ventre Butte), P.O. Box 4780, Jackson, WY 83001. © 800/443-6139 or 307/733-8833. 125 units. $210 double; $375–$1,200 condo. AE, MC, V. **Amenities:** Restaurant; outdoor pool; tennis court;

spa; Jacuzzi; complimentary shuttle; room service. *In room:* A/C, TV/VCR, kitchenette, fridge, coffeemaker.

IN TETON VILLAGE

You can take advantage of the attractions of Jackson, to the south, and Grand Teton, to the north, without suffering the crowds by journeying to Teton Village, which is approximately equidistant from both. Located at the foot of the ski hill, the village and surrounding area offer several fine eating and dining establishments, and activities nearby include skiing, ballooning, and hiking in Grand Teton National Park. During winter months, this is the center of activity in the valley. While lodging in the town of Jackson tends to be a little cheaper in the winter than the summer, at Teton Village the ratio is reversed—rooms by the ski hill get more expensive after the snow falls. Accommodations on this side of the valley run the gamut from pricey dude ranches and resorts to less expensive ski lodges that offer good value during the less hectic summer months. For a wide range of basic condos and deluxe vacation homes, contact **Jackson Hole Resort Lodging,** 3200 McCollister Dr., P.O. Box 51087, Teton Village, WY 83025 (℃ **800/443-8613** or 307/733-3990; www.jhresortlodging.com). All establishments are open year-round unless otherwise indicated.

Alpenhof Lodge ⍟   No other spot in the village has quite the Swiss chalet flavor of this longstanding hostelry, which has a prize location only 50 yards from the ski resort tram. Four stories tall, with a pitched roof and flower boxes on the balconies, it offers a little old-world atmosphere, as well as excellent comforts and service. The management continues to upgrade, most recently redoing the dining room and deluxe accommodations with brightly colored alpine fabrics, newly constructed handcrafted Bavarian furnishings, and tiled bathrooms with big, soft towels. Among the accommodations, you can choose from two junior suites with wet bars and five rooms with fireplaces, and many rooms have balconies or decks. Economy rooms offer two doubles or one queen-size bed, while deluxe units are larger.

3255 W. McCollister Dr., Teton Village, WY 83025. ℃ **800/732-3244** or 307/733-3242. Fax 307/739-1516. www.alpenhoflodge.com. 42 units. Dec–Apr $119–$258 double, $183–$538 suite; May–Oct $88–$168 double, $118–$408 suite. AE, DC, DISC, MC, V. Closed Nov. **Amenities:** 2 restaurants, lounge. *In room:* A/C, TV, kitchenette.

Hostelx ⍟ *Value*   If you came to Wyoming to ski, not to lie in the lap of luxury, get yourself a room at Hostelx and hit the slopes.

Called "the soul of Jackson Hole," it's a great bargain for skiers who don't need the trimmings, and it's not a dormitory, either—comfortable private rooms (above the caliber of a roadside motel) with king-size beds hold up to four people. There's also a good place to prep your skis, a library, and a common room with a fireplace and TV. You can walk to the Mangy Moose and other fun spots, and nobody will be able to tell you apart from the skiers staying at the Ritz.

Box 546, Teton Village, WY 83025. ⓒ **307/733-3415.** Fax 307/739-1142. www. hostelx.com. Summer $48–$54 double; winter $47–$60 double. MC, V. **Amenities:** Game room; self-serve laundry. *In room:* No phone.

Snake River Lodge & Spa ✵

Major renovations on what was once the Renaissance were completed in 2002, and this perpetually changing establishment looks to have gained some stability under the ownership of Vail Resorts. Wooden walls, stone floors and fireplaces, and a stuffed bison accent the main reception area. The main lodge provides accommodations where classy overshadows rustic, with exposed wooden-beam ceilings, down comforters, and luxurious furnishings. There are three levels of suites, from oversize versions of the standard rooms to three-bedroom versions with top-of-the-line kitchens, good sound systems, and Jacuzzi tubs. The 17,000 square foot **Natura Spa** is a new addition, featuring everything from hydrotherapy to free weights. Winter visitors can ski directly to a locker room with whirlpool and sauna, and drop their skis off for an overnight tune-up.

7710 Granite Loop Rd. (Box 348), Teton Village, WY 83025. ⓒ **800/445-4655** or 307/732-6000. Fax 307/732-6009. www.snakeriverlodge.com. 135 units. May–early June and Sept–mid-Dec $169–$299 double, $300–$900 suite; June–mid-Sept $229–$329 double, $400–$1000 suite; mid-Dec–Apr $340–$380 double, $450–$1050 suite. AE, MC, V. **Amenities:** Restaurant, lounge; indoor/outdoor pool; health club and spa; Jacuzzi; concierge; children's programs; room service; dry cleaning. *In room:* TV, kitchenette, coffeemaker, hair dryer, safe.

Teton Pines Resort ✵

Arnold Palmer and Ed Seay designed the challenging 18-hole golf course attached to this luxury resort. Don't expect to improve your handicap on this course, but you can soothe your frustrations on the green in the comfortable rooms, which feature, among other things, his and her bathrooms, one with a tub and one with a shower. There is also a pair of condo units, complete with kitchens and washer/dryer combinations. An upscale resort like this offers a range of recreation (although some cost extra): tennis, heli-skiing, fly-fishing and more.

3450 N. Clubhouse Dr., Jackson, WY 83001. © **800/238-2223** or 307/733-1005.
18 units. Summer $395–$750 suite; rest of year $100–$675 suite. AE, MC, V.
Amenities: Restaurant; outdoor pool; golf course; tennis courts; access to nearby
health club; Jacuzzi; activities desk; room service; dry cleaning. *In room:* TV, kitchen.

WHERE TO DINE

Jackson has more dining options than all of the other towns in this
book combined, running the gamut of cuisine and price. You'll find
the predictable steak/seafood/pasta menus—usually injected with a
few de rigueur wild game dishes, too—but you'll also find more
unusual choices. In addition to the choices reviewed below, you can
get a quick bite at **The Merry Piglets,** 160 N. Cache St. (© **307/
733-2966**), a snug Mexican restaurant that also serves Thai chicken
wraps. Another popular Mexican joint is **Vista Grande,**
2550 Moose-Wilson Rd. (© **307/733-6964**), with a festive atmosphere and killer margaritas. **Harvest Bakery and Natural Food
Cafe,** 130 W. Broadway (© **307/733-5418**), serves smoothies, vegetarian meals, and other organic breakfast and lunch entrees. At the
other end of the spectrum is **Bubba's Bar-B-Que,** 515 W. Broadway
(© **307/733-2288**), a late-night hangout dishing out ribs and other
meats. If you need a good shot of espresso with your morning paper,
stop at the **Betty Rock Coffee House & Cafe,** 325 W. Pearl St.
(© **307/733-0747**), where you can sit outside on the deck.

EXPENSIVE

The Blue Lion ✪✪ ECLECTIC   In the fast-moving, high-rent
world of Jackson dining, the Blue Lion stays in the forefront by staying the same. On the outside, it's a two-story blue clapboard building across from the town park that looks like a comfy family home.
On the inside, in intimate rooms accented with soft lighting, diners
enjoy slow-paced and elegant meals. The menu features rack of
lamb and wild game specialties, such as grilled elk loin in a pepper-
corn sauce. Fresh fish is flown in daily for dishes such as the wine-
basted rainbow trout stuffed with snow crab.

160 N. Millward. © **307/733-3912.** Reservations recommended. Main courses
$15–$28. AE, DC, MC, V. Wed–Mon 5:30–10pm.

The Cadillac Grille CALIFORNIA ECLECTIC   The 1950s
neon and hip American cuisine give this restaurant a trendy air that
attracts see-and-be-seen visitors more than locals. The chefs work
hard on presentation, but they also know how to cook, despite the
wide-ranging variety of dishes, from fire-roasted elk tenderloins to
garlic-painted Chilean sea bass. A *Wine Spectator* favorite, the wine
list is equally long and varied. The menu in this Art Deco restaurant

changes regularly, but the place itself has become one of Jackson's longer-lived establishments.

55 N. Cache. ✆ **307/733-3279.** Reservations recommended. Lunch $5–$18; dinner $15–$25. AE, MC, V. Daily 11:30am–3:30pm and 5:30–10:00pm.

Snake River Grill ✿✿✿ CONTEMPORARY AMERICAN

This is a popular drop-in spot for locals, including some of the glitterati who sojourn in the area—Harrison Ford and Uma Thurman, to name but a couple. The front-room dining area overlooks the busy Town Square, but there's a more private, romantic room in the back. It's an award-winning restaurant for both its wine list and its menu, which features regular fresh-fish dishes (ahi tuna is a favorite), crispy pork shank, and some game meat entrees such as venison chops and Idaho trout. The pizzas—cooked in a wood-burning oven—are topped with exotic ingredients such as duck sausage or eggplant with portabello mushrooms.

Town Square, Jackson. ✆ **307/733-0557.** www.snakerivergrill.com. Reservations recommended. Main courses $20–$40. AE, DC, MC, V. Daily 5:30–9:30pm. Closed Nov and Apr.

Stiegler's *Finds* AUSTRIAN/CONTINENTAL

Austrian cuisine isn't exactly lurking beyond every street corner, waiting to be summoned with a Julie Andrews yodel, but the discerning Austrian will certainly appreciate Stiegler's. Since 1983, Stiegler's has been confusing, astonishing, and delighting customers with such favorites as venison St. Hubertus, bratwurst, and schnitzel, as well as less recognizable (but equally tasty and heavy) delicacies. You'll be familiar with the desserts, at least: apple strudel and chocolate bread pudding. Peter Stiegler, the Austrian chef, invites you to "find a little Gemütlichkeit"—the feeling you get when you're surrounded by good friends, good food, and, of course, good beer.

Teton Village Rd. at the Aspens. ✆ **307/733-1071.** Reservations recommended. Main courses $18–$30. AE, MC, V. Tues–Sun 4–9:30pm. Closed Mon.

Sweetwater Restaurant ✿ AMERICAN

Although this little log restaurant serves American fare, it does so in a decidedly offbeat way. The eclectic menu includes, for example, a Greek salad, a Baja chicken salad, and a cowboy grilled roast beef sandwich. During the summer, there's outside dining. The dinner menu is just as quirky and livened by nightly specials; try the unique smoked buffalo carpaccio before diving into a giant grilled salmon fillet. Vegetarians will want to sample the spinach-and-feta casserole that is topped with a cheese soufflé.

85 King St. ✆ **307/733-3553.** Reservations recommended. Lunch $5–$8; dinner $13–$22. AE, DISC, MC, V. Daily 11am–3pm and 5:30–10pm; shorter hours in winter.

MODERATE

Anthony's *Kids* ITALIAN   There was a time when Anthony's was *the* Italian restaurant in Jackson, and you would stand in line for a table in an atmosphere of friendly frenzy. The menu has changed a bit since those days, but Anthony's is no longer the pinnacle of fine dining in Jackson. It's still a very respectable eatery, and many locals swear by it, but the competition has gotten so stiff over the years that Anthony's has suffered a bit by comparison. The menu offers selections of pasta, veal, poultry, and seafood, alongside the requisite antipasti selections and a kid's menu. A personal favorite: the rich lasagne verde, an arresting concoction with layers of grilled egg-plant, Italian cheeses, and roasted red peppers.

62 S. Glenwood St. ✆ **307/733-3717.** Main courses $10–$17. AE, MC, V. Daily 5:30–9:30pm.

Koshu Wine Bar *Finds* ECLECTIC   A relatively new entry in Jackson's frenetic dining scene, the Koshu Wine Bar has quickly emerged as one of the hippest restaurants in town. Both locals (including the area's resident celebrities) and tourists crowd the small, sleek dining room for chef Joel Holland's ingenious, addictive creations. His ever-changing menu reads "Asian-inspired food," but the Far East is just a starting point for Holland, who melds dozens of other influences into dishes such as tamarind pork with coconut milk, green onions, and rice; sweet miso-marinated black cod with spinach and mushrooms; and an out-of-this-world ahi sashimi. Thanks to its location in the Jackson Hole Wine Company, patrons can choose from 800 varieties of wine at retail price (plus a nominal corking fee). The brunch has quickly become a favored hangover cure for locals—the wok-fried catfish is sure to roust the cobwebs on one's brain.

200 W. Broadway in the back of the Jackson Hole Wine Company. ✆ **307/733-5283.** Reservations not accepted. Main courses $12–$18; brunch dishes $6–$11. AE, MC, V. Tues–Sat 6pm–midnight, Sun 11am–2pm and 6–10pm. Bar open later. Closed Mon.

Mangy Moose *Kids* AMERICAN   Coming off the slopes at the end of a hard day of skiing or snowboarding, you can slide right to the porch of this Teton Village institution. Good luck getting a seat inside, but if you like a lot of noise and laughter, a beer or a glass of wine, and a tasty dish such as buffalo meat loaf, you'll be patient—it beats getting into your car and driving into town. The decor matches the pandemonium: It looks like an upscale junk shop, with bicycles, old signs, and, naturally, a moose head or two hanging from the walls and rafters. The food is customary Wyoming fare (steak, seafood, and pasta), with a good salad bar and a smattering of Mexican dishes. Try the hot spinach and artichoke-heart dip as an appetizer, and move on to the elk fajitas or buffalo prime rib. There is often live music on weekends in the bar.

1 McCollister Dr., Teton Village. ℂ **307/733-4913.** Reservations recommended for larger parties. Main courses $15–$35. AE, MC, V. Daily 5:30–10pm.

Nani's Genuine Pasta House ℛ *Finds* ITALIAN

The setting is simple, but the food is extraordinary at Nani's, where you are handed two menus: *a carta classico* featuring pasta favorites such as *amitriciana* (tomato, onion, pancetta, and freshly ground black pepper) and a bowl of mussels in wine broth, or a list of specialties from a different featured region of Italy, which might include veal seared in a Marsala sauce or swordfish stuffed with bread crumbs, Parmigiano Reggiano cheese, capers, and garlic. Your only problem with this restaurant might be finding it—it's tucked away behind a rather run-down motel, and rarely does it fill to the rafters.

240 N. Glenwood. ℂ **307/733-3888.** www.nanis.com. Reservations recommended. Main courses $10–$17. MC, V. Tues–Sat 5–10pm.

Nora's Fish Creek Inn ℛ *Finds* AMERICAN

If you like to eat among locals, and if you like to eat a lot, Nora's is the place to hang out in Wilson, 6 miles (9.5km) northwest of Jackson—just look for the 15-foot trout on the roof. Rough but pleasant to look at, it's an institution, and if you come here often, you'll start to recognize the regulars, who grumble over their coffee and gossip about doings in the valley. Breakfast is especially good, when there are pancakes and huevos rancheros that barely fit on the huge plates. Prices are inexpensive compared to those at any of the other restaurants in town. Dinner is fish, fish, and more fish, namely fresh Idaho trout.

5600 W. WY 22, Wilson. ℂ **307/733-8288.** Breakfast $5–$8; lunch $4–$9; dinner $12–$21. AE, DISC, MC, V. Daily 6am–1:30pm and 5–9:30pm.

Rendezvous Bistro AMERICAN/SEAFOOD

Taking over a building that once housed a Denny's franchise, the Rendezvous opened in 2001 and garnered a fast local following. It's easy to see why: The place is contemporary yet casual, the food is affordable but very good, and the service is well above average. Climb into one of the intimate booths and order a dozen oysters on the half shell and slurp away, but save some room for a main course, ranging from grilled New York strip *frites* to whole Maine lobster. It might sound formal, but it's really not—the beauty is that the food is top-notch, while the atmosphere is laid-back and friendly.

380 W. Broadway. © **307/739-1100**. Reservations recommended. Main courses $9–$20. AE, MC, V. Daily 5:30–10:30pm. Closed Nov.

INEXPENSIVE

Billy's Giant Hamburgers (Value) BURGERS   If you take a wrong turn while entering the posh Cadillac Grille (right instead of left), you'll find yourself in a cramped 1950s-style lunch booth and counter shop—and you might just stay. Big, juicy burgers are what you'll get, cooked right in front of you. You can actually sit in here and order from the fancy Cadillac, perhaps a Maine lobster and a fine Sauvignon Blanc, or go easy on your wallet and order a giant cheeseburger with a pile of fries on the side.

West side of town square. © **307/733-3279**. Reservations not accepted. Most dishes $4–$6. AE, MC, V. Daily 11:30am–11pm. Closed Nov.

Jedediah's House of Sourdough (Kids) AMERICAN   You feel like you've walked into the kitchen of some sodbuster's log cabin home when you enter Jedediah's—the structure was built in 1910 and now resides on the National Register of Historic Places. Bring a big appetite for breakfast, and a little patience—you might have to wait for a table, then you might have to wait for food while you stare at the interesting old photos on the wall. But it's worth it, especially for the rich flavor of the sourjacks (sourdough pancakes) served with blueberries. During summer months, Jedediah's also serves dinners: steaks, BBQ chicken, rainbow trout, and the like.

135 E. Broadway. © **307/733-5671**. Reservations not accepted. Breakfast $4–$8; lunch $5–$9; dinner $8–$18. AE, DC, DISC, MC, V. Year-round daily 7am–2pm; summer daily 5:30–9pm.

JACKSON AFTER DARK

Talented musicians from well-known orchestras participate in the **Grand Teton Music Festival** (G) (© **307/733-1128**) held in summer in the amphitheater next to the tram lift. Tickets are usually available on short notice, especially for the weeknight chamber music performances, which are often terrific.

The summer-only **Jackson Hole Playhouse,** 145 W. Deloney Ave. (© **307/733-6994;** www.jacksonholetheatre.com), and the year-round **Pink Garter Mainstage Theatre,** 50 W. Broadway

(© **307/733-3670**), produce musicals, melodramas, and other light fare. Tickets for all shows should be reserved.

Those less impressed with dramaturgy should head down to the **Silver Dollar Bar,** at 50 N. Glenwood in the Wort Hotel (© **307/ 733-2190**), for a drink with one of the real or wannabe cowpokes at the bar. And, yes, those 1921 silver dollars are authentic. At the very famous **Million Dollar Cowboy Bar** on the Town Square, at 25 N. Cache St. (© **307/733-2207**), you can dance the two-step to live bands. If you want some high-octane dancing fun led by some talented local hoofers, head west to Wilson and the **Stagecoach Bar** (© **307/733-4407**) on Wyoming 22 on a Sunday night. It's the only night there's live music in this scruffy bar and hamburger joint, and the place is jammed wall to wall.

5 Cody, Wyoming ⊛⊛

Cody is 53 miles (85km) from the east entrance to Yellowstone.

Almost from the moment trappers first reported the unworldly marvels of Yellowstone, would-be entrepreneurs were setting up shop. However, none could match the vision of William F. "Buffalo Bill" Cody, the famed scout and showman who in 1887 set about building a hunting resort, an irrigation project, and a city on the eastern edge of the park. Today Cody is one of the most beautifully situated communities in Wyoming, near the juncture of rivers that pour from the rugged Absaroka Range. The drive from the east entrance of Yellowstone to Cody cuts through the magnificent East Yellowstone (Wapiti) Valley, a drive Theodore Roosevelt once called the most scenic 50 miles (80km) in the world.

The town oozes Western charm year-round, but it's at its best during the summer: The daytime skies are cloudless, and the longest-running rodeo in the country provides nightly entertainment under the stars. Museums, a re-created Western town, and retail shops supply plenty of diversions. Cody's friendly residents preserve and promote their particular brand of Western heritage to visitors the world over. And it's not too hard of a sell: Jackson might be the state's most renowned mountain paradise, but Cody's Western charm feels much more authentic.

ESSENTIALS

Information on air service to Cody and rental car agencies is discussed in "Getting There," in chapter 2.

GETTING THERE If you're driving from Cheyenne, travel north on I-25 to Casper and then west on U.S. Highway 20/26 to Shoshoni, where U.S. Highway 20 turns north to Thermopolis. From there, it's another 84 miles (135km) to Cody on Wyoming 120. From Jackson, take U.S. Highway 191 to the West Thumb Junction in Yellowstone, drive east along the northern boundary of Yellowstone Lake, and continue on U.S. Highway 14/16/20 to Cody. If you enter Wyoming from the west on Interstate 80, drive north from Rock Springs on U.S. Highway 191 to Farson, Wyoming 28 to Lander, Wyoming 789 to Thermopolis, and Wyoming 120 to Cody. Call ✆ **888/WYO-ROAD** (in-state) or 307/772-0824 for **road and travel information.**

VISITOR INFORMATION For printed information on this area of Wyoming, contact the **Park County Travel Council,** 836 Sheridan Ave. (P.O. Box 2454), Cody, WY 82414 (✆ **307/ 587-2777;** www.pctc.org), or the **Wyoming Business Council Travel and Tourism Division,** I-25 at College Drive, Cheyenne, WY 82002 (✆ **800/225-5996** or 307/777-7777; www.wyoming tourism.org).

GETTING OUTSIDE

Because of its proximity to Yellowstone, the best place to get outdoors near Cody is the park itself, but be aware that the town's only access to Yellowstone during the winter months is by snowmobile over dizzying Sylvan Pass. Once you're outside the park, Cody doesn't have the plethora of activities that Jackson Hole does, but it's still a bustling community. **Buffalo Bill State Park,** located along the canyon and reservoir 6 miles (9.5km) west of Cody, is a hot spot for lovers of the outdoors, with opportunities for hiking, fishing, and a variety of water sports. Its **Buffalo Bill Reservoir** is regarded as one of the premier spots for windsurfing in the United States. The park also has facilities for camping and picnicking. In the winter, cross-country and downhill skiing, ice climbing, and snowmobiling are popular in the Cody area.

If you'd rather not be a driver in the park's heavy summer traffic, guided Yellowstone National Park tours are available locally through **Grub Steak Expeditions,** P.O. Box 1013, Cody, WY 82414 (✆ **800/527-6316** or 307/527-6316; www.grubsteak.com) and **Powder River Tours** (✆ **800/442-3682, ext. 114** or 307/527-3677). Bob Richard, Grub Steak's proprietor (and one of the most knowledgeable guides you'll find), is a third-generation Cody resident and former Yellowstone ranger.

BIKING   If you want to explore the area on two wheels, mountain bike rentals ($12 to $20 a day) and local trail information are available at **Olde Faithful Bicycles,** 31 16th St.(© **307/527-5110;** bikecody@wyoming.com). Although there isn't a marked network of bike paths in the Cody area, you can ride on the Forest Service trails west of town off U.S. Highway 14/16/20 in the Shoshone National Forest. For specific trail information, call Olde Faithful Bicycles or the **Forest Service** at © **307/527-6921.**

CROSS-COUNTRY SKIING   If you favor a groomed course for cross-country skiing, try the **North Fork Nordic Trails** in Shoshone National Forest near the east entrance to the park off U.S. Highway 14/16/20. You can circuit 25 kilometers of trails adjacent to the Sleeping Giant downhill area (see below) and the Pahaska Tepee resort.

DOWNHILL SKIING   Near the east entrance to the park, 50 miles (80km) west of Cody, is an inexpensive, family-oriented ski area, cheap and not challenging: **Sleeping Giant Ski Area,** 349 Yellowstone Highway, Cody, WY 82414 (© **307/527-SNOW;** www.skisleepinggiant.com).

FISHING   Yellowstone's legendary fly-fishing waters are a short drive away, but you should try the smaller but excellent angling streams west of Cody: **The Clark's Fork of the Yellowstone, the North and South Forks of the Shoshone,** and **Sunlight Creek.** To the east, the warmer and slower **Big Horn River** and **Big Horn Lake** nurture catfish, walleye, and ling for boat fishers. For advice on the trout streams near Cody, ask at **North Fork Anglers,** 1107 Sheridan Ave. (© **307/527-7274;** www.northforkanglers. com), which stocks gear and clothing and also offers guides short day trips or longer, overnight excursions. If you like to troll or cast from a boat, **Buffalo Bill Reservoir** has produced some big Mackinaw, as well as rainbow, brown, and cutthroat trout. You have a shot at landing a 10-pound rainbow at **Monster Lake** (© **800/ 840-5137;** www.monsterlake.com), a private 150-acre pond on the Deseret Ranch 10 miles (16km) south of Cody. It's strictly catch-and-release for these gargantuan trout, and there's a hefty fee per rod.

FLOAT TRIPS   One of the most popular things to do in Cody in summer is to float along the Shoshone River, the major eastern drainage of the Yellowstone River. The mild Class I and II rapids make it an enjoyable trip for almost anyone. Contact **Wyoming**

River Trips, 1701 Sheridan Ave. (© **800/586-6661** or 307/587-6661; www.wyomingrivertrips.com), which also runs rafts on the smoother Class II waters below the dam, along with **River Runners,** 1491 Sheridan Ave. (© **307/527-RAFT;** www.westwyoming.com/rafting). Prices run from about $18 to $50, depending on the length and difficulty of the trip.

GOLF The **Olive Glenn Golf and Country Club,** 802 Meadow Lane, is an 18-hole PGA championship that is open to the public daily from 6am to 9pm. Greens fees are a modest $20 for 9 holes, and $35 for 18. Call © **307/587-5551** for tee times.

SNOWMOBILING The most popular Cody snowmobiling trails originate from nearby **Pahaska Teepee Resort,** located 51 miles (82km) from Cody on U.S. Highway 14/16/20 (see "Where to Stay," below). Don't take the Pahaska Tepee Trail over 8,541-foot Sylvan Pass if you're afraid of heights; but if you're not, it connects to the Yellowstone National Park trails and the lengthy Continental Divide Snowmobile Trail, and it offers breathtaking views, including Avalanche Peak (10,566 ft.) and Cody Peak (10,267 ft.). The **Sunlight trail system** is located 36 miles (58km) north of Cody and winds through the wilds to a stunning view of the Beartooth Mountains. Sledders start from a parking area at the junction of Wyoming 296 and U.S. Highway 212 and follow the Beartooth Scenic Byway east for 16 miles (26km) to a warming hut. To the east, there are 70 miles (113km) of snowmobile routes in the Bighorn Mountains. Snowmobiles can be rented at **Pahaska Tepee Resort** and in Cody at **Mountain Valley Engine Service,** 422 W. Yellowstone Ave. (© **307/587-6218**).

WINDSURFING According to *Outside* magazine, the 8-mile-long (13km), 4-mile-wide (6.5km) **Buffalo Bill Reservoir,** which receives wind from three mountain gorges, is one of the top 10 windsurfing destinations in the continental United States. It's best experienced in the warmer months of June to September. There is a boat ramp near the campground on the north side of the reservoir just off U.S. Highway 14/16/20. There are no places to rent a windsurf board in the vicinity.

SPECIAL EVENTS

The Buffalo Bill Historical Center is a tremendous resource for unique events in Cody. The April festival of **Cowboy Songs and Range Ballads** features storytelling, poetry, and some fine yodeling and balladry. In mid-June, the **Plains Indian Powwow** brings the

Robbie Powwow Garden on the south end of the Buffalo Bill Historical Center parking lot alive with whirling color. Traditional dance competitions are coupled with craft shows and Native American food, and non-Indians are welcomed into round dances. Call the **Buffalo Bill Historical Center** (© **307/587-4771**) for exact dates of these and other events and special exhibits.

Every July 1 to July 4, during the **Cody Stampede,** the streets are filled with parades, rodeos, fireworks, street dances, barbecues, and entertainment, capped by a top-notch rodeo. Call © **800/ 207-0744** or 307/587-5155 for tickets (also see www.codystampede rodeo.org). For 2 days in July, the cool rhythms of jazz and the brassy sound of big band and swing music take over the lawn of the Elks Club at 1202 Beck Ave. (next to the Cody Convention Center) during the **Yellowstone Jazz Festival.** Featured musicians come from afar, playing varieties of jazz from 11am until dark. Call © **307/587-3898** for additional information.

Late in August, the Buffalo Bill Historical Center (see above) stages the **Buffalo Bill Celebrity Shootout,** where celebrities and local shooters test their skills in trap, skeet, sporting clays, and five-stand shooting. It's a more serious test of marksmanship than the melodramatic shoot-out staged every summer evening at 6pm in front of the Irma Hotel.

SEEING THE SIGHTS

Buffalo Bill Historical Center ★★   This vast museum is top-drawer, casting a scholarly eye on the relics of the West's young history while offering some flash and entertainment for the easily distracted. From its beginnings in a rustic log building, it's grown into a sprawling modern edifice that now houses five different museums in nearly 300,000 square feet of space.

The **Buffalo Bill Museum** is a monument to one of the earliest manifestations of America's celebrity culture, displaying the wares that turned a frontier scout and buffalo hunter into a renowned showman. Posters trumpet his world-famous Wild West shows featuring "Custer's Last Rally" and "Cossack of the Caucasus," and there are some grainy film clips of the show itself. The **Whitney Gallery** showcases work by the adventurous artists who carried their palettes to the frontier to record firsthand the wilderness beauty, the proud Indian cultures, and the lives of trappers and cowboys in the 19th century. Bygone Western artists such as Frederic Remington, Charlie Russell, Albert Bierstadt, and Gutzon Borglum share exhibition space with contemporary practitioners. The **Plains Indian**

Museum is devoted to the history of Plains tribes, including the Blackfeet, Cheyenne, Crow, Gros Ventre, Shoshone, and Sioux. Interactive exhibits explain the migrations and customs of the tribes and display art and artifacts, including cradleboards, ceremonial dresses and robes, pipes, and beadwork. Situated in an eye-catching rotunda surrounded by a herd of bison statues, the **Draper Museum of Natural History** is the center's newest addition, opening its doors in June 2002. The $17 million museum focuses on man's investigation of nature over time, with specific attention on the Greater Yellowstone ecosystem. The **Cody Firearms Museum** displays weaponry dating back to 16th-century Europe in its collection of more than 5,000 pieces.

The center also features rotating special exhibitions, and its research library is an unparalleled resource for all things Western. Additionally, numerous educational programs are held throughout the year.

720 Sheridan Ave. © 307/587-4771. www.bbhc.org. Admission $10 adults, $6 students (18 and over), $4 youth (6–17), free for children under 6. Admission is good for 2 consecutive days. Group tour rates available by request. Open daily year-round, peaking at 7am–8pm Jun to mid-Sept; call for seasonal hours.

Tecumseh's Old West Miniature Village and Museum *Finds*

You have to pass through a trading post of ordinary Western tourist plunder to get to this finely detailed miniature diorama of Wyoming and Montana history. Described by proprietor Jerry Fick as his "lifetime work," the room-size landscape depicts everything from fur trappers floating the rivers to Custer's last moments at Little Big Horn. There is also a sizable collection of Indian and pioneer artifacts.

142 W. Yellowstone Ave. © 307/587-5362. Admission $3 adults, $1 students, children under 6 free. June–August daily 8am–8pm; call for hours in winter.

Cody Nite Rodeo *Kids*

If you want to see an authentic Wyoming rodeo, Cody offers a sure thing: a nightly tussle between bulls, broncs, and cowboys, as well as roping, cutting, and kids' events such as the "calf scramble." Pay an extra $2, and you get a seat just above the chutes in the Buzzard's Roost. The 6,000-seat stadium sits out on an open terrace above the Shoshone River west of town—not a bad place to be on a cool Wyoming evening beneath the stars. Once a year, some of the nation's top rodeo competitors show up for the Fourth of July Cody Stampede (see "Special Events," above).

Stampede Park (on U.S. 14/16/20 as you head west of town toward the Wapiti Valley). © 800/207-0744. Admission $11 adults, $5 children 7–12, free for children under 7. Memorial Day–Labor Day nightly at 8:30pm.

Old Trail Town *(Kids)*   Walking the creaky boardwalks here, you'll pass by gray storefronts and clapboard cabins gathered from ghost towns around the region and assembled on the original town site of Cody City, a short jog from the rodeo grounds. Soft-spoken archaeologist Bob Edgar hasn't wasted any paint on these relics, which include an 1883 cabin from Kaycee where Butch Cassidy and the Sundance Kid once conspired, a saloon decorated with bullet holes, and what must be the largest collection of worn-out buckboard carriages in the U.S. Also onsite: the relocated graves of a number of Western notables, including John "Liver-eatin'" Johnston, the model for Robert Redford's *Jeremiah Johnson*.

1831 Demaris Dr. ℂ 307/587-5302. www.oldtrailtown.com. Admission $5. May 15–Sept 15 daily 8am–8pm; call ahead for hours at other times of year.

Buffalo Bill Reservoir   The **Buffalo Bill Dam** drops like a slim concrete knife 328 feet into the gorge carved by the Shoshone River west of Cody, and you can walk out atop the dam and look down the steep canyon or back across the deep blue water of the reservoir. Several workers died building it, and when it was completed in 1910, it was the tallest dam in the world. The lake behind it serves anglers, boaters, and windsurfers while providing irrigation water to farmers downstream. An octagonal visitor center perched next to the dam provides exhibits on the reservoir, wildlife, and area recreation. There is a boat launch along the north lakeshore off U.S. Highway 14/16/20 and a clean, spacious campground that lacks only adequate shade.

6 miles (9.5km) west of Cody on U.S. Hwy. 14/16/20 at the top of Shoshone Canyon. ℂ 307/527-6076 for visitor center. Free admission. May–Sept daily 8am–8pm.

WHERE TO STAY

If you want to book lodging before you arrive, contact **Cody Area Central Reservations** (ℂ 888/468-6996), which can set you up at a myriad of different properties, from chain motels to frontier-style lodges. Another good accommodations resource is **Cody Guest Houses,** 927 14th St. (ℂ 800/587-6560 or 307/587-6000; www.codyguesthouses.com), which manages a dozen properties, from Victorian B&Bs to three-bedroom houses.

Buffalo Bill Village Resort: Comfort Inn, Holiday Inn & Buffalo Bill Village Historic Cabins *(Æ)*   This is not exactly a "resort" but an oddly matched cluster of lodgings with a convenient downtown location. The Holiday and Comfort Inns are similar to their chain brethren elsewhere, while the village of aged cabins offers a rustic exterior and a more Western feel, with modern conveniences inside. Family cabins provide two bedrooms. There is also a boardwalk where you can shop for curios or sign up for tours and river trips, and there's an outdoor heated pool and several restaurants.

Two of the standout properties in town, the Comfort Inn and Holiday Inn are priced nearly identically and have similar amenities (the rooms at the Holiday Inn are slightly newer, but the Comfort Inn includes continental breakfast in the rate). The cabins at Buffalo Bill Village are simply equipped—not much beyond a bed, phone, and TV—and resultantly less expensive.

17th and Sheridan Ave., Cody, WY 82414. ℂ 800/527-5544. Fax 307/587-2795. Comfort Inn: 75 units. $75–$140 double. Holiday Inn: 189 units. $75–$150 double. Buffalo Bill Village Historic Cabins: 83 units. $50–$130 double. AE, DC, DISC, MC, V. Buffalo Bill Village closed Oct–Apr. **Amenities:** 2 restaurants; outdoor pool. *In room:* Comfort Inn and Holiday Inn: A/C, TV, coffeemaker, hair dryer. Buffalo Bill Historic Cabins: TV.

The Irma Hotel *(Overrated)*   Buffalo Bill's entrepreneurial gusto ultimately left him penniless, but it also left us this century-old hotel (named for his daughter) in the heart of town. Cody hoped to corral visitors who got off the train on their way to Yellowstone, and one of his lures was an elaborate cherry-wood bar, a gift from straight-laced Queen Victoria. You can still hoist a jar on Her Royal Majesty's slab in the Silver Saddle Saloon or spend the night in a renovated room that might have once housed a president or prince.

Suites are named after local characters from the town's early days: The Irma Suite, on the corner of the building, has a queen-size bed, a writing table, a vanity in the bedroom area, a small sitting area, and an old-fashioned bathroom with a tub-shower combination. While the Irma's aura will surely please history buffs, those acclimated to ultramodern convenience will probably want to look elsewhere.

1192 Sheridan Ave., Cody, WY 82414. ℂ 800/745-4762 or 307/587-4221. www.irmahotel.com. 40 units, including 15 restored suites. $69–$92 double; $96–$119 suite. AE, DC, DISC, MC, V. **Amenities:** Restaurant. *In room:* A/C, TV.

The Mayor's Inn *(★)*   This two-story A-frame, built in 1905 for Mayor Frank Houx, found itself in the path of a wrecking ball in 1997. However, before it was demolished, it was sold and moved on a truck to its current location, just a few blocks away. It's now one of Cody's best B&Bs, with rooms such as the Yellowstone, featuring a lodgepole-pine bed frame and black-and-white photos of the park's early years, and the Hart Mountain Suite, with romance and floral decor in spades. There's also a well-equipped guest kitchen and a fully licensed bar on the enclosed back porch, the perfect spot to unwind after a day of sightseeing. The breakfasts here are a hearty treat, featuring sourdough flapjacks and buffalo sausage.

1413 Rumsey Ave., Cody, WY 82414. ℂ **888/217-3001** or 307/587-0887. www. mayorsinn.com. 5 units, including 1 suite. $80–$155 double; $205 suite. MC, V. *In room:* A/C. No phone.

Pahaska Tepee Resort ⚔ Buffalo Bill's hunting lodge, only a mile (1.5km) from the east entrance to Yellowstone, was dubbed with his Lakota name, Pahaska (longhair), when he opened the lodge to park visitors in 1905. Near the top of the beautiful Wapiti Valley along U.S. Highway 14/16/20, Pahaska is a popular stop for people visiting the Yellowstone area in both summer and winter. The cabins scattered on the hill behind the lodge close in the winter, while the A-frames by the lodge are open year-round. Accommodations have limited amenities and might best be described as "mini-motels" with two to five rooms, each with a private entrance. Some bathrooms have only showers, some have tubs—it's best to ask in advance.

183 Yellowstone Hwy., Cody, WY 82414. ℂ **800/628-7791** or 307/527-7701. Fax 307/527-4019. 48 units. Mid-June to August $100–$130 double, $895 lodge, $450 condo; off-season $65–$99 double, $650 lodge, $295 condo. DISC, MC, V. Closed Nov and Apr. **Amenities:** Restaurant; self-serve laundry. *In room:* No phone.

WHERE TO DINE

For its size, Cody may have more good restaurants than any of the gateways, especially considering that the town virtually shuts down from November to May. The town's finest restaurants aren't all meat-and-potatoes operations, either, although there's no shortage of good prime rib. Note that all the restaurants listed in this section are open year-round.

If you need something less than a formal meal, such as a plateful of fuel food or a jolt of caffeine for a busy day, Cody has a good supply of familiar fast-food joints and a few informal, inexpensive places. **Peter's Cafe Bakery,** at 1191 Sheridan Ave. (ℂ **307/ 527-5040**), across the street from The Irma, serves a full breakfast starting at 6:45am, with fresh-baked bagels, pastries, and espresso, plus subs and burgers for lunch and dinner. There is also the **Cody Coffee Co. & Eatery,** 1702 Sheridan Ave. (ℂ **307/527-7879**), for coffee drinks, fresh-made pastries, soups, and sandwiches. One of the best places day or night to get a beer-and-burger (or Rocky Mountain oysters!) is the thoroughly Western **Proud Cut Saloon,** 1227 Sheridan Ave. (ℂ **307/527-6905**).

Cassie's Supper Club ⚔ WESTERN   Cassie's is the sort of place you might expect and look for in the West: big platters of beef, four bars serving drinks, and ornery roadhouse decor with taxidermy, antelope skulls, and assorted cowboy ephemera. This place has the routine down, having been in business since 1922. Located along the highway west of town in what was once a "House of Ill Fame," Cassie's is now very respectable and very busy. Besides the requisite steaks, there's seafood (including a great rainbow trout dinner), pasta, and chicken, plus a full menu of specialty drinks. In the Buffalo Bar, a 20-foot mural depicts horses, cowboys, and shoot-outs. Hesitant dancers are lured onto the floor by free Western swing lessons several evenings a week, and there's live country music every night in summer.

214 Yellowstone Ave. ℂ **307/527-5500.** Main courses $16–$30. AE, DISC, MC, V. Mon–Sat 11am–2pm and 5–10pm; Sun 5–10pm.

The Gardens ⚔⚔ MEDITERRANEAN   Chef-owner John McCormack's splashy new entry into the Cody culinary scene is worlds apart from the region's typical meat-and-potatoes establishments. Trained in Paris and at some of the finest restaurants in New York and Las Vegas, McCormack now stamps the Gardens' menu with his indelible style: wild game and seafood prepared with French and Italian flair. This combination results in pheasant ravioli, boar and elk sausage, and incredible seafood pasta dishes. Likewise, the restaurant looks a lot different from the norm, a melding of Old West and funky cosmopolitan, with a sinfully red wine bar, an adjacent Internet bar, Victorian furnishings, and three stages for live music, including one on the big, breezy patio.

1313½ Sheridan Ave. ℂ **307/587-1101.** Reservations recommended on weekends. Main courses $8–$25. AE, MC, V. Daily 11am–10pm (bar open later).

Mack Bros. Brew Co. *Value* BURGERS/BBQ   Formerly the Silver Dollar Bar & Grill, this down-and-dirty establishment is a Cody institution. A stuffed cougar stands guard over the eclectically decorated room, where the walls are plastered with the likes of Woodstock posters and longhorn skulls. The menu is equal parts gourmet burgers and Southern-style barbecue, and the beers—brewed nearby in Red Lodge, Montana—are first-rate. Try the Sundance Wheat with a lemon wedge after a day in the great outdoors.

1313 Sheridan Ave. ℂ **307/587-3554.** Reservations not accepted. Most dishes $7–$14. AE, MC, V. Daily 11am–10pm (bar open later).

Maxwell's Restaurant *(Kids* ECLECTIC AMERICAN   A family restaurant in which "family" does not translate to "bland," Maxwell's has some spicy chicken and pasta dishes to go with its salads, seafood, and beef. The gourmet pizzas (especially the garlicky Margherita) aren't a bad choice, nor is the pork tenderloin marsala, sautéed in a light wine sauce with shitake mushrooms. You can even order a Philly cheese steak for lunch, uncommon in Wyoming. The low-backed booths and varnished wood tables are sometimes packed with boisterous families, raising the noise level and waitress stress, but it's a friendly crowd.

937 Sheridan Ave. ✆ **307/527-7749.** Lunch $7–$10; dinner $10–$20. AE, DISC, MC, V. Mon–Sat 11am–9pm.

Stefan's Restaurant *★★* CONTEMPORARY   Stefan Bennett is a restless chef, so the menu of his restaurant today is almost completely different from what he began with in 1997. However, everything is still made from scratch with an eye for invention. A sign reads, WE DON'T DO GIDDY-UP HERE, and it's right: This eatery—mild yet sleek in its appearance—serves truly gourmet fare that bears little resemblance to typical Wyoming cuisine. Among the entree survivors are a filet mignon stuffed with Gorgonzola cheese, sun-dried tomatoes, and portabello mushrooms; an "Untraditional Meatloaf" with spicy buffalo; a crustless chicken pot pie; andStefan's delectable honey-soy salad dressing. There are separate lunch and Sunday brunch menus—on the latter, Stefan smokes his own salmon and even makes hollandaise sauce from scratch—and a "little bites" menu with $4 to $5 children's meals.

1367 Sheridan Ave. ✆ **307/587-8511.** Reservations recommended. Lunch $5–$9; dinner $10–$23. AE, DISC, MC, V. Summer daily 11am–10pm; off-season Mon–Sat 11am–8pm.

9

A Yellowstone & Grand Teton Nature Guide

Although they are often linked in people's minds, Yellowstone and Grand Teton national parks couldn't be much more different. One is an immense wilderness plateau that sits atop a caldera seething with molten lava; the other is a striking set of peaks rising from a broad river plain. One encloses some of the most remote backcountry in the Lower 48 and provides crucial habitat for rare species such as grizzly bears and wolves; the other is only a quick drive away from a chic resort town and includes an airport and grazing cattle in its mixed-use approach.

What they *do* share is the affection of millions of visitors who come here annually to renew their ties to the natural beauty of the northern Rockies. Many Americans make the pilgrimage to see these shining mountains, alpine lakes, majestic elk, and astonishing geysers.

Unfortunately, mining, logging, and housing developments have diminished the area known as the **Greater Yellowstone Ecosystem** that surrounds the parks. The ecosystem is an interdependent system of watersheds, mountain ranges, wildlife habitat, and other components that extends beyond the two parks into seven national forests, an Indian reservation, three national wildlife refuges, and nearly a million acres of private land. To put it into perspective, the 18 million acres that comprise the ecosystem span an area that is as big as Connecticut, Rhode Island, and Delaware combined. It is one of the largest intact temperate ecosystems on the planet.

It's also a massive and important source of water. West of the Continental Divide, snowmelt trickles into creeks, streams, and rivers through Yellowstone before draining into the Snake River, traveling through Grand Teton National Park and Idaho before running into the Columbia River, which winds it way west through Oregon and into the Pacific Ocean.

Water on the eastern slopes of the Divide passes through Yellowstone in the form of the Madison and Gallatin rivers, which meet the Jefferson River west of Bozeman, Montana, merging into the Missouri. Then, as the song lyrics tell us, the Mighty Mo runs "down the Mississippi to Gulf of Mexico."

As if that weren't enough, the headwaters of the Yellowstone River are in the remote Thorofare country south of Yellowstone Lake. After running north the length of the park, the Yellowstone meanders across Montana as the longest undammed river in America, until it converges with the Missouri in North Dakota.

1 The Parks Today

It has long been difficult for park managers to both provide the public with a good vacation and protect the natural wonders of the parks. One challenge is making the parks accessible to 3 million annual visitors, many with different, even contradictory, expectations of a wilderness excursion. This brings about the construction of new facilities and ongoing road maintenance and repair. At the same time, the parks are wild preserves, and the Park Service must cope with the impact of six million feet on the forests, meadows, and thermal areas, as well as on the day-to-day lives of the millions of animals that inhabit the area.

It's a tough balancing act. Some of the pivotal issues in the parks today include: the impact of snowmobiles; the reintroduced wolves and the livestock losses of ranchers in and around the parks; the inadequacy of the park's infrastructure—sewage is the latest problem—to cope with 3 million annual human visitors; increased winter use despite no studies of the impact on wildlife; and the reduction of habitat surrounding the parks, coupled with a growing population of elk and bison seeking forage beyond park boundaries and possibly infecting domestic animals with a disease called brucellosis. And that's the short list.

Often possible solutions are a case of too little, too late, layering complex management strategies on an ecosystem that might do better if it were simply allowed to work things out naturally. The problem is, Grand Teton and Yellowstone have already been altered significantly by humans, so "natural" becomes a relative concept.

A good example is the reintroduction of a natural predator of the overpopulated elk: gray wolves, which were eliminated in the 1920s. These days, ranchland surrounds the parks, so the Defenders of Wildlife offers payments to anyone who loses a calf to a lupine— and ranchers do because wolves haven't read the management plan. When wolves wander down to Grand Teton, park officials put out roadkill carcasses to keep them well-fed and away from cattle, which are legally allowed to graze in the park. It's no picnic for park managers, although it is one for the wolves—literally.

Yellowstone's artificial boundaries also cause problems for bison. The state of Montana now allows hunters to shoot bison when they stray outside the park. Ranchers fear bison because of brucellosis, a disease that, when transmitted to cattle, causes cows to abort fetuses. Now there is talk of mass vaccinations of elk and bison, although, so far, there are less than 10 documented cases of either species infecting livestock.

As for the proliferation of snowmobiles and cars, most agree that there will have to be changes as visitation continues to grow. Snowmobilers arrive in the park in flocks as soon as the snow starts falling and remain until late February. While the popularity of the sport has had a positive affect on the tourism industry in the gateways of West Yellowstone, Jackson, and Gardiner, park officials are studying the long-term environmental impact of the machines. In their opinion, the snowmobiles create their own types of problems. First, the machines are noisy. Second, they share the same narrow trails as wildlife during months when the animals' energy levels are depleted by bad weather and a lack of food. Third, engine emissions create air pollution, which some say presents a health hazard. Finally, snowmobilers tend to drive the crowded paths at high speed, which can lead to accidents. As a consequence, a 3-year phaseout of snowmobiles was agreed upon in 2000, although litigation has since placed a potential ban in purgatory, pending the conclusions of additional research.

Then there's the traffic issue. Park roads are narrow and twisty, so the intrusion of 30-foot-long motor homes and pickup trucks towing trailers creates congestion, especially during the peak summer months. There have been studies of transportation alternatives to unclog park roadways, even a costly monorail that would wind through Yellowstone, but no decisive action has been taken.

As the world awakens to the accelerating loss of vital species in shrinking wild habitat, it becomes ever more imperative to find ways in which to preserve the relatively unspoiled ecosystems, like that of Greater Yellowstone. Recently, park scientists have battled to protect the native cutthroat trout in Yellowstone Lake from the impact of lake trout introduced by man. They have also recognized the enormous value of the microbes evolving in Yellowstone's super-hot thermal areas and have signed a unique agreement with a private company giving it exclusive rights to collect and market resident microbes, with an agreement that returns benefits that stem from commercial success to the park.

2 Landscape & Geology

The Yellowstone and Grand Teton region is one of the most dynamic seismic areas in the world—racked by earthquakes, cracked by water boiling to the surface, and littered with the detritus of previous volcanic eruptions. Today the bowels of the Yellowstone caldera are again filling with magma. Geologic studies show that, for the last two million years, the plateau has blown its top every 600,000 years or so—and the last explosion was about 600,000 years ago. That means that a titanic blow—bigger than anything seen in recorded history—could happen, well, any century now. The geological time frame is a long one, by human standards.

As you'll learn when you visit the exhibits on the park's geology at Moose, Mammoth, and the various geothermal areas, what you see on the surface—great layers of ash and the core of volcanic vents, such as Mount Washburn and Bunsen Peak—is only a fraction of the story of Yellowstone and Grand Teton.

Situated on 2.2 million acres, Yellowstone is significantly larger than its sister to the south. Encompassing 3,472 square miles, Yellowstone boasts 370 miles (596km) of paved roads and 1,200 miles (1931km) of trails, and is home to more geysers and hot springs than the combined total in the rest of the world.

Although it can't match Yellowstone's size, Grand Teton National Park is nothing to sneeze at. It has towering mountain spires reaching almost 14,000 feet skyward that have been compared to cathedral towers, picturesque glacial lakes, and a great deal of interesting topography. The 485 square miles of Grand Teton contain 159 miles (256km) of paved roads and 230 miles (370km) of hiking trails.

THE FACES OF YELLOWSTONE NATIONAL PARK

By the completion of the 1872 Hayden expedition, explorers had identified several distinct areas in the park, each with its own physical characteristics. Less spectacular than the craggy mountain scenery of Grand Teton and less imposing that the vast expanses of the Grand Canyon of Arizona, Yellowstone's beauty is subtle, reflecting the changes it has undergone during its explosive past.

Although Yellowstone has its share of mountains, much of the park is a high mountain plateau. The environment changes dramatically as you ascend the mountain slopes from the foothill zones in the valleys—the elevation at the entrance at West

Geysers, Hot Springs, Mud Pots & Fumaroles: What's the Difference?

Here's a way to identify the four most common types of thermal attractions in Yellowstone.

Geysers, the most prominent and spectacular of the thermal features in the park, are formed by the marriage of three elements: heat in the center (mantle) of the Earth, water, and pressure-resistant rock. Here's how they work together: The water source comes in the form of snowmelt that sinks into the earth, reaching depths of 10,000 feet—that's 2 miles (3km), but, remember, thermal areas in Yellowstone are that close to the surface. The second element is heat, which is provided by the cauldrons of magma. When water moves toward the center of the Earth, the heat brings it to a boil and sends it back toward the surface, often with traces of numerous minerals. The third element, pressure-resistant rock, acts like a geologic traffic cop by guiding the water toward the surface. Because the geyser's plumbing system does not have a way to diffuse energy, pressure builds, the boiling water is converted to steam, and boom! Plumes of steam are spewed forth from vents in the Earth's surface. Following the eruptions, silica that once was a component of the magma returns down the pathway to form a lining through which more snowmelt will travel, and the process repeats itself.

Hot springs are closely related to geysers but don't display the same eruptions because they don't develop the same subsurface pressures. Their colorful appearance is a result of different minerals, algae, the absorption of light by colloidal particles—tiny, suspended particles of liquid—and reflections.

Mud pots are hot springs on the Earth's surface that are formed as heated water mixes with clay and congealed minerals. Some mud pots are very colorful; others are unsightly and smelly.

Fumaroles are steam vents known as "dry geysers," from which gases rush into the air; they are considered hot springs that lack a liquid component.

Yellowstone is 6,600 feet, for example, compared to 5,300 at the Gardiner Entrance. Because the park lies about halfway between the equator and the North Pole, its summers consist of long, warm days that stimulate plant growth at the lower elevations.

As you walk the park trails, you'll find that plant distribution changes with the elevation. At the lowest elevations, down around 5,000 feet above sea level, you'll find **grassy flats** and sagebrush growing on dry, porous soils, with creeks and rivers cutting through to form wildlife-rich **riparian zones.** Next up: the **foothills,** sloping upward toward peaks, sometimes dotted by deposits of glacial moraine. Douglas fir, pine, and other conifers, as well as aspen, clad these slopes, and there are marshes and ponds fed by the spring snowmelt. Shrubs and flowers such as huckleberry and columbine favor these wet, shady spots.

Then comes the **mountain zone** (6,000–7,600 ft.), thickening forests dominated by lodgepole pine, broken by meadows where deer, elk, and moose often graze. The transition area between the highest forest and the bare surface above timberline is known as the **subalpine zone** (between 7,600 and 11,300 ft. of elevation). Finally, we come to the bare rock at the very top of the continental shelf, where small, hardy plants such as glacier lilies and sky pilot bloom briefly after the annual thaw.

Although the park is most famous for its geysers, visitors can choose among very different environments, reflections of the long-term effects of geologic activity and weather.

The limestone terraces at **Mammoth Hot Springs** give testimony to the region's subsurface volcanic activity. The park sits atop a rare geologic hot spot where molten rock still rises to within 2 miles (3km) of the Earth's surface, heating the water in a plumbing system that still mystifies scientists.

The **northern section of the park,** between Mammoth Hot Springs and the Tower–Roosevelt area, is a high plains area that is primarily defined by mountainous regions, forests, and broad expanses of river valleys that were created by ice movements.

The road between the Tower–Roosevelt junction and the northeast entrance winds through the **Lamar Valley,** an area that has been covered by glaciers three times, most recently during an ice age that began 25,000 years ago and continued for 10,000 years. In geologic terms, that was yesterday. Because this area was a favorite spot of Theodore Roosevelt, it is often referred to as "Roosevelt Country." The beautiful valley where elk, bison and wolves interact is still dotted with glacial ponds and strewn with boulders deposited by moving ice.

Farther south are **Pelican** and **Hayden valleys,** the two largest ancient lakebeds in the park. They feature large, open meadows with abundant plant life that provides food for a population of bison and elk.

In the warm months, you'll enjoy the contrast between the lush green valleys and **Canyon Country,** in the center of the park. Canyon Country is defined by the Grand Canyon of the Yellowstone, a colorful, 1,000-foot-deep, 24-mile-long (39km) gorge—in many opinions, just as dramatic as its cousin in Arizona. The Yellowstone River cuts through the valley, in some places moving 64,000 cubic feet of water per second, creating two waterfalls in the process, one of which is more than twice the height of Niagara Falls.

When you arrive at the **southern geyser basins,** you might feel that you've been transported through a geologic time warp. The cratered landscapes here are unlike any other in the park. Here you will find the largest collections of thermal areas in the world—there are perhaps 600 geysers and 10,000 geothermal features in the park—and the largest geysers in Yellowstone. The result: boiling water that is catapulted skyward and barren patches of sterile dirt; hot, bubbling pools that are unimaginably colorful; and, of course, the star of this show, Old Faithful geyser. Plan on spending at least 80 minutes here because that's the typical period between eruptions that send thousands of gallons of boiling water through the sky at a speed exceeding 100 mph.

You'll see the park's volcanic activity on a 17-mile (27km) journey east to the **lake area,** the scene of three volcanic eruptions that took place more than 600,000 years ago. When the final eruption blasted more than 1,000 square miles of the Rocky Mountains into the stratosphere, it created the Yellowstone caldera, a massive depression measuring 28 by 47 miles (45 by 67km), and Yellowstone Lake basin, some 20 miles (32km) long and 14 miles (23km) wide, reaching depths of 390 feet. You'll notice as you travel the roads here that the landscape consists of flat plateaus of lava that are hundreds of feet thick.

THE SPIRES OF GRAND TETON NATIONAL PARK

Your first sight of the towering spires of the **Cathedral Group**—the *trois tetons* (three breasts), as lonesome French trappers called them—will create an indelible impression. A bit of history makes them even more interesting.

Their formation began more than 2.5 billion years ago when sand and volcanic debris settled in an ancient ocean that covered this entire area. Scientists estimate that roughly 40 million to 80 million years ago, a compression of the Earth's surface caused an uplift of the entire Rocky Mountain chain from Mexico to Canada. This was just the first step in an ongoing series of events that included several periods during which a miles-thick crust of ice covered the area. Then, 6 million to 9 million years ago, the shifting of the Earth's plates caused movement along the north-south Teton fault that produced a tremendous uplift. The movement pushed the rock that is now the **Teton Range** to its present site from a position 20,000 to 30,000 feet *below* what is today the floor of the valley.

The west block of rock tipped upward to create the Teton Range, and the eastern block swung downward to form the valley that is now called **Jackson Hole**—kind of like a pair of horizontal swinging doors that moved the earth 5 miles (8km).

At this conclusion of the upheaval, and after eons of erosion and glacier activity, the **Grand Teton peak,** centerpiece of this 40-mile-long (64km) fault area, towered 13,770 foot above sea level, more than a mile (1.5km) above the visitor's center at Moose Junction. Eleven other peaks over 12,000 feet high are in the park today, with conditions that support mountain glaciers. As you gaze upward at this magnificent range, you will notice that many of the cliffs are more than half a mile (1km) in height.

During geologic explorations of **Mount Moran** (elevation 12,605 ft.), which gets less attention than it deserves, it was discovered that erosion has removed some 3,000 feet of material from its summit, so it once must have been more than 15,000 feet high. Equally remarkable is the fact that the thin layer of Flathead sandstone on the top of this peak is found in the valley below, buried at least 24,000 feet below the surface—further evidence of the skyward thrust of the mountains.

Although this is the youngest range in the Rockies, in yet another geologic anomaly, the rocks here are some of the oldest in North America, consisting of granitic gneisses and schists, which are the hardest and least porous rocks known to geologists.

The Teton area experienced a cooling trend about 150,000 years ago, during which time glaciers more than 2,000 feet thick flowed from higher elevations and an ice sheet covered Jackson Hole. When it melted for the final time, some 60,000 to 80,000 years ago, it gouged the 386-foot-deep, 16-mile-long (26km) depression now known as **Jackson Lake.**

The receding layers of ice also left other calling cards. Several beautiful **glacial lakes** were created, including Phelps, Taggart, Bradley, Jenny, String, and Leigh. The sides of **Cascade Canyon** were polished by receding ice. Glacial lakes called **cirque lakes** were carved at the heads of canyons, and the peaks of the mountains were honed to their present jagged edges. Five glaciers have survived on Mount Moran. The best trail for glacial views is the Cascade Trail, which leads to the Schoolroom Glacier. But you shouldn't walk on the Mount Moran glaciers unless you are experienced; it's very dangerous.

3 Plant Life in the Parks

When it comes to the variety of plants in the two parks, the only limiting factor is the high altitude—otherwise, the diversity of terrain, weather, and soils permits a fairly wide range of vegetation. Estimates vary, but in the ecosystem known as Greater Yellowstone, there are more than 1,500 plant varieties. In an area larger than many of our states on the eastern seaboard—more than 3,900 square miles between the two parks—there's plenty of room for them to stretch their roots and branches. Because of the diverse terrain, some species are found living on the dry valley beds in hostile soil, close to other species that predominate in lush meadows and riverbeds. Some thrive in thermal areas, while others do well in alpine areas, near mountain lakes, and in cirques near glaciers.

The history of the parks' plant life makes for interesting reading. Examination of plant fossils indicates that life began during the Eocene epoch, approximately 58 million years ago, and continued for 25 million years. The inspection of petrified tree stumps in Yellowstone's Lamar Valley led to the identification of 27 distinct layers of forests, one atop the other.

Climatic conditions during the Eocene period were similar to those in the southeastern and south-central United States. Difficult as it might be to imagine, the area was once a warm temperate zone in which rainfall might have averaged 50 to 60 inches per year at what was then an elevation of 3,000 feet above sea level.

These days, the elevation ranges from 5,000 to 13,000 feet, the average low temperature is approximately 30° F, and hundreds of inches of snow fall each year. Plants have adapted to a growing season that is merely 60 days in duration. As a consequence, forests once populated with hardwoods (such as maple, magnolia, and sycamore) are now filled with conifers, the most common of which are pine, spruce, and fir. A smattering of cottonwood and aspen also thrive in the cool park temperatures.

Some experts speculate that during the glacial periods, the tallest mountains in the Lamar Valley of Yellowstone were islands amid a sea of ice, thus providing refuge for some species of plant life.

The parks have several growing zones. Above 10,000 feet in the alpine zone, plants adapt to wind, snow, and lack of soil by growing close to the ground, flowering soon after the snows melt. You'll find such flora on trails near Dunraven Pass in Yellowstone and in Cascade Canyon in Grand Teton.

In Yellowstone, the Canyon and subalpine regions, at 7,000 to 10,000 feet, are known for **conifer forests** and open meadows of **wildflowers.** As elevation increases, wildflowers are abundant and healthy, while trees are stunted and shrub-like.

In the valley in Grand Teton, at 6,400 to 7,000 feet, the porous valley soil supports plants that are capable of tolerating hot and dry summertime conditions. **Sagebrush, wildflowers,** and **grasses** thrive and predominate. Plants bloom in a pageant of colors from early June until early July.

Identifying the plants described below does not require a degree in botany. However, a copy of Richard J. Shaw's book *Plants of Yellowstone and Grand Teton National Park* (Wheelright Press) will simplify the task, as will Jean L. Seavey's laminated identification card, *Wildflowers of the Yellowstone Area.* If you can't find these at your local bookstore, they can be purchased by mail from the Yellowstone Association (its complete address and telephone number are given in chapter 2, "Planning Your Trip to Yellowstone & Grand Teton National Parks").

TREES

Coniferous trees are most common in the parks because of the high altitude and short growing season, but there are some hardy deciduous trees as well, such as cottonwood and aspen. The most common cone-bearing trees in the parks are lodgepole pines, which cover as much as 80% of Yellowstone, and Douglas fir, subalpine fir, Engelmann spruce, blue spruce, and whitebark pine. The key to identification is the trees' basic shape, the shape of their needles, and their cones.

LODGEPOLE PINE   This familiar tree grows tall and slender, with bare trunk at the bottom and needles near the top resulting in dense stands that look like the spears of a closely ranked army. The needles of the lodgepole are clustered in pairs, typically around 3 inches long. You'll see logs from this tree supporting teepees and in the construction of cabins.

Lodgepole Pine

Douglas Fir

DOUGLAS FIR   "Doug fir" is actually a member of the pine family, with prickly cones and dark, deeply etched bark. This tree has flat, flexible, single needles that grow around the branch, giving the tree the appearance of fullness. Another giveaway is that its cones hang downward and do not disintegrate aloft, but litter the forest floor. These trees like the north-facing side of the mountain.

SUBALPINE FIR   You can usually distinguish firs by their needles, which sprout individually from branches instead of in clusters, like a pine; and by their cones, which grow upright on the branch until they dry out and blow away. Look for the slender, conical crown of this tree. When heavy snows weigh down the lower branches, they often become rooted, forming a circle of smaller trees called a snow mat. You'll find subalpine fir at high elevations near timberline.

Subalpine Fir

ENGELMANN SPRUCE   This tree also likes the higher elevations, growing in shaded ravines and in the canyons of the Teton Range above 6,800 feet and sometimes much higher. Look for it near Kepler Cascades, Spring Creek, and the south entrance of

Yellowstone National Park. It is distinguished by single needles that are square and sharp to the touch, and cones with papery scales that are approximately 1.5 inches long.

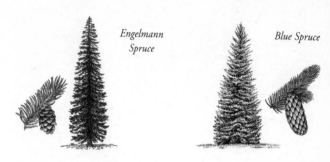

Engelmann Spruce

Blue Spruce

BLUE SPRUCE   The Englemann Spruce's cousin, this is most commonly found along the Snake River near Jackson. True to its name, it is characterized by its bluish appearance; rather stiff, sharp needles; and cones that are twice the size of the Englemann's.

OTHER PLANTS

Here's a brief listing of some of the most common and interesting plants found in the ecosystem.

GLACIER LILY   A member of the Lily family with a nodding bloom on a 6- to 12-inch stem, this bright yellow spring flower is found in abundance in both parks at elevations of more than 7,500 feet. Also known as the fawn lily, trout lily, and adders tongue, it is especially common near Sylvan Pass and on Dunraven Pass.

Glacier Lily

Indian Paintbrush

INDIAN PAINTBRUSH   This is the Wyoming state flower. It exhibits a distinctive narrow, brightly colored, scarlet bloom that is most commonly found from mid-June to early September in the

Snake River bottomland. Other species are white, yellow, orange, and pink.

PLAINS PRICKLY PEAR   This member of the cactus family is only one of two such species found in the park, most frequently in the Mammoth area and near the Snake River. It is distinguished by thick, flat green stems armed with spines and a conspicuous yellow flower with numerous petals during midsummer. American Indians, who recognized prickly pear's medicinal qualities, treated warts by lacerating them and then applying juice from the plant.

*Plains
Prickly Pear*

*Fringed
Gentian*

FRINGED GENTIAN   This member of the Gentian family is the official flower of Yellowstone Park, where it is common and blooms throughout the summer. The purple petals are fused into a 2-inch-long corolla and sit atop 1- to 3-foot-tall stems. It is also found below Jackson Lake Dam in Grand Teton.

ROUNDLEAF HAREBELL   This delicate herbaceous perennial is abundant in the forests and along roadsides, primarily in July and August. Perched atop 1-foot-tall stems, its heart-shape basal leaves are prominent because buds grow erect, but the purple blossoms tend to droop or grow horizontally, nature's way of protecting pollen from rainfall.

*Roundleaf
Harebell*

Silky Phacelia

SILKY PHACELIA   Silky is one of the most photogenic and easily recognized species in the parks. Growing in purple clumps alongside the road at Dunraven Pass, the flower derives its name from the silvery pubescence that covers stems and leaves. The best time for photographing this star is July and August.

SHOOTING STAR   The shooting star is characterized by pinkish 0.5- to 1-inch long flowers that dangle earthward like meteorites from a 12-inch stem; they bloom in June. It is commonly found near thermal areas, streambeds, and Yellowstone Lake.

*Shooting
Star*

*Yellow
Monkey-Flower*

YELLOW MONKEY-FLOWER   The monkey-flower exhibits a bright yellow petal that, together with orange spots, attracts insect pollinators near stream beds at elevations of 7,000 to 9,000 feet all summer. It is also commonly found near thermal areas and Yellowstone Lake.

FAIRYSLIPPER (also known as the **Calypso Orchid**)   Finding this beautiful orchid might require some serious detective work, but the payoff is worth the effort. It is one of 15 orchid species found in the parks and is considered by many to be the most beautiful and striking. Commonly seen during May and June, it usually has one small, green leaf and a red-pink flower that resembles a small lady's slipper, hence the name. It is found in cool, deep-shaded areas and is becoming rare because its habitat is disappearing.

Tips **Photo Tip**

To successfully record your discovery of the parks' flora, consider adding a microlens to your arsenal of camera gear that will allow you to focus within 6 inches of blossoms. Film speeds of 200 ISO will add to the chances of proper exposure, even on cloudy days.

*Fairyslipper
(a.k.a. Calypso
Orchid)*

Bitterroot

BITTERROOT The state flower of Montana, the bitterroot, with its fleshy rose and white petals, which extend to 1 inch in length, makes its first appearance in early June in dry, open, sometimes stony soil and in grassy meadows. It was a source of food for Indians, who introduced it to Capt. Lewis of Lewis and Clark fame, hence its botanical name.

*Columbia
Monkshood*

COLUMBIA MONKSHOOD This is a purple, irregularly shaped flower with a hood-shape structure that has two sepals at its side and two below (these make up the calyx, the leafy parts that surround the flower). Its stem varies in height from 2 to 5 feet. You'll find these flowers in wet meadows and on stream banks from June through August, often near thermal areas, streambeds, and Yellowstone Lake.

4 Wildlife in the Parks

For many, the primary reason for a visit to these parks is the wildlife: bear, bighorn sheep, bison, elk, bald eagles, river otters, and moose all wandering free, often within roadside view of travelers. Yellowstone and Grand Teton are home to the largest concentration of free-roaming wildlife in the Lower 48. This includes one of the largest herds of elk in North America, the largest free-roaming herd of bison in the country, and the only significant population of grizzly bears south of the Canadian border.

Tips **Photo Tip**

Photographers need to be armed with a telephoto lens, preferably a zoom, to get good shots of wildlife. Even the biggest animals in the park present minimal risks to humans, unless you move in for a close-up of a grazing bison or a grizzly bear. Invest in a 300-millimeter lens, or 100- to 300-millimeter zoom, and you should get some good shots without disturbing the wildlife or putting yourself at risk.

But it doesn't stop there. Also in Yellowstone/Grand Teton are 8 species of ungulates (hoofed mammals), black bears, and 3 species of wildcats, as well as coyotes, wolverines, pine martens, 70 smaller species of mammals, and 290 species of birds. Add to that the wolves reintroduced in 1995—and now reproducing prolifically—and you have a rich array of wildlife intermingling throughout the parks. Most of these creatures will steer clear of humans. But humans, never shy, want to get ever closer to the animals, and that can cause problems. Unlike the critters that inhabit petting zoos, the animals in the Greater Yellowstone Ecosystem are wild and pose a constant threat to the safety of visitors.

There might be shocks, too, for tourists not familiar with animals in the wild. In 1998, wolves in Slough Creek attacked a coyote that wandered into their new territory, sending a message to coyotes—and to people with spotting scopes on the hill across the creek—that this would now be a coyote-free zone. It was not a pretty death. But death is a day-to-day affair in the parks. In the spring, you'll see carcasses of elk and bison that died during the long winter, attracting bears and other carnivores looking for a free lunch. That's part of the picture when you vow to interfere as little as possible with nature's way.

Park naturalists generally agree that every major vertebrate wildlife species that was present during the most recent ice age (over 10,000 years ago) is a resident of the parks today, as are several rare or endangered species, the most notable being the grizzly bear and the bald eagle.

MAMMALS

BEAR (BLACK & GRIZZLY)   In recent years, grizzly bears have been quite visible, including a pair that foraged daily in a meadow just off the road over Dunraven Pass while dozens of photographers clicked away. That's unusual. Unless you have the patience to spend weeks outdoors in bear country such as the Lamar and Hayden valleys, your chances of seeing a grizzly in Yellowstone or Grand Teton aren't all that good—you might have to go to the grizzly zoo in West Yellowstone. But it's the bears that tourists are always asking to see, and they've mounted a comeback after nearly dying off once park garbage dumps were closed in the early 1970s.

Estimates vary, but there are probably more than 600 grizzly bears in the Greater Yellowstone Ecosystem today, and an equal or greater number of black bears. Rangers say you're most likely to spot the black bears, especially during spring months after they emerge with new cubs from their winter dens. However, the black bears are probably more visible because they are not as reticent to venture near human development as grizzlies are, which means that an encounter with a grizzly is most likely to occur in the backcountry. Neither type of bear sits along park roads the way both once did, begging for food or wrestling over park lodge garbage while tourists sat watching on bleachers. Bears who get a taste for human food or get too comfortable around human campsites are relocated to the depths of the wilderness. Black bears are most commonly sighted in the Canyon–Tower and Madison–Old Faithful areas, where they feed on green grass, herbs, berries, ants, and carrion.

Grizzly bears are most commonly seen in the northeast area of the park, in the meadows on the hillsides of the Lamar Valley, or wandering the Hayden Valley north of Yellowstone Lake. They also feed on trout spawning in Yellowstone Lake tributaries during the late spring (campgrounds by these streams are closed during spawning times). They are most active in the spring, when they emerge from hibernation hungry, and in the fall, fattening up for winter.

Grizzly bears can do you the most damage, particularly when their cubs are around or when they think you're after their food.

Black
Bear

Grizzly
Bear

Black Bear or Grizzly?

Because a black bear can be black, brown, or cinnamon, here are some identifiers. The grizz is the larger of the two, typically, 3.5 feet at the shoulder with a dish-face profile and a pronounced hump between the shoulders. The black's ears are rounder, just like those you see on stuffed animals. The grizzly's color is typically more yellowish-brown, but the coat is sometimes recognized by its cinnamon color, often highlighted by silver tips.

Caution: Park rangers attempt to keep track of grizzlies to avoid human/bear incidents. However, because the bears don't follow prescribed pathways, it is best to assume that they are always in the area; always make noise when traveling in isolated areas.

BIGHORN SHEEP   If there's a hint of a foothold, a bighorn sheep will find it. Its hooves are hard and durable on the outside but soft and clamplike able underneath, the perfect design for steep, rocky terrain. You'll often hear them clattering before you spot their stocky, gray-brown bodies and white rumps. Six feet long, the males weigh up to 300 pounds. Their horns are coiled; the females' are straight. The Greater Yellowstone Ecosystem probably contains the largest concentration of bighorns in the United States. Look for them on Mount Washburn, along Specimen Ridge, and in the Gallatin Range in Yellowstone; they are also seen occasionally in the Heart Mountain area in southern Yellowstone. In Grand Teton, smaller herds are found in the Gros Ventre Valley, as well as the western slopes of the Tetons. East of the Tetons, in the Wind River Range, a large herd of bighorn sheep congregates in the winter south of the town of Dubois in Whiskey Basin.

BISON   Bison (or buffalo) appear indifferent to humans as they wander the roads and go about their grazing, but don't think for a minute that they're docile. Their prodigious size, cute calves (which look like cattle calves), and fearless nature ensure that bison are very visible symbols of Yellowstone. On ballerina-thin ankles, these burly brown animals carry as much as 2,000 pounds, concentrated in thick shoulders and massive chests. Those big heads helps them clear snow for winter browsing, but during harsh winters they instinctively migrate to lower elevations (some biologists insist that both grizzlies and bison were driven up on the plateau from their natural home on the prairie). If their wanderings take them into Montana, they're in trouble; ranchers are legally allowed to shoot them in order to protect their livestock from brucellosis. Bison are very easy to spot in the summer; you'll see them munching grass and rolling in dust pits in Hayden Valley, Pelican Valley, the Madison River area, and the geyser areas near the Firehole River. In the winter, snowmobilers often have to make way for the shaggy beasts because bison take advantage of the snow-packed roads to travel around.

Bighorn Sheep

Bison

COYOTE   The wily coyote is the predator most often spotted by park visitors. Looking something like a small, lanky shepherd dog with grizzled, gray-brown coat, the coyotes number around 450, living in 65 packs that make their homes in burrows and caves. Numbers have dropped some since wolf reintroduction, but coyotes are very adaptable. Active hunters year-round, they feast on small animals such as squirrels and rabbits, as well as the carcasses of animals that died naturally or were killed by larger carnivores, such as bears and wolves. They are seen near most park roads, in the meadows and the sagebrush. Coyote pups are considered a delicacy by great horned owls, eagles, cougars, and bears.

Coyote

Wolf

Wolf or Coyote?

Wolves and coyotes both bear a striking resemblance to large dogs. Here are some ways to distinguish them.

- Coyotes are the more delicate-looking; wolves are sturdy, almost massive.
- Coyotes grow to a height of 20 inches; wolves often grow to 34 inches.
- Coyotes have long, pointed ears; wolf ears are rounded and relatively short.
- Coyotes have thin, delicate legs, similar to those of a fox; wolves' legs are thick and long.

WOLF In a controversial move, gray wolves were reintroduced to Yellowstone in 1995 for the first time since the 1920s, when they were eliminated by hunters operating under a federal predator control program designed to protect cattle herds. The population of Canadian gray wolves is thriving in its new environment; well over 150 animals have spread from Montana down to Grand Teton, where they're now denning in the Gros Ventre and the valley. They are high-profile occupants of the Lamar Valley and are under constant observation by visitors with binoculars or spotting scopes who travel the area.

ELK It is estimated that 63,000 elk (wapiti) populate the Greater Yellowstone Ecosystem, 40% of which live in the two parks. The most common large animal in the parks, elk are rather sociable and travel in small groups. Males are easily identifiable by a massive set of antlers. Although they shed them every spring, by early summer bulls are beginning to display prodigious racks that, by year's end, are the envy of their cousins in the deer family. Their grayish-brown bodies, which typically weigh as much as 900 pounds, are accented by chestnut brown heads and necks, a shaggy mane, a short tail, and a distinctive tan patch on their rumps.

One herd can usually be located in the vicinity of Mammoth Hot Springs, often on the lawn of the main square. Others are found throughout each park. During winter months, the northern Yellowstone herd heads to a winter grazing area near Gardiner, while their cousins in Grand Teton head for the National Elk Refuge, just north of Jackson, where the Forest Service supplements their diet with bales of alfalfa.

Elk

Moose

MOOSE   Perhaps because of their size, their homely appearance, or the broad antler racks that can grow to 6 feet across, moose sightings provide park visitors with unequaled excitement. The largest member of the deer family, a typical adult male weighs 1,000 pounds and is most easily recognizable by a pendulous muzzle and fleshy dewlap that hangs beneath its neck like a bell.

Moose sightings are most frequent on the edges of ponds and in damp, lush valley bottoms where they feed on willows and water plants, especially along the Moose–Wilson Road and near the Jackson Lake Lodge in Grand Teton.

The plodding, nibbling moose in a meadow is not to be approached—and is not likely to budge if you do. Although it appears ungainly, a moose is capable of traveling at 30 mph; cows will charge any perceived threat to a calf, and bulls become particularly ornery in the fall, so giving them a wide berth is recommended.

MULE DEER   Not to be outnumbered by their larger cousins, an estimated 120,000 mule deer live in the ecosystem, thousands of them within the park borders. They are most often spotted near forest boundaries or in areas covered with grass and sagebrush. Their most distinguishing characteristics are their huge ears and a black tip on their tail that contrasts with their white rump. When they run, they bounce, with all four legs in the air. Fawns, often in pairs, are typically born in late spring.

Mule Deer

Pronghorn Antelope

Antlers or Horns?

Most of the larger, four-legged animals roaming the parks have lavish headpieces that are either horns or antlers. But what's the difference?

Antlers are shed every year; horns last a lifetime. Male deer, elk, and moose shed their *antlers* every spring, so they're as bald as cue balls when the parks open. By early June, though, new velvet-covered protuberances are making their appearance.

In comparison, both sexes of bison and pronghorn grow only one set of horns during their lifetimes.

PRONGHORN   The often-sighted pronghorn graze near the north entrance to Yellowstone and on the valley floors of Grand Teton, but they are shy and difficult to approach or photograph because of their excellent vision and speed. Often mistakenly referred to as antelope—they're actually unrelated to true African antelope—the pronghorn is identified by its short, black horns, tan-and-white bodies, and black accent stripes. They can run 45 mph, but they can't clear fences.

5 Birds in the Parks

The skies above the parks are filled with predators on the wing, including eagles and 27 species of hawks, not to mention ospreys, falcons, and owls. Here are descriptions of some of the birds you might want to look for.

BALD EAGLE   The bald eagle holds a position in the pecking order that parallels that of the grizzly. Of all the birds in the park, visitors are most interested in spotting this endangered species, once almost wiped out by the pesticide DDT. The Yellowstone/Grand Teton area is now home to one of largest populations of eagles in the continental United States; more than 200 of these magnificent birds make their homes in the parks. Bald eagles are most recognizable by a striking white head, tail feathers, and wingspans up to 7 feet. They typically live within 2 miles (3km) of water, so the Yellowstone Plateau, Snake River, Yellowstone Lake, and headwaters of the Madison River are prime spotting areas for this spectacular bird.

Tips **Birding Spot**

Take a picnic lunch, or plan a relaxing break at the **Oxbow Bend** overlook in Grand Teton. Weather permitting, you can soak up some sunshine and observe the great blue herons, osprey, pelicans, cormorants, and, just maybe, a bald eagle. Although it's a popular spot, there's always room for one more vehicle.

GOLDEN EAGLE   The bald eagle's cousin, the golden eagle, is similar in appearance, although it is smaller and does not have a white cowl—sometimes it is confused with an immature bald eagle. The golden eagle goes after small mammals such as jackrabbits and prairie dogs. It works out in the open country; sometimes you'll find one feeding on roadkill.

Bald Eagle

Golden Eagle

OSPREY   The osprey, which is nicknamed the "fish eagle" (on account of its diet), is a smaller version of the eagle, growing from 21 to 24 inches and with a white underbody and brown topsides. It is recognizable by a whistling sound it makes while hunting. Ospreys tend to create large nests made of twigs and branches that are found on the tops of trees and power poles. Look for this handsome, interesting bird in the Snake River area and the Grand Canyon of the Yellowstone River, a popular nesting area.

TRUMPETER SWAN   The trumpeter swan, one of the largest birds on the continent, has chosen the Greater Yellowstone Ecosystem as a sanctuary. Easily recognizable by their long, curved necks; snowy white bodies; and black bills, they are found in marshes and on lakes and rivers. Odds of a sighting are excellent on the Madison River near the West Yellowstone entrance and on Christian Pond, Swan Lake, and Cygnet Pond in Grand Teton.

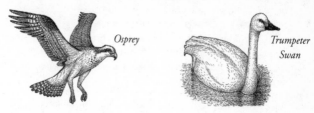

Osprey

Trumpeter Swan

OTHER RAPTORS **American Kestrels, Prairie Falcons,** and **Red-Tailed Hawks** are seen on Antelope Flats–Kelly Road in Grand Teton, most often over hay fields, where they search for small rodents.

American Kestrel

Prairie Falcon

Red-Tailed Hawk

OTHER AQUATIC BIRDS The **Great Blue Heron,** a skinny, long-legged wading bird, is found in wetlands and rocky outcrops, especially near the end of Jackson Lake. Yellowstone Lake is a prime viewing area for the best fishers in the park, the **American White Pelicans** that capture fish in their long, yellow-pouched bill. The **American Dipper,** the only aquatic songbird in North America, revels in cold, fast-flowing mountain streams. The slate-gray dipper is tiny, only 7 to 8 inches tall, and is recognized by its long bill and stubby tail.

Great Blue Heron

American White Pelican

American Dipper

Index

See also Accommodations and Restaurant indexes below.

ACCOMMODATIONS

RESTAURANTS

FROMMER'S® COMPLETE TRAVEL GUIDES

Alaska
Alaska Cruises & Ports of Call
Amsterdam
Argentina & Chile
Arizona
Atlanta
Australia
Austria
Bahamas
Barcelona, Madrid & Seville
Beijing
Belgium, Holland & Luxembourg
Bermuda
Boston
British Columbia & the Canadian Rockies
Budapest & the Best of Hungary
California
Canada
Cancún, Cozumel & the Yucatán
Cape Cod, Nantucket & Martha's Vineyard
Caribbean
Caribbean Cruises & Ports of Call
Caribbean Ports of Call
Carolinas & Georgia
Chicago
China
Colorado
Costa Rica
Denmark
Denver, Boulder & Colorado Springs
England
Europe
European Cruises & Ports of Call
Florida
France

Germany
Great Britain
Greece
Greek Islands
Hawaii
Hong Kong
Honolulu, Waikiki & Oahu
Ireland
Israel
Italy
Jamaica
Japan
Las Vegas
London
Los Angeles
Maryland & Delaware
Maui
Mexico
Montana & Wyoming
Montréal & Québec City
Munich & the Bavarian Alps
Nashville & Memphis
Nepal
New England
New Mexico
New Orleans
New York City
New Zealand
Nova Scotia, New Brunswick & Prince Edward Island
Oregon
Paris
Philadelphia & the Amish Country
Portugal
Prague & the Best of the Czech Republic
Provence & the Riviera

Puerto Rico
Rome
San Antonio & Austin
San Diego
San Francisco
Santa Fe, Taos & Albuquerque
Scandinavia
Scotland
Seattle & Portland
Shanghai
Singapore & Malaysia
South Africa
South America
Southeast Asia
South Florida
South Pacific
Spain
Sweden
Switzerland
Texas
Thailand
Tokyo
Toronto
Tuscany & Umbria
USA
Utah
Vancouver & Victoria
Vermont, New Hampshire & Maine
Vienna & the Danube Valley
Virgin Islands
Virginia
Walt Disney World & Orlando
Washington, D.C.
Washington State

FROMMER'S® DOLLAR-A-DAY GUIDES

Australia from $50 a Day
California from $70 a Day
Caribbean from $70 a Day
England from $75 a Day
Europe from $70 a Day

Florida from $70 a Day
Hawaii from $80 a Day
Ireland from $60 a Day
Italy from $70 a Day
London from $85 a Day

New York from $90 a Day
Paris from $80 a Day
San Francisco from $70 a Day
Washington, D.C., from $80 a Day

FROMMER'S® PORTABLE GUIDES

Acapulco, Ixtapa & Zihuatanejo
Amsterdam
Aruba
Australia's Great Barrier Reef
Bahamas
Baja & Los Cabos
Berlin
Big Island of Hawaii
Boston
California Wine Country
Cancún
Charleston & Savannah
Chicago
Disneyland

Dublin
Florence
Frankfurt
Hong Kong
Houston
Las Vegas
London
Los Angeles
Maine Coast
Maui
Miami
New Orleans
New York City
Paris

Phoenix & Scottsdale
Portland
Puerto Rico
Puerto Vallarta, Manzanillo & Guadalajara
San Diego
San Francisco
Seattle
Sydney
Tampa & St. Petersburg
Vancouver
Venice
Virgin Islands
Washington, D.C.

FROMMER'S® NATIONAL PARK GUIDES

Family Vacations in the National Parks
Grand Canyon

National Parks of the American West
Rocky Mountain
Yellowstone & Grand Teton

Yosemite & Sequoia/ Kings Canyon
Zion & Bryce Canyon

Frommer's® Memorable Walks

Chicago
London

New York
Paris

San Francisco

Frommer's® Great Outdoor Guides

Arizona & New Mexico
New England

Northern California
Southern New England

Vermont & New Hampshire

Suzy Gershman's Born to Shop Guides

Born to Shop: France
Born to Shop: Hong Kong,
  Shanghai & Beijing

Born to Shop: Italy
Born to Shop: London

Born to Shop: New York
Born to Shop: Paris

Frommer's® Irreverent Guides

Amsterdam
Boston
Chicago
Las Vegas
London

Los Angeles
Manhattan
New Orleans
Paris
Rome

San Francisco
Seattle & Portland
Vancouver
Walt Disney World
Washington, D.C.

Frommer's® Best-Loved Driving Tours

Britain
California
Florida
France

Germany
Ireland
Italy

New England
Scotland
Spain

Hanging Out™ Guides

Hanging Out in England
Hanging Out in Europe

Hanging Out in France
Hanging Out in Ireland

Hanging Out in Italy
Hanging Out in Spain

The Unofficial Guides®

Bed & Breakfasts and Country
  Inns in:
  California
  New England
  Northwest
  Rockies
  Southeast
Beyond Disney
Branson, Missouri
California with Kids
Chicago
Cruises
Disneyland

Florida with Kids
Golf Vacations in the
  Eastern U.S.
The Great Smoky &
  Blue Ridge Mountains
Hawaii
Inside Disney
Las Vegas
London
Mid-Atlantic with Kids
Mini Las Vegas
Mini-Mickey
New England & New York
  with Kids

New Orleans
New York City
Paris
San Francisco
Skiing in the West
Southeast with Kids
Walt Disney World
Walt Disney World for
  Grown-ups
Walt Disney World for Kids
Washington, D.C.
World's Best Diving Vacations

Special-Interest Titles

Frommer's Adventure Guide to Australia & New
  Zealand
Frommer's Adventure Guide to Central America
Frommer's Adventure Guide to India & Pakistan
Frommer's Adventure Guide to South America
Frommer's Adventure Guide to Southeast Asia
Frommer's Adventure Guide to Southern Africa
Frommer's Britain's Best Bed & Breakfasts and
  Country Inns
Frommer's France's Best Bed & Breakfasts and
  Country Inns
Frommer's Italy's Best Bed & Breakfasts and Country
  Inns
Frommer's Caribbean Hideaways

Frommer's Exploring America by RV
Frommer's Gay & Lesbian Europe
Frommer's The Moon
Frommer's New York City with Kids
Frommer's Road Atlas Britain
Frommer's Road Atlas Europe
Frommer's Washington, D.C., with Kids
Frommer's What the Airlines Never Tell You
Israel Past & Present
The New York Times' Guide to Unforgettable
  Weekends
Places Rated Almanac
Retirement Places Rated